What to Feed Your Baby

What to Feed Your Baby

Cost-Conscious Nutrition
for Your Infant

Stan Cohen, MD

ROWMAN & LITTLEFIELD PUBLISHERS, INC.
Lanham • Boulder • New York • Toronto • Plymouth, UK

Published by Rowman & Littlefield Publishers, Inc.
A wholly owned subsidiary of The Rowman & Littlefield Publishing Group, Inc.
4501 Forbes Boulevard, Suite 200, Lanham, Maryland 20706
www.rowman.com

10 Thornbury Road, Plymouth PL6 7PP, United Kingdom

Distributed by National Book Network

British Library Cataloguing in Publication Information Available

Library of Congress Cataloging-in-Publication Data
Cohen, Stanley A., 1947–
   What to feed your baby : cost-conscious nutrition for your infant / Stan Cohen.
      pages cm
   Includes index.
   ISBN 978-1-4422-1920-5 (pbk. : alk. paper) — ISBN 978-1-4422-1921-2 (electronic)
   1. Infants—Nutrition.   2. Children—Nutrition.   I. Title.
   RJ206.C64 2013
   618.92'02—dc23   2012047855

∞ ™ The paper used in this publication meets the minimum requirements of American
National Standard for Information Sciences—Permanence of Paper for Printed Library
Materials, ANSI/NISO Z39.48-1992.

Printed in the United States of America

To my children (David and Bernice, Adam and Mindy, and Lauren),
their children (Sam, Nathan, Ashton, and Kobe), and yours

Contents

Acknowledgments

Writing a book is a daunting but rewarding task. With *What to Feed Your Baby*, it has truly been the latter. I'm now able to explain my thoughts and recommendations in greater depth for the parents in my practice and for the physicians and medical personnel whom I have (and have had) the opportunity to speak to throughout the country. *What to Feed Your Baby* also allows me to expand my practice, hopefully helping a wider audience of parents and physicians sort through the challenge of providing healthy, cost-conscious nutrition for their infants.

I've asked some of the wonderful, committed dieticians and physicians I respect and work with to review the concepts and help with the content. They have been kind and generous with their time and information. In particular, Bailey Koch, registered dietitian (RD) and certified specialist in pediatrics (CSP), provided constant encouragement and up-to-the-minute nutritional insights and guidelines that she uses in our practice daily. Kylia Crane, RD, was my coauthor on the algorithm created for Georgia physicians and Special Supplemental Nutrition Program for Women, Infants and Children (WIC) officers and helped to ensure that what may be complex is decoded into readable material for parents as well as for health-care professionals. Aruna Navathe, RD, was my coauthor on several medical textbook chapters on feeding children with developmental disabilities (better stated as *differently abled children*), and her support was appreciated.

I would also like to thank the numerous mentors I have had over the years at Ohio State, Johns Hopkins, and Mass General; the parents and patients who have taught me as well; and colleagues who have shared their time and knowledge to make *What to Feed Your Baby* a better book. In particular, Ben Gold and Seth Marcus at GI Care for Kids and the SouthEast Eosinophilic Disorder (SEED)

Center; Luqman Seidu at the SEED Center and Georgia Allergy, Immunology and Asthma; Mel Heyman and Jatinder Bhatia, from the University of California, San Francisco, and the Medical College of Georgia, respectively, and both former members of the Committee on Nutrition of the American Academy of Pediatrics; and my other associates at Children's Center for Digestive Health Care, better known as GI Care for Kids, who endured my thousand questions. Elaine Harbin, the medical librarian at Children's Healthcare of Atlanta's Scottish Rite campus, was invaluable in ensuring I had all the references I needed. Myra Atkinson, Nancy Chambers, Jamie Cohen, and Monika Malik all contributed in ways beyond measure. And Bill Tomassi crafted clear, direct figures that illustrate the points well. Anne Devlin, Suzanne Staszak-Silva, and others at Rowman & Littlefield pushed and pulled to present this material optimally—which earns my great appreciation.

As the book progressed, I came to realize that this legacy would be short-term unless I could continue to update the information and expand the focus. The website www.what2feedyourbaby.com is intended to serve this purpose. While it won't have the depth of this reference or its successors, it will provide a mechanism for you and me to interface as new products come onto the market, as new information becomes available, and as nutritional thinking evolves. Hopefully, we'll also be able to provide an ongoing dialogue to meet your needs.

One of the real joys in writing this book and conceiving the website has been the opportunity to work with my children. It's been almost astonishing that the three children huddled around me in the picture on the back cover of *Healthy Babies, Happy Kids* have become thoughtful, diligent contributors to *What to Feed Your Baby*. Lauren was the research assistant who tracked down references, formatted the text, and created some of the tables. David is the mastermind of www.what2feedyourbaby.com, and Adam looked over our shoulders as legal advisor. And they all patiently endured seemingly endless discussions. I love you all and appreciate everything you have done, including providing me with cheerful, engaging grandchildren who hopefully will grow into as thoughtful, intelligent, and loving adults, like you have become, with spouses who are also wondrous, adept parents and children.

My hope is that my efforts and those of everyone involved will assist you pleasurably as you feed your babies and nourish their lives.

Stan Cohen, MD
Atlanta

1

~~~

First Decisions

Two young mothers shared a room in the hospital when each delivered a healthy little boy. A month later, the mothers sat talking over coffee while their infants quietly slept, with their older children playing where they could be watched easily. Mrs. Whitman's three-year-old son, Wallace, and Mrs. Moore's four-year-old daughter, Maya, had been playing with their dolls. But now they began to fight, struggling over one of the dolls.

"Wallace won't play right!" Maya said, nearly crying as the mothers went over.

"No, no, no, no!" Wallace shrieked.

"What's wrong?" both mothers wanted to know.

"We were playing house," Maya started, "and we were going to feed the dolls, but he won't do it right."

"Yes, I did! I did it just like my mommy," interjected Wallace.

"No, he didn't. I took a bottle and fed 'Tasha [the doll], but he wanted to pull up his shirt and put the doll under there," Maya said, pointing at Wallace's immature nipples.

Fortunately, this funny situation was easily remedied by Mrs. Whitman's showing Maya how her infant son was breastfed. It also points out, rather charmingly, how our children learn.

A question remains: Was one child right and the other wrong in the way they were feeding their dolls? Another way to ask that question might be this: Can I give my baby a healthier start? And in these times, an additional question is often added: What's the least expensive way to feed my baby?

What to Feed Your Baby: Cost-Conscious Nutrition for Your Infant provides those answers. Based on the book I wrote over 30 years ago, *Healthy Babies, Happy Kids: A Commonsense Guide to Nutrition for the Growing Years* (a book

1

that I've been repeatedly asked to update), and the information I've learned and provided to parents and physicians since, *What to Feed Your Baby* addresses these significant issues, providing valuable information about nutrition during infancy and about how that may impact your child as he or she grows.

Think about your role as a parent for a moment, if you will. The entire concept of parenthood is based on nourishing and nurturing your children during every aspect of their development. It makes sense, then, to examine and possibly improve the nutrition you provide. Most expectant mothers actually begin this process the moment they learn they are pregnant. They avoid alcohol and various foods, change their eating habits, and take prenatal vitamins. This understandable obsession with having a healthy pregnancy and a healthy infant seems new to some, but it is not. Generations of pregnant mothers in some areas of India have been instructed to eat fish during their last trimester, a concept that's been validated by contemporary research (showing that at least one component in fish oil enhances the baby's brain development,[1] as you'll soon learn). Obviously, that commitment to raising healthy, happy children who thrive in their world continues after delivery and throughout your and their lives.

What to Feed Your Baby shares the findings of recent research and some sidebars of cultural wisdom to assist you as you seek to provide the best for your baby and your growing children. The book takes its name in part from the British version of my earlier book, which was titled *Start Right: Feeding Babies and Young Children* to emphasize *the critical window* in infancy and young childhood, when what and how we nourish babies and toddlers greatly affects their entire lives.[2] A baby's brain and body grows enormously, almost doubling in size, during the first year of life,[3] and what his[4] organs are fed in large part dictates how they function not just in that first year but for years and decades after—so the nourishment and nurturing you provide during those early growing years is absolutely crucial.

The subtitle of this book is also important, with a real focus on value and cost-effectiveness—not simply on the dollars spent but on what those dollars are buying. In essence, the *nutritional value* of foods is considered in light of the traditional model of value. Nutritional value is really a reflection of what the food you're eating offers you nutritionally. Take an orange, for example. That orange is loaded with vitamin C, potassium, fiber, and sugar. Make it into orange juice, and most, if not all, of the fiber is lost. While you still have an excellent source of potassium and vitamin C, you are consuming a large quantity of sugar (approximately what you would get in the same amount of Coca-Cola) at the same time. What happens if you just have an orange soda? Then all the nutritional value is lost, and you just have the flavor and a detrimental amount of sugar—10 teaspoons in a can.

Now, combine that concept with the definition of value, which is really a relationship between quality and monetary cost. The various factors that make up quality (here, the nutritional value of the food) are then considered in terms of what the cost is. In the example of the juice, the nutritional cost of the vitamin C and potassium is the sugar you are getting at the same time. But we are not just talking about that alone. What does the juice actually cost you in the grocery store?

Thus, we want to consider the various factors that make up quality to determine if it justifies the cost. With any product, if the cost is low, but you're not satisfied with the quality, it still isn't worth what you paid. On the other hand, if you like a particular product much better for any number of reasons, quality, performance, or appeal, you will be happier paying slightly more since the value, in your experience, is greater—noting that if it does not meet your expectations, you are unlikely to purchase it again.

With infant nutrition (as with all nutritional products), we need to consider another layer—and that's *outcome*. Nutritional outcome is often taken for granted as a factor in nutritional value. Yet certain aspects are often ignored, and we need to be more mindful of those because they provide greater satisfaction and a better result for your baby.

Let's take the example of the orange again. The potassium is an essential element in cellular structure, muscle contraction, and heart health. The vitamin C contributes to bone and tissue structure and immune function. The sugar is necessary for energy, and we are just beginning to learn about all that fiber does in the intestinal tract and in nurturing the intestinal flora. So the outcomes are clear. When the orange is squeezed into juice, the fiber's filling is lost. The juice is more likely to result in gastroesophageal reflux in my experience, especially because more juice is often consumed and the relatively higher sugar content adds considerable calories—equivalent to those in an orange soda.

Babies aren't usually fed oranges or orange juice because of the potential for allergy. But consider apples and apple juice instead, and the same factors apply, though with less chance of allergy. And the juice, when it's given as a nighttime or naptime bottle, is infamous for causing cavities and dental problems.

Change the juice to prune, and it brings up a second issue: tolerability. Some infants and toddlers like prune juice; others hate it. In small quantities, it becomes a traditional assistant for relieving or preventing constipation—but not if the baby or child won't drink it or consumes too much and develops diarrhea.

A third factor is often assumed in the US, and that's food safety, because the Food and Drug Administration (FDA) is mandated to oversee food preparation and protect us. But, as was recently seen, when salmonella contaminated peanut butter, the FDA finds out after the fact. And when spoiled milk or formula is consumed, the manufacturer is rarely at fault. Nor can the FDA be as vigilant as you need to be.

So safety and tolerability (which, for the infant, often means taste) are also very much a part of purchasing and offering a food. Thus outcomes need to be considered together with nutritional value in establishing cost-conscious nutrition, which can be put into a summary equation (figure 1.1).

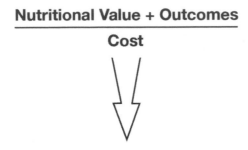

Figure 1.1.
Cost-conscious nutrition.

Very real examples exist and will become evident as we examine different infant formulas. One type of formula can actually cost three times as much as the others (as much as $6,000 in the first year of life, and some children are placed on this for even longer). That amount is justified when treating children suffering from certain conditions, which we'll talk about, because without those formulas, the children would spend more time in the hospital and less time at school and in age-appropriate activities when they're older. However, when one of those formulas is used to treat a milder condition, the value is lost because a less expensive product, costing far less than half, could be used with the same result.

A DIFFERENT KIND OF FOOD FIGHT

Formula manufacturers have a number of products that might suit your infant's needs, and they want to sell them to you, fighting for shelf space and for your attention and your pediatrician's recommendation,[5] because in 2007, just 1 percent of the formula market represented $35 million in sales to the manufacturers.[6] The same is true for foods that are intended to appeal to children, where the billions of dollars spent each year have each sector of the food-supply chain eyeing your budget and trying to convince you to spend your money on their products, sometimes with little regard for your child's nutrition or health (consider all the calorie-dense, low-nutritional-value snack foods on grocery store shelves).

All that competition makes it difficult for you to make the best choice. Walk into any grocery store, pharmacy, or discount store and try to pick the right formula for your baby, the one that provides the greatest value (not just the best price, because that can be misleading). It's a real challenge.

What to Feed Your Baby is here to help. This book sorts through common situations and pediatric conditions, offering advice that can guide you as a parent while you are in the store and when talking with your primary care providers (the fancy term for your doctors and their assistants) and coming to reasonable conclusions about what to feed your child—what might help and what could get in the way. In other words, a one-size-fits-all approach isn't appropriate; targeted categories are, but even with those groupings, individual needs can vary substantially.

Yes, I'm going to recommend breastfeeding, but that doesn't work for all mothers, and even when it does, the mother may need to supplement or introduce other foods because her infant's needs might be specific.

Questions and issues can arise. Some infants and children have their own specific needs, in addition to the general nutritional needs of all children (for example, the child who has reflux or isn't gaining weight well). Those needs change dramatically as infants and children age, acquire new needs and skills, or develop particular problems. So those aspects are addressed.

The reason for writing this book now is that I recently created an algorithm to help physicians in Georgia select the appropriate formula for each baby receiving vouchers from the Special Supplemental Nutrition Program for Women, Infants and Children (WIC). As you may know, the WIC program provides nutritional assistance through the US Department of Agriculture (USDA) to ensure that these vulnerable populations receive adequate nutrition when they might not be able to afford it otherwise. I first worked with the WIC program when I became chairman of the nutrition committee of the state chapter of the American Academy of Pediatrics approximately 15 years ago. The WIC program was struggling to provide clients with routine formulas under its guidelines for healthy infants. The processes I put in place for them saved over $1.6 million in the first six months, which translated into thousands more families the program could serve. Over the next dozen years, with the modifications that we nuanced and promoted, the WIC program credited these efforts with saving over $52 million.[7]

However, the problem is that not all babies thrive on routine formulas. Some have issues as simple as reflux; others have more complex needs. The selection of the best formula for each baby can make a huge difference in the infant's life and in the taxpayer's pocketbook. As a result, I devised a tiered system to help providers when thinking about which formula to offer. I expect that to save the WIC program and the USDA even more.

But I also want you to benefit, even if you don't live in Georgia, and particularly if you are paying for your infant's formula and foods. And because you are an interested, involved parent, grandparent, or caregiver working to provide the best for your child as he is growing, we (recognizing the many people who have helped create this book for you) have looked carefully through the parents' lens to ensure this book is focused on the information you need and want. Tables, diagrams, and a point-by-point summary at the end of each chapter should make this information accessible. An appendix with growth charts and helpful tables is also there for your reference.

Using these features and the input of many thoughtful colleagues, *What to Feed Your Baby* should help you improve the quality, while lowering the cost, of the foods you offer your infant. To take it a step further, our website, www.what2feedyourbaby .com, provides additional information and resources that can support your efforts.

As I said in the introduction to *Healthy Babies, Happy Kids*, "I realized I was writing with three hats on. As a researcher in pediatric gastroenterology (diseases of the liver and intestinal tract) and nutrition, I tried to bring together and evaluate the important developments that have an impact on your child's nutrition. As a pediatrician, I remembered the children who had been in my office and the problems that they had. For your benefit, I have tried to retell illustrative stories (compiled from many of these parents), recalling, as I could, concerns and questions that parents have faced. And as a parent myself, I was among you, the readers, empathizing with you and trying to make sure that the message came across." And now, as a grandparent, I want to provide you with some perspective and an arm around your shoulder, helping you create a positive approach to healthy nutrition while supporting your efforts with a useful reference should problems develop.

However, no book can replace the good medical care of a practitioner who has seen your infant firsthand. You should discuss the recommendations here with your physician before embarking on any of them, since neither I nor the publisher can accept any risk or responsibility without having examined your child. Some of the recommendations are controversial. They are based on my personal experiences and my interpretation of the medical literature with which I'm familiar. I have tried to indicate why the controversy exists and the arguments on both sides. Your physician may have come to a different conclusion for equally good reasons. Hopefully, this book will give you sufficient information to allow you to understand any differing views and actively participate in making decisions with your practitioner.

Products are mentioned to help you make decisions. Similar products may come on the market and others may be modified over time. I do not intend to demean any products when I recommend others. The formulas and the products mentioned couldn't be sold if they didn't meet the standards set by the Food and Drug Administration. Again, discuss the recommendations with your physician and, if you'd like, explore our website, www.what2feedyourbaby.com, where we will try to keep you current with new recommendations and evolving research.

SUMMARY

- A critical window exists in infancy and early childhood, when the brain is growing and the body is developing. What you feed your child can greatly influence how he will grow and develop.
- Numerous nutritional options are available for your infant or child.
- Some of the options are more nutritious than others, and some are far less expensive.
- Certain infants and children have more specialized needs than others.
- Nutritional needs change as children grow, gain skills, or develop problems.
- *What to Feed Your Baby*, www.what2feedyourbaby.com, and www.nutrition 4kids.com can help you make thoughtful choices that will contribute to your child's health and development.
- *What to Feed Your Baby* is intended to help you understand the basis for the decisions your primary care provider is making and actively participate in the discussion, but, like any medical guide, it cannot replace the good medical care of someone who is evaluating your child.
- Tables, diagrams, and other features make the main points instantly accessible.

2

⌒

Back to the Breast

In the United States, approximately three out of every four infants are being breastfed when they leave the hospital.[1] Among educated middle- and upper-middle-class women, the figure is even higher, with closer to 80 to 85 percent of their infants being breastfed initially (an increase of over 10 percent over the last 20 years).[2] This represents a resurgence of sorts, a "back-to-the-breast" movement. As recently as 1970, only one in every five infants received breastmilk, and among those, three-fourths had been weaned by five months of age.[3] While we are making progress, one in four breastfed infants is introduced to infant formula within two days of age, and at six months, less than half of the children who start on the breast have continued.[4]

Worldwide, encouraging breastfeeding is a more pressing problem. Almost 9 million children under the age of five die each year. A third of those deaths are related to malnutrition, with two-thirds occurring in the first few months of life. Yet Dr. Elizabeth Mason, director of the World Health Organization's Department of Maternal, Newborn, Child and Adolescent Health and Development, estimates that fewer than 35 percent of infants breastfeed exclusively until six months of age and take advantage of this natural resource—despite the fact that their families cannot afford the formulas we take for granted in privileged societies.[5] These families obviously do not understand the short- and long-term impact of that initial decision.

THE CRITICAL WINDOW

Infant nutrition exists within a critical window. A baby's body and brain grow rapidly in the last months before birth and for the first years afterward. In that last

7

trimester of pregnancy, the brain grows 260 percent (measuring by weight). In
the first year after birth, the brain grows another 175 percent. During the whole
next year, the brain grows approximately 18 percent, achieving only 10 percent of
the growth the year before. The brain will only grow another 10 percent during
the rest of that child's lifetime, indicating that those last months of pregnancy and
those first years of life represent a critical period to nourish the brain and enhance
the baby's growth and function.[6]

Having a greater understanding of infants' needs and the potential to nourish
them better, parents and health-care providers have become more cautious about
formulas and other processed foods and re-enamored with the natural aspects of
breastfeeding. Healthy People 2020[7] is a national health promotion and disease
prevention initiative that brings together government agencies at different levels,
as well as individuals, to address major public health issues. The initial report,
Healthy People 2010, released by the Department of Health and Human Services
in January 2000,[8] emphasized that breastfeeding is one of the many areas considered essential to improving health in the United States, setting forth national
objectives on breastfeeding. The Surgeon General's Call to Action[9] and Healthy
People 2020 continue that effort, targeting specific goals for breastfeeding (and
numerous other initiatives as well) for various organizations and government
agencies (see table 2.1).

The question, of course, is why? If we consider the economics alone, the
government's position makes sense. The current estimate is that 1,000 deaths
would be prevented and $13 billion would be saved in medical costs annually if
90 percent of the infants in the United States were breastfed.[10] Breastmilk is free
and always ready to use as long as the mother is available. No mixing, heating,
or cleaning required! Even the least expensive formula costs more than $1,000
for the year. But the real savings comes from the health benefits. Babies who are
formula-fed have a tendency to require more doctors visits, prescriptions, and
hospitalizations, are at greater risk of infections and sudden infant death syndrome, and have a higher incidence of diabetes and obesity later.[11]

Table 2.1. Healthy People 2020 Goals

Mothers Who Breastfeed	1998 Baseline (%)	2006 (%)	Target for 2020 (%)
In early infancy	64	74	82
At six months	29	43	61
At six months, exclusively		14	25
At one year	16	22	34

Source: Healthy People, "Maternal, Infant, and Child Health," http://www.healthypeople.gov/2020/
topicsobjectives2020/objectiveslist.aspx?topicId=26.

WHAT ARE THE ADVANTAGES OF HUMAN MILK?

To breast- or bottle-feed is the mother's choice, but the decision should be an informed one, with the recognition that breastfeeding is not just one of the ways of feeding infants but the gold standard—the normal method—and ongoing research continues to find benefits of breastmilk that formula companies try to simulate. As a result, the American Academy of Pediatrics, American Academy of Family Physicians, American Dietetic Association, American Public Health Association, World Health Organization, and UNICEF all recommend that an infant be exclusively breastfed until six months of age.[12, 13, 14, 15, 16] The reasons are legion and important (see table 2.2).

First, nursing provides for strong mother-child bonding. It is now even believed that hormones released encourage mothering behaviors. To promote breastfeeding, nursing should start immediately after birth. Even mothers who have just had a Caesarian (C-section) often have their babies placed on their chest to initiate skin-to-skin contact that nurtures the baby, lowers his heart and breathing rates, and fosters the mothering experience. The skin contact actually stimulates a hormone, oxytocin, which improves the flow of milk and relaxes the mother. That pattern should then continue with the mother feeding (by breast, preferably) and comforting her infant when he is hungry or distressed.

Second, breastfed babies have decreased incidence of infection, reducing their medical costs and in turn reducing the number of sick days that a parent must take to care for a sick child. And that advantage to the infant is far more significant than just the economics. At birth, an infant's immune system is incompletely developed; he is unable to fight infection effectively, largely because of the lack

Table 2.2. Advantages of Breastfeeding for the Baby

Short-term/Immediate Benefits	Long-term Benefits
Decreased incidence of infections such as • diarrheal disease • influenza • necrotizing enterocolitis (NEC) • herpes simplex • respiratory synctial virus (RSV) • ear infections • respiratory infections (i.e., bronchitis) • bacterial meningitis	Decreased risk of developing • diabetes • asthma • childhood cancers • rheumatoid arthritis • osteoporosis • vision defects • obesity
Decreased incidence of illnesses such as • sudden infant death syndrome (SIDS) • gastroesophageal reflux (GER) • multiple sclerosis	Enhanced development and intelligence: • higher IQ • cognitive and social development
Protection from allergies	Improved dental health

Source: Bailey Koch, RD, CSP, www.nutrition4kids.com.

of protective factors. Although he receives a small quantity of gamma globulin across the placenta from his mother, the infant is slow to begin making his own disease-fighting globulins in large quantities. Breastmilk, however, transfers some of the mother's antibodies and immune factors to the infant, especially in the dense first milk, or *colostrum*.

The antibodies remain in the baby's gastrointestinal tract, protecting the infant against many bacteria and viruses, and their toxic products, that would otherwise be absorbed or could establish an infection in the baby's intestinal tract. An enzyme, *lysozyme*, also crosses to an infant from the mother through her milk. The lysozyme acts together with the immune globulins to further enhance protection against certain bacteria.

The growth of *Lactobacillus* (the same probiotic found in yogurt), *Bifidobacteria*, a number of other protective bacteria, and yeast is encouraged by poorly digestible carbohydrates, collectively called prebiotics, contained in breastmilk. These prebiotics (discussed in more detail along with probiotics in chapter 5) constantly reconstitute the intestinal flora with protective organisms that then compete with and lessen the growth of other potentially detrimental bacteria in the infant's intestinal tract.

In addition, thousands of the mother's own cells pass through her breastmilk to the baby each day. These cells, similar to those in our bloodstream or lymph nodes, continue to live in the infant and retain the capacity to produce more immune globulins and other infection-fighting proteins. A number of other growth factors, enzymes, and immunologically active proteins are present in human milk, and help the baby's immune system develop.[17] Lactoferrin, for example, is a binding protein for iron that prevents bacteria from using the iron for their growth. These immunological advantages are considered so important that many children's hospitals have developed human-milk banks. These are similar in concept to Red Cross blood banks. The idea is for milk banks to act as institutional wet nurses, providing human milk to critical care nurseries for premature infants at risk for infections, when their mothers' milk is not available or usable. The processing of this milk often destroys the donor mother's living cells, but the proteins in the human milk remain functionally unimpaired, providing nutrition and some immune defenses for these infants.

Another major difference between breastmilk and formula is the ability to prevent the development of allergies. As we will detail later, the protein components of cow's milk, even though modified, can contribute to or directly cause allergies. The immune globulins and lysozyme found in human milk have an additional function here as well. They may digest and prevent the absorption of milk proteins that may not have been broken down. There is research showing that the absorption of cow's milk and other "foreign" proteins in infancy may increase some individuals' risk of developing allergies and other intestinal diseases later in life.[18]

Breastfeeding may prevent, or at least delay, those exposures to a time (around six months) when the infant's intestinal cells knit together and prevent those proteins from penetrating the intestinal barrier. (If the proteins can't penetrate the surface layer of cells, they can't provoke an allergic response.[19])

One of the other benefits of breastfeeding is that breastfed infants are at a decreased risk of obesity later in life. The Centers for Disease Control indicate that babies who breastfeed for nine months have 30 percent less chance of obesity.[20] With obesity at epidemic proportions, this is a major advantage for breastfed babies. Part of this benefit comes from the composition of human milk. The first part of the milk coming from a mother's breast, otherwise known as foremilk, is high in protein, which decreases toward the end of the feeding. The last part of the feeding contains hindmilk, which is higher in fat content. The high fat content slows the stomach's emptying of the milk and slows its intestinal passage, producing a full and satisfied infant. Even if the baby still wants to stay at the breast to satisfy his sucking needs, little milk is coming out because the flow of breastmilk also diminishes at the end of the feeding.

The formula-fed baby can be equally full and satisfied, but his interest in sucking fills the stomach with more formula and more calories for his body. Any mother would have a difficult time telling the difference between a child who, like most infants, is still hungry but pauses to relax before several more gulps of breastmilk or formula and the infant who is completely nourished but continues to suck for neurological and psychological reasons. The tendency for overfeeding to occur with bottle feeding is further worsened by our instinctive desire to provide adequate nutrition for our young. A mother sees that her baby usually takes 3 to 4 ounces of formula at each feeding. When that infant only takes 1 or 2 ounces of formula, she will jiggle the bottle around in the infant's mouth to encourage the baby to take more, even though the baby may be full. That situation can't happen as easily with breastfeeding.

Fortunately, there are no ounce markers on the breast. The infant, not the mother or pediatrician, will decide how much milk he should drink. (Admittedly, fat breastfed babies exist, too, but they are rarer by far and appear to come from mothers trying too hard to satisfy their babies' desire to suck. Every time the child begins to fret, the breast is offered as a pacifier. But that problem can be improved by making the mother aware of the situation and its dangers.)

An often overlooked and incompletely understood aspect of breastfeeding is that hormones also pass to the baby and may affect gastrointestinal function and body composition. They also enhance DNA synthesis in concert with the nucleotide building blocks that also pass from mother to baby.

A BETTER BRAIN

Babies who breastfed for only four to six months demonstrated higher IQs when they were tested at four years of age, compared to formula-fed infants—not just by a little but by 13 points in several studies by E. E. Birch and others in Texas.[21] The average IQ for these formula-fed infants was 99, but the breastfed infants averaged 112 points. While that may not sound like much, while I was writing this book, there were many nights when I would have been grateful for extra IQ points. (And Craig Jensen, a researcher in the field based at Texas Children's Hospital, remarks that he often wants to ask the pilots of the flights he's on whether they slept well the night before and whether they were breastfed as infants.)

Another finding in these studies sponsored by the National Institutes of Health (NIH) is that vision improves for these infants as well. Factors in breastmilk help the receptors on the back of the eyeball mature, but they also may help the neuro-transmission to the brain and, in doing so, help researchers get another important picture of the brain's activity.[22]

Two of the most convincing studies further emphasize the importance of breastfeeding. One, in New Zealand, found that children who breastfed scored higher on their school exams from the time their IQ was first assessed at eight to nine years, through the time of their math and reading comprehension tests, all the way through their exit exams from secondary schools.[23] You could question that, recognizing that women who breastfeed are more likely to have intact families, smoke less, and have higher education and better socioeconomic standards, but because the researchers studied over 1,000 children in Christchurch, where the population tended to stay in the area, they could statistically eliminate those confounding factors and demonstrate that breastfeeding was the important element. Another study in Denmark goes one step further and shows that individuals who breastfed for at least four to six months had higher IQ scores when they entered the army at an average of 18.7 years of age.[24]

BRAIN FOOD FOR BABIES?

One of the responsible factors seems to be the docosahexaenoic acid (DHA). When it's added to infant formula in sufficient amounts (as it now is in most varieties—more about this later), NIH-sponsored studies have shown that it parallels the effect of breastmilk in raising IQ and visual tracking in infants, which could be the result of improving vision itself or improving the signals that get to the brain.[25] But please note, not all formulas add equal amounts of DHA (as discussed in chapter 5), so its mere presence may not make the difference, and there are in fact numerous other differences between breastmilk and formula, as well as differences in terms of maternal infant bonding, that could contribute.[26]

Where does DHA come from? It is one of fatty acids among the omega-3 oils from fish, so mothers can take omega-3 oils or DHA from the third trimester, when it begins to cross the placenta, through the time they are breastfeeding, or they can eat fish approximately three times a week to get the fatty acids to cross through their breastmilk. (Eggs contain DHA as well, but you'd have to eat around 20 eggs, at 65 milligrams each, to get the same benefit as 3 ounces of salmon, with its 1,350 milligrams.)[27] The problem, of course, is that some game fish (swordfish, king mackerel, tile fish, shark) are tainted with increased amounts of methyl mercury and should not be eaten, particularly by pregnant and breastfeeding women, since the mercury can also cross the placenta and breastmilk to your infant. Some tuna contains intermediate amounts of methyl mercury and may pose a hazard if eaten frequently or in quantity (so the recommendations are for pregnant and breast-feeding mothers to eat less than 4 ounces of tuna three times a week).[28]

Another long-chain fatty acid, arachidonic acid (ARA), is in a wide variety of foods, meat, eggs, and milk. It is sufficient in most diets. It helps to regulate triglyceride and cholesterol metabolism, immunity, and blood clotting, and in the infant, it is important in balancing the DHA in order to optimize the infant's growth and weight gain.

ANY OTHER ADVANTAGES?

Science speaks of only some of the advantages of breastfeeding—those that can be tested and proven. Other benefits exist as well, but they are more subjective, if not indefinable. The most obvious is the warm relationship of a mother with her child. This serene bonding experience always evokes the warmest, most tender emotions. The mother joyfully feeding her infant, with the infant's hand stroking her or wrapped around her finger as she lovingly watches, remains the appropriate symbol of the nurturing of society as well as the nourishment of the infant.

Another interesting feature of breastmilk is that it changes daily, depending on what the mother is eating. That may vary the flavor of the milk, and as a result some experts think that breastfed infants are therefore more willing to try a wider variety of foods when they are older. And with the immunological tolerance that the breastfed intestinal flora provides, these children may become less picky eaters. Notice, I keep saying "may," since this is simply supposition at this time.

There are also benefits for the breastfeeding mother (see table 2.3). Evidence shows that women who breastfeed have a decreased risk of some cancers (most particularly ovarian and breast), and they have an easier time losing the weight gained during their pregnancies (though even then, it isn't easy).

Table 2.3. Benefits of Breastfeeding for the Mother

Helps shrink uterus after childbirth
Promotes postpartum weight loss
Decreased insulin requirements in diabetic mothers
Increased sleep for mom
Protects mom against anemia
Improved emotional health
Stronger mother-child bond
Decreased risk of developing • breast cancer • uterine cancer • ovarian cancer • endometrial cancer

Source: Bailey Koch, RD, CSP, www.nutrition4kids.com.

THE OTHER ADVANTAGE: COST

How much does breastfeeding cost? This is a tricky question, actually, because it depends on what you consider. Breastmilk costs nothing in and of itself; it's a free gift from God, so to speak. However, breastmilk can be deficient in vitamin D, particularly if the mother is not getting enough herself, so pediatricians routinely recommend vitamin D drops or a routine infant multivitamin, bringing the real cost to about $5 a month (a bargain compared to formula, which costs approximately $150 for a month when the baby is taking a full quart per day).

However, the mother herself has to take vitamins (not for the baby but to replenish her own stores), and if she isn't eating enough fish to supply the baby with DHA, she'll have to take fish oil or supplement with DHA itself. So there's a small cost there, but again, far less than for formula. There's also the cost for nursing bras, nipple shields, breast pumps, and freezer bags, but one could argue that these are balanced by the cost of the paraphernalia used for bottles and for washing them, which entails a cost as well. You can also account for the time away from work to do the pumping and storage, as well as for the extra diapers that some babies require because breastfeeding often produces more bowel movements daily, but if you do that, you probably should credit needing fewer doctor visits and less time away from work for those visits for the working, breastfeeding mother. Some mothers also concede that they have an increased appetite during the first few months (which, of course, costs more, but they often lose weight without the normal amount of exercise it would take to balance the increased calories—providing a real benefit despite that extra cost).

So, stir it together, and breastfeeding seems to entail a small fraction of what it costs to feed a baby with formula. In addition, the many benefits and advantages of human milk and breastfeeding have led us "back to the breast." Even some mothers of adopted children want to attempt suckling their infants. Some are successful—especially those who have had previous pregnancies. Women who are unable to lactate have benefited from using artificial nursers. These are feeding systems that have a straw connecting a thin tube to a pouch containing formula. When the other end is placed in the infant's mouth along with the mother's nipple, breastfeeding can be simulated. Quite obviously, this is done for the mother's emotional fulfillment. But it may be very worthwhile for the mother who has not had nine months of pregnancy to become attached to her infant or for the mother who feels otherwise cheated of the opportunity to breastfeed.

Mothers who wish to breastfeed can face other difficulties as well. Many of the solutions are discussed in the next chapter, but all of this renewed emphasis should not demean, or in any way cause guilt among, those mothers who choose not to or cannot breastfeed. They can certainly provide adequate nutrition for their infants, and their options are addressed beginning in chapter 4.

IS BREASTFEEDING EVER INAPPROPRIATE?

Some mothers should not breastfeed for a number of reasons. Perhaps the most common reason is that the mother is taking certain medications. Just as in pregnancy, nutrients and medications gain access to an infant from his mother. A mother's nipple is just like an umbilical cord. This is a real threat, because certain drugs are selectively concentrated in the fat of the mother's milk, and even small doses should be avoided by the breastfeeding mother. In this case, bottle-feeding breastmilk pumped prior to initiating the particular medication or exclusive formula feeding would be recommended. For all medications, mothers should check with their obstetricians or pediatricians before nursing to make sure that any drugs they take will be safe for their infant.

The best advice is to avoid medicines whenever possible, especially those listed in tables 2.4 and 2.5. At the same time, mothers should recognize that their own good health is important (and absolutely necessary in order to take care of their children), and they should not stop taking needed medicines in order to breast-feed. To get the most up-to-date advice, mothers can consult the same references doctors and lactation specialists do, including Thomas Hale's *Medication and Mother's Milk*,[29] and links through www.womenshealth.gov.

Table 2.4. Medications that Require Careful Monitoring while Breastfeeding

Consult with your physician prior to administering the following:	
Antidepressants	Metoclopramide
Aspirin	Metronidazole
Codeine	Morphine
Demerol	Oral contraceptives
Ergots	Paxil
General anesthesia	Phenobarbital
Indomethacin	Prozac
Isoniazid	Valium
Lithium	Zoloft

Source: Bailey Koch, RD, CSP, www.nutrition4kids.com.

Table 2.5. Medications that Preclude Breastfeeding

Anticancer drugs	Mysoline
Cyclosporine	Methotrexate
Lindane	Radioactive drugs
Parlodel	Narcotics and barbiturates

Source: Bailey Koch, RD, CSP, www.nutrition4kids.com.

Just as medications may be transferred, bacteria, viruses, and other infectious agents can cross the breast to the infant. These can enter the baby's system and allow an infection to develop in the child as well as the mother. Fortunately, there are only a few absolute contraindications to breastfeeding for these reasons:

- Mothers with active tuberculosis. These mothers must be separated from their infants and suspend any breastfeeding until both mother and baby are receiving appropriate medical treatment.
- Mothers infected with HIV. (Mothers who have access to an affordable, sustainable, and safe food source for the baby should opt for it. In countries like Haiti, where HIV is endemic and the cost of formula is often prohibitive, mothers are still encouraged to breastfeed as their best choice.)
- Mothers with active herpes lesions on their breasts.
- Mothers with human lymphotropic virus HTLV-1 and HTLV-2, which are associated with adult T-cell leukemia and lymphoma.

Complications of a difficult or problematic delivery may also dictate that formula be substituted for human milk. These complications, which may afflict either the mother or the infant, are usually only temporary. Serious, chronic diseases or prolonged emotional fatigue may diminish a mother's ability to feed her baby. In addition, severe malnutrition from illness may result in suboptimal nutrition for an infant, even though nutrients are preferentially transferred to the breastmilk rather than being used to improve the mother's own malnourished state. Most mothers are able to breastfeed their baby once the problem has resolved.

Rare genetic conditions preclude breastfeeding. Galactosemia is one of those. A baby's inability to metabolize lactose or galactose can lead to liver failure and mental retardation. This and other abnormalities are detected with prenatal or genetic testing, allowing an affected infant to be placed on a formula that compensates for the defect.

Various social and emotional pressures and vocations may also interfere with a desirable breastfeeding experience. The increase in women in the workforce has led to a federal law that now requires companies to have time and private spaces (not bathrooms) for breastfeeding mothers. Some employers even offer day care at or near the workplace so that attending to her baby's needs will not interfere with the breastfeeding mother's occupation (with higher productivity and morale and less absenteeism being the result of breastfeeding support programs).[30]

On a broader basis, some breastfeeding advocates contend that WIC itself may lessen breastfeeding rates among some populations. WIC (along with other government agencies) actually espouses breastfeeding and provides breastfeeding education and support, but the free formula it provides to ensure nutritional adequacy can make formula feeding seem like more of an advantage for some mothers.

A SPOUSE'S SUPPORT

A controversial aspect of the emphasis on breastfeeding is the displacement of the other parent. In bygone days, husbands would have been content to have their wives relieve them of child-care responsibilities. But with the advent of feminism and the sharing of parenting roles, is the father going to feel thwarted in his desire to participate in the feeding of his child? The answer certainly can be yes, but it should be no. With more women going back to work after childbirth, more women are pumping and storing their breastmilk for times when they are not available to nurse. The bottle of either breastmilk or formula (when the mother wants or needs to be away from her infant at feeding time) will permit the father to enjoy the pleasure of feeding his infant.

A husband's, the family's, and the pediatrician's encouragement provide an optimum environment for successful breastfeeding, since lack of encouragement can destroy any mother's ability to relax in order to feed her baby. My office has seen many women in tears, unable to produce milk, because of the tensions that evolve when the woman's wishes to breastfeed are met with direct or indirect opposition by her family. With the increase in breastfeeding and an increasing number of parents attending prenatal classes, fewer women have complained of that lack of support. Some still suffer embarrassment when breastfeeding in public, though they do so discreetly. Usually that can be remedied by finding a private area, using a cover, and, mostly, recognizing the beauty and naturalness of breastfeeding.

Quite the opposite can occur when encouragement to breastfeed begins to feel like coercion, and subtle pressure is applied by peers and pediatricians alike. A mother who cannot breastfeed, or chooses not to, may begin to feel guilty that she is not providing good nourishment for her infant and that she is not meeting everyone else's expectations.

Perhaps the costs involved in bottle-feeding formula will convince both parents that successful breastfeeding is not only a sound scientific concept but a sound financial one as well. A family pays for the formula company's profits and advertising, as well as the high costs of the various ingredients that must be added to cow's milk in order to make it more like human milk. With each ingredient, the price goes up a bit more. In the ready-to-feed formulas, you even pay to ship the water that has been added so you don't have to add it to the slightly less convenient powdered or liquid concentrate form.

The bottle-feeding mother needs support, too. With commercial infant formula and good medical advice, she will be supplying her infant with quality nutrition—including the protein, fat, calories, vitamins, and minerals her infant needs. And in fact, many breastfed infants may have formula supplements from time to time.

The decision of how to feed can benefit from the guidance of a physician and the support of the family, but clearly the decision should usually reside with the mother, since she must determine whether she is comfortable with the idea of breastfeeding. While this remains the optimal method for the majority of infants, each woman's decision is her own. Hopefully, it will be met with the support and love of her mate and the rest of her extended family.

In either case, an understanding of basic techniques and potential problems (detailed in the next chapter) will help the family create a successful and gratifying feeding experience.

SUMMARY

- Breastfeeding is again becoming the preferred option for many more mothers.
- Immunological factors in breastmilk lessen infection rates and doctor visits, particularly for ear and respiratory infections.
- The intestinal flora and these immunological factors may also enhance food tolerance and lessen allergy later in life.
- Docosahexaenoic acid and perhaps other as-yet-unrecognized breastmilk components increase visual function and brain development, with a substantial improvement in IQ.
- Breastfeeding lessens the potential for obesity.
- The costs of breastfeeding are only a small fraction of the costs of formula feeding.
- Additional benefits for the baby and mother are noted in tables 2.2 and 2.3, respectively.
- Certain mothers should not breastfeed because of underlying illnesses (listed above) or the medications they may need to take (tables 2.4 and 2.5).
- The family and employer should support a mother's efforts to breastfeed or her decision not to.

3

~~

Breastfeeding Is Almost as Simple as It Looks

Techniques and Guidelines

When you, as a new mother, are lying on the bed in the delivery room, and the doctor or nurse hands you your new baby, you are understandably excited and overwhelmed with emotion. But one of those emotions may be uncertainty or terror, because suddenly you may have the feeling that you are supposed to know what to do with that infant. You have read and certainly thought about your role as a mother; you may have even discussed it with your significant other, friends, or your prospective pediatrician. Now the baby is here. You feel as if you are expected to breastfeed ever so naturally—by the doctor, by the nurse, by your husband, by your parents and in-laws, and by the baby.

In fact, neither the doctor nor the nurse expects that of you, though they sometimes pull you down from the clouds a little. Hopefully, your husband and all your family and friends are supportive and will try to keep you up there.

Don't worry about the baby either. He needs little nourishment in those early hours. Besides, he is just as new to this as you are. The baby can guide you with his mouth searching for your nipple. You may have certain, basic instincts, but his reflexes are adapted to obtaining nourishment. And you have at your disposal a cavalry of lactation consultants, nurses, doctors, and supportive websites to accelerate you through the learning curve and provide accurate information, if this book and the other resources you consult can't provide you with an answer for your particular question.

HOW SOON CAN YOU BEGIN? AND HOW?

Hopefully your delivery went well (congratulations are in order, of course), and hopefully you and your baby are awake and alert. If so, you can put your infant to the breast right there on the birthing bed or in the recovery room.

Little first milk, or *colostrum*, will be available to the infant at that time, but he does not need any immediate nourishment or fluid; he still has plenty from the womb, and his stomach only has the capacity of a small marble. These early feedings are simply to help establish your milk flow as soon as possible. And when your baby does get that colostrum, its nutritional benefits, laxative properties, and immunological content will help the baby in those first several days until your breastmilk comes in fully.

If your labor or delivery required sedation, the baby may have received some of that medication as well. As a result, he may be less responsive right away. His interest and ability to suck will be reduced at first. You can still place the baby on your chest for that skin-to-skin contact that will ease his heart and breathing rates while also stimulating the release of oxytocin for all its beneficial effects.[1] Then the baby will usually be taken to the nursery to recover and to be observed. Feedings will be withheld until the infant is more alert, generally at two to six hours of age.

Most importantly, make certain as you begin that both you and your baby are comfortable. Pamper yourself and your infant. Find a comfortable position with your elbow resting on several pillows or an armrest.

When you are both ready, place your baby in front of you, resting his head in your arm. You needn't be afraid of the baby: his movements won't be smooth—his head will snap back unexpectedly, and his arms may jerk forward—but this *moro reflex* is normal in the first months of life. Make sure that the baby is awake and anxious to feed. If he's not, you can put the baby on your bare chest. He may inch down to your breast after feeling the skin-to-skin contact. If he doesn't, delay the feeding for a while and enjoy (and admire) this wonderful life that's just arrived.

Once your baby is actively interested, your gentle stroking of his cheek will cause him to turn his head to that side, and he will start to move his mouth until he finds something to put his mouth around. If you simply touch your breast under his nose or tickle the middle of his lip, he will latch onto the nipple instinctively. One of the best ways to offer your breast is by letting it hang naturally while you support his head and bring his chin into the underside of your breast (the tissue under your nipple and the areola around it; see figure 3.1). He will open his mouth, and you can gently lift and bring his head forward so that he fills his mouth with the nipple and sometimes the entire areola and more. That usually works well. If it doesn't, you can try an older technique, placing your first finger and thumb on top and the rest of your fingers under the breast, supporting it. Your fingers should be at the back part of the colored areola with little pressure applied. Either latching-on technique also helps to keep the infant's nose clear of your breast so that his breathing is not obstructed.

You may find that he has taken too little of the nipple into his mouth. Usually the baby will readjust this himself. If he does not, you can do it for him by slipping your finger alongside the nipple, breaking the suction. Then gently offer your breast again, watching and listening until he begins to suck effectively.

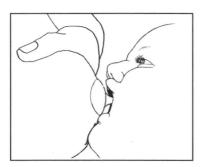

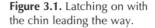

Figure 3.1. Latching on with the chin leading the way.

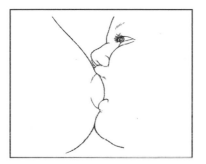

While this relaxed, sitting position is the most common, others may be tried or even preferred. You may like to have the baby lying on the pillows under your arm as you sit up or angling his body on your side in what is called the "football hold," or you may prefer to lie alongside your baby stretched out in bed. One mother I know occasionally likes to lay her infant on her lap, while she leans forward letting her breast drop into her baby's mouth. No one position is better than any other. Just use the positions that relax both you and the baby, allowing the two of you to enjoy each other. Please know that any anxiousness may lessen your initial enjoyment, but as you become more comfortable with the practice, ease and contentment often replace any concerns or quandaries.

HOW LONG SHOULD EACH FEEDING BE?

In the first few days, very little colostrum is produced. But importantly, small amounts of your cells and immune proteins (antibodies and the immune globulin IgA, which protects against intestinal and respiratory infections) are passed to the infant in that thick, golden liquid.

These feedings allow you and the baby to adjust to each other while they stimulate your milk flow. Few babies have very strong sucking needs at this time, so feedings are often brief, perhaps three to five minutes on each side, giving the baby the marble-sized feedings in those first days and then walnut-sized feedings by the end of a week. You may appreciate the brevity of these initial feedings, since prolonged feedings can make you feel very sore or exhausted, as you will want to have eight to twelve feedings for each of those first days.

If your nipples themselves are sore, you may want to get the baby to latch on to more of the areola (the dark area around the nipple) rather than just the nipple itself. The techniques described should help you do that.

Do take time to see your baby's primary care provider within three days after the baby's discharge and again by two weeks to check the baby's weight and over-all health. As the weeks become a month, most mothers and babies become quite proficient at breastfeeding, but there is a learning curve, and it does take time for babies' appetites and stomachs to grow so that they can begin taking more at each feeding and extend the time between feedings. Then the feedings may last 5–20 minutes or longer. And even then, the pattern will vary. Often babies will feed every hour or two during the day and then go longer between feedings at night. Some babies go through periods when they want to feed frequently again and other times when they take less, in terms of both time on the breast and the number of times they want to be fed. Believe it or not, most babies will even let you sleep through the night again—eventually.

ANY BEST PATTERNS FOR ONCE THE BREASTMILK ITSELF COMES IN?

As the mature milk comes in (at approximately day four) and the baby begins to suck longer, he will increase those feedings gradually. Continue to offer your breast frequently, and let your baby tell you when he wants to feed (he may not have read the same books you did). Look for early signs of interest: the baby putting his hand to his mouth, making sucking sounds, or rooting for (trying to find) a nipple. These hunger cues help you recognize his need and lessen the frustration and difficulty with latching that often comes a short time later when your baby is crying to be fed.

That unscheduled, frequent pattern usually works. Offer to feed when he seems hungry or you think he might be. You can further this by not offering a pacifier or other feedings of water or formula (it's best not to use a pacifier for a month or more) and by ensuring your own fluid supply by drinking plenty of fluids (a good way to remember is a glass of water or other fluid at the time of each breast-feeding). When the techniques and patterning don't work, you needn't give up. My suggestion is to place the baby on one breast for five to seven minutes, then transfer the baby to the other breast, allowing him to take as much as he desires there, assuring the baby gets the hindmilk from the second breast to fill him comfortably.

This schedule takes advantage of several physiological factors. First, most of the milk is expressed from each breast in the first few minutes, with dimin-ished quantities available to the infant after that. Second, emptying one breast completely promotes more milk production than only partially emptying both breasts. And finally, the last part of the milk (the hindmilk) in each breast contains more fat and is part of the reason that breastfed infants are satisfied and tired at the end of their feedings.

Thus, a five-minute feeding on one side gets most of the milk, but milk that is low in fat, so the baby will remain awake and not need to be stimulated. Feeding on the other side will then promote more milk, an adequate supply in general, and should produce a full and satisfied customer. Should the baby still be hungry, you can progressively lengthen the time spent on the first breast. If he doesn't stay on the second breast long, then you will want to reverse the process, going longer on the first breast to get the hindmilk of that breast, then letting him finish off on the second side.

Attaching a safety pin to the bra strap on the side where you finished nursing will help you to remember where to begin the next feeding. You should try to alternate between breasts when you start feedings unless you have sore nipples or mastitis (discussed later). And do know that your *letdown reflex* is variable. At times you will begin expressing milk even before the baby latches on; at other times, it may take a few minutes for milk to begin flowing.

Please note that my suggestion differs from that of many lactation experts, who will continue to press on with frequent feedings, feeling that your baby will eventually get the hang of it. I offer mine as an alternative, since I have seen it work well in the rare situation when the other approach fails.

You can judge if your baby is getting enough by inspecting his diapers. By the third or fourth day, he should have six or more wet diapers. And most babies will have three dirty diapers a day, though that can vary considerably. (Please see the section on bowel movements; if you still have questions, there's an entire chapter on bowel movements titled "Pooping Problems." Please don't be embarrassed; poop is one of those subjects I talk about all day in my practice—lucky me.)

HOW FREQUENTLY SHOULD I NURSE?

The La Leche League is an organization that promotes breastfeeding and serves as an excellent resource for the nursing mother with problems or questions.[2] They encourage breastfeeding whenever the baby appears to be hungry, "on demand," whenever that is, in order to satisfy the baby.

My own feelings differ slightly. I am concerned with the mother not having enough milk—for several reasons. First, prolactin, one of the major hormones that stimulate milk production, apparently has a recycling time of 2½ hours.[3] This time between feedings appears necessary for adequate milk production. Second, mothers who are feeding their infants every hour or two for an extended period have complained to me of exhaustion and frustration. They feel as if their infants are always hungry. Their own fatigue alone is enough to diminish milk supply. As a result, their babies are, in fact, often hungry.

A cycle develops. The baby is hungry and fed. Two hours later, the baby cries and is fed again. But the baby is not full because the hormones haven't recycled or the mother is tired. And when the baby is fed again two hours later, he is still not full and demands to be fed more and more.

The mother may not recognize the problem, or may not be able to, because the infant is feeding as long or longer than previously (and trying to drain every drop). She becomes progressively more exhausted trying to meet the baby's needs. If the baby has older siblings who have their own needs, the mother's exhaustion can reach catastrophic proportions.

Do not automatically assume this cycle is occurring; you can check. Write down when you are feeding the baby and for how long. Babies can have cluster feedings, taking the breast every hour or two for a period, then sleeping longer. You do want to get in at least 8 to 12 feedings during those early months and generally to feed at intervals of 2½ to 3 hours. If you are doing that and still tired, you may need to look at your own schedule and determine whether your exhaustion is because your life is loaded when you are not feeding the baby or you're not sleeping for other reasons. If possible, make the needed adjustments, though that can require help from your husband or your own doctor.

Most importantly, look at the baby's weight gain. After the baby's first few days, when babies typically lose weight, your infant should be gaining at least half an ounce each day. Moreover, you should be able to see an appreciable weight gain in the baby if he is weighed (with the same diaper and clothes) before and after a feeding. If the baby is not gaining weight well or not urinating frequently, a feeding problem may exist. The usual problem is similar to the one I have just described.

The solution is simple. During the first few weeks, put the baby to the breast whenever he seems hungry. Once your milk flow is established, try to maintain a 2½- to 4-hour feeding schedule (still on demand). If your baby is wailing before that, the baby is often not hungry—just uncomfortable. Changing his diapers or cuddling the baby will often help. If the baby is over a month old, a pacifier can be offered. If the baby is not soothed, give the baby a few ounces of water (or 1 ounce of water with 1 teaspoon apple juice—but only if he will not drink plain water) *just one time* to try to reset his feeding intervals. The intent is that the bottle will hold him off for a brief while. Then he will usually be hungrier at the next feeding, get more hindmilk, and extend the interval between feedings slightly, giving you an opportunity to make more milk and give him more nutrition in the process.

You will still have the work of giving the baby that water bottle (unless you are able to coax someone else into doing it), but your own body's stores can be replenished and enough milk can be produced.

Do check your diet to make sure it is adequate for both you and the baby—particularly your fluid intake and nutritional balance. And try also to save a little time in your day for your own relaxation. Taking care of a newborn can be time-consuming, and if your energy is depleted by other responsibilities as well, remember that the only way you can take care of your baby is if you also take care of yourself. If you do not see an improvement in a day or two, do see your pediatrician as soon as possible to check the baby's hydration and for any underlying problem.

IF THE BABY GOES BEYOND FOUR HOURS, SHOULD I WAKE HIM?

In the early weeks of life, when you are trying to establish your milk flow, and even later if the baby is having difficulty gaining weight, you should wake the baby and then feed, whether he's breast- or bottle-fed. Once a good feeding pattern is established and he is gaining weight well, allow the baby to sleep as long as possible through the night (which generally occurs at three to four months of age, whether solids are added or not). But during the day, wake the baby if five hours pass between feedings. Again, go by the baby's urine output and weight gain: stimulate him at five hours (massaging his back or providing skin-to-skin contact). If he is lagging in either his urine production or gaining weight, wake him at 3½ to 4 hours. If you have any concern, or if you're not sure about how the baby is gaining, consult your baby's primary care provider.

WHAT IF I HAVE TWINS (OR MORE)?

First of all, further congratulations on having a successful pregnancy and delivery. Often, multiple births are delivered earlier, so you may want to read the section on premature infants as well (chapter 11). If the babies are in the intensive care area, your best choice for breastfeeding will be to pump and store your breastmilk so it can be used when they are ready to begin feedings. The neonatologist may arrange for it to be dripped slowly through a tube into their stomachs, depending on their general condition.

When your doctors think it is advisable to begin breastfeeding directly, alternate the breast you feed each one (again, the bra strap safety pin will identify which breast you fed Johnny so that he will go to the other breast the next time and Joanna will go to that one).

As you will probably hear repeatedly, maintain good fluid intake, nutrition, and sleep so that you can provide sufficient feedings for them and maintain your own health to continue their care. Also, please recognize that you may need to use a formula to supplement your milk. If they are premature, you will need a milk fortifier to adapt your milk to their needs (discussed in more detail in chapter 11). Some mothers do well feeding twins, with sufficient milk for both, but you will rarely be able to feed triplets or more with your breastmilk alone.

DO I NEED TO STOP BREASTFEEDING IF I HAVE A COLD OR VIRUS?

If you have a high fever or significant infection, stored breastmilk or formula can be used. Do note, however, that you generally do not have to stop breastfeeding if you have a cold or flu symptoms without fever—and some experts feel that breastfeeding through a viral infection can actually help the baby. The baby was already exposed to the virus when it was tracking through your body, even before you developed the runny nose and cough, and the antibodies your own body develops will pass to the baby, assisting him in fighting the infection, so it is often better if you can continue to breastfeed.

SHOULD SUPPLEMENTS AND SUBSTITUTES BE AVOIDED?

Supplements of water or formula are useful in several selective situations. As indicated, the child who wishes to feed more frequently can be given a water bottle occasionally to extend the time between feedings to see if the longer interval will allow you more milk production. The exception is in the first few days of life; then you should put the infant to the breast whenever he seems hungry because the stimulation will help to establish your milk production and to produce the syrupy colostrum that will provide immune benefits for your baby.

Formula should not be used as a substitute for water. Even water is rarely needed. And while water usually will not interfere with the infant's appetite if it is given an hour or so before a regular feeding, formula will suppress the baby's feeding interest. The protein and fat in the formula will slow the stomach's emptying and will satiate the infant in a manner similar to breastmilk, so the baby may not be hungry for the next feeding.

For that reason, if you are not opposed to using formula, it can be substituted for a regular feeding and is an acceptable substitute in almost all situations (if you don't have stored breastmilk): if the baby has prolonged jaundice from breastmilk (discussed in more detail below), if weight gain is not adequate, if you are working, or even if you want or need to be away from the baby during a feeding (especially for a restful evening out occasionally, which is my personal prescription for new and old parents alike).

For most infants, a routine, cow's-milk-based formula will work as a substitute for a breastmilk feeding. For an infant from a family with a significant history of allergies or a baby with reflux or any number of problems, this book will help you understand and choose the right formula, so please refer to the section(s) appropriate to your infant.

Particularly for breastfed infants, the best and most cost-sensitive version for supplementing are the powdered forms, no matter which actual formula is used. Until mixed, the powdered forms are stable and do not become contaminated easily, though they are still more likely to become contaminated than the other varieties (so please read that section in chapter 4). Since small, occasional amounts are all that are used for breastfeeding supplementation, the powders can be prepared as needed and do not lead to the waste and expense that occurs when opening a can of liquid concentrate or ready-to-feed formula, as the unused portion (once the baby has put his mouth on the bottle) or any formula made from the powders should be discarded within 24 hours.

ISN'T STORED BREASTMILK PREFERRED?

Properly stored breastmilk is preferred, if available. Breastmilk can be expressed and stored when your milk exceeds the baby's demands (such as at the end of a feeding or when you are engorged) or when you are at work.

To express breastmilk, the entire breast can even be massaged downward toward the nipple, eventually bringing the thumb and forefinger around the areola. Manual suction pumps are inexpensive, but they are only a little more effective and occasionally difficult to operate. They should be meticulously cleansed or sterilized between use, per the manufacturer's instructions.

Electric pumps are often more productive, quicker, and easy to use (again, they should be cleaned according to the manufacturer's recommendations). They may be particularly worthwhile if you are returning to work or if you delivered a premature infant who requires a prolonged hospitalization. Several videos (by Stanford[4] and Ameda[5]) are now available that show you how to hand-express after (or in place of) pumping, producing several ounces more even after using an electric pump.

Since your baby will not be giving you normal stimulation to begin your flow, you will want to time your expressing to when you are feeling full. Pleasant thoughts of the baby, a picture, or something with his scent is often enough to bring on a letdown response. You can use a warm compress, gentle massage, or just a few minutes of quiet relaxation, and usually you will be able to begin.

The milk is best stored in plastic nursing bags, since the immune cells in breastmilk are thought to adhere to glass bottles. (This may be an area of mild controversy since some milk banks have now returned to glass.) Remember to carefully label the container with the date, swirl it to mix the fatty cream with the rest, provide enough room in the container for the breastmilk to expand once it freezes, and again tighten the cap if you are using a bottle. Place the milk in the back of the freezer. See table 3.1 below for storage guidelines.

Table 3.1. Storage Guidelines for Breastmilk

Location	Temperature	Duration	Comments
Countertop	Room temperature	6–8 hours	Must be covered
Insulated cooler	5–39°F or –15–4°C	24 hours	Keep with ice packs
Refrigerator	39°F or 4°C	5 days	Keep at the back of fridge; use oldest first
Freezer compartment of refrigerator	5°F or –15°C	2 weeks	Store at back of freezer where temperature is more constant
Freezer compartment of refrigerator with separate doors	0°F or –18°C	3–6 months	
Deep freezer	–4°F or –20°C	6–12 months	

Source: Bailey Koch, RD, CSP, www.nutrition4kids.com.

CAN I MICROWAVE FROZEN BREASTMILK?

Microwaving can create hot spots that can burn the baby's mouth. It's best to place frozen breastmilk in the refrigerator overnight to allow it to thaw. If you can't do that, run warm water over the container or allow the container to sit in warm water to bring it to room temperature.

Use the thawed breastmilk within 24 hours, and do not refreeze. It's often best for milk goddesses who make buckets of breastmilk to store the milk in portion sizes of 2 to 4 ounces.

HOW WILL I KNOW IF MY BREASTMILK IS ADEQUATE, AND IF IT IS NOT, WHAT CAN I DO?

This is a far greater concern for most women than it is an actual problem. Rare is the woman whose breastmilk is not adequate for her child. And according to the World Health Organization, only 2 percent of the women who breastfeed have difficulty in doing so.[6] Yet well over 60 to 70 percent of the new mothers I see are concerned.

You can maintain your confidence knowing that breastfeeding is the most naturally nurturing experience for both you and the baby, but it is a learned skill. Breastfeeding at the outset often requires a (brief) learning period for you and the baby, with both of you getting used to the process. You have a number of resources available to you, personally or through educational material on the Internet (see "Resources"). If it still seems too confusing or overwhelming, ask your or your baby's primary care provider to help or to refer you to a supportive lactation consultant. However, if breastfeeding is not fulfilling and comfortable, with the adequate alternatives that are available, there is no need to continue to do something that you find unpleasant or exceedingly difficult.

Physically, there are several things you can do to help yourself gain success in breastfeeding. The most obvious is to drink plenty of liquids, maintain an adequate diet, continue to take your prenatal vitamins (as recommended by your doctor), and if your intake of fish is minimal, take a docosahexaenoic acid (DHA) supplement. The nutritional aspect, however, is far less important than simply establishing a pattern of frequent nursing, particularly in the first few days with your infant. Nothing will stimulate the hormones and secrete as much milk as simply having the baby's suction at your breast. So if it is at all possible, maintain availability to your infant and let the nurses know your desire to have the infant accessible to you while you are still in the hospital. Birthing hospitals and women's centers are quite sensitive to this and will accommodate and support your efforts. And, of course, continue that same pattern once you are at home.

Again, an adequate milk supply can be achieved easily for most mother-baby pairs on an "on-demand" feeding basis. That is, feed the baby when he is hungry and demands it (approximately every two to three hours in those first few days). If your infant requires additional care in the nursery, however, and he cannot stimulate your breasts, numerous alternatives are available, including the manual and electric suction pumps already discussed.

The addition of rest and relaxation will enhance your ability to have a positive letdown reflex, which will help the milk flow more readily to your infant as well. Therefore, make sure you take care of your infant and yourself during his first days of life and limit visitors and other commitments, if necessary.

Should feedings still be slow in establishing themselves in the first few days, supplementation with an infant formula may be appropriate. The decision to provide this support should be made in conjunction with your pediatrician or primary care provider and will most probably be made on the basis of your infant's weight gain and state of hydration. When supplementation is required, it should immediately follow breastfeeding and should only occur if the infant is still hungry. When these feedings take place more than an hour after your breastfeeding, they can fill the baby up and interfere with the baby's interest in feeding the next time he is brought to your breast.

If you are one of the mothers for whom the problem of inadequate milk supply continues, your physician may recommend beer (an old remedy) or herbal tea (along with a relaxed time to drink it) or prescribe metaclopramide (Reglan), domperidone (not available in the United States), or another *galactogue* (breastmilk stimulant) to stimulate milk flow. These medications may be successful when all else fails. Usually, they are needed only temporarily to bring forth an appropriate letdown reflex, and they allow you to feed the baby as originally intended. The Academy of Breastfeeding Medicine is not convinced that enough solid evidence justifies their use, but for the brief time they are needed, it is at least a consideration to discuss with your primary care provider.

WHAT IF I HAVE AN OVERSUPPLY OF BREASTMILK?

Breastmilk goddesses[7] who have more than ample milk are the envy of those who have struggled with the opposite problem. But they, too, have challenges and concerns. The simplest solution is to feed the baby entirely on one side at a feeding and express the other side if you are experiencing discomfort. Try to feed at the first signs of your baby's hunger and use a position where he gets the fullest flow. If that flow is too rapid at the beginning and he has some gagging when the milk lets down, you can either express the first portion or slow the flow with your first two fingers, forming a valve above and below the areola and nipple.

HOW SHOULD I TAKE CARE OF MY NIPPLES AND BREASTS?

Fortunately for the breastfeeding mother, the containers themselves are sterile and quite portable. And the recommendations are now much more relaxed than they used to be. The skin needs to be cleansed well. Bathing once a day should keep your breasts clean, and some say that is all that is needed because the *Montgomery glands* (around the edge of the areola) moisturize the area. If you are at home, you can wash your nipples and areola with warm water before and after each feeding. If you are out, you generally don't need to do so, and you can begin the feeding immediately rather than waiting and frustrating your baby. In all cases, avoid alcohol or drying agents, including soaps that remove natural oils and cause chafing or cracking. Breastmilk reportedly helps heal sore nipples, so you can rub a few drops on your nipples after each feeding and let them dry before putting your bra back on.

Between feedings, nursing pads, sterile gauze, or cloth may be placed against the breast inside your bra or blouse to keep the nipples and breast dry. This too will reduce chapping and cracking. If problems develop, do not hesitate to call upon your obstetrician.

Should your nipples become cracked, make sure that they are kept dry after feedings. When you end a feeding, you can slip your finger in alongside the nipple into the baby's mouth to break the suction; otherwise the baby will continue to suck as you are pulling him off your breast, and this may engorge the tip. Purelan or Lansinoh creams or any other lanolin-like substance may help the nipple feel more comfortable. If the feeding time is nearly equal on both breasts, begin your feedings on the less sore nipple, but do not avoid the affected breast in your feedings.

CAN I DO ANYTHING ABOUT FLAT, SMALL, OR INVERTED NIPPLES?

Quite frankly, your baby probably won't notice. Many infants will latch onto the breast even if a nipple is not present at all. Just make sure that the baby's mouth is well around the areola so that he can get good suction. Should that not be effective, soft, silicone nipple shields can often be used. Most often, the shields are a temporary measure, with the baby able to go back to the breast when he becomes more competent at sucking and is able to stimulate a greater flow. A certified lactation consultant can be a great resource if breastfeeding is difficult.

WHAT IF I HAVE HAD BREAST SURGERY?

Breast surgery does not usually interfere with milk production, supply, or delivery. Breast augmentation is done under the breast tissue and is not a problem unless there has been silicone leakage that can interfere with the function of the baby's esophagus, which is one of the reasons silicone is now rarely used. Breast reduction usually leaves the glands' duct structure intact, so most often breastfeeding can be done, assuming the nipple was moved only a short distance (or not at all) and the ducts to it were left attached.

WHAT IS MASTITIS, AND WHAT CAN BE DONE?

Mastitis signifies inflammation within the breast that usually comes from engorgement—stored milk that is unable to drain. This process often begins with plugged ducts and leads to caking, with greater pressure against the other ducts that drain the breast. Inflammation and swelling are the result. The treatment for this in the 1950s was to lessen the breastfeedings on that side and allow the inflammation to subside. However, it is now recognized that the inflammation is due to prolonged blockage in the ducts caused by the milk itself.

Therefore, this milk is best drained on a regular basis by placing the infant to that breast even more frequently. Should that not relieve the developing tension, the milk can be expressed between feedings or before the next feeding to prevent further obstruction from developing. Taking hot showers or massaging your breasts with warm, wet towels will help the milk flow and temporarily relieve the pain from the engorgement, but pain medications such as ibuprofen (Motrin) or acetaminophen (Tylenol) are occasionally required. However, if redness develops or the condition doesn't quickly resolve, see your doctor as soon as possible, since you can be harboring a resistant bacteria or an abscess that needs attention and possibly an antibiotic.

WILL BREASTFEEDING PREVENT CANCER OR CHANGE THE BREAST'S SHAPE?

Women who breastfeed for at least six months are at a decreased risk of developing certain types of breast, uterine, and ovarian cancer. Breastfeeding also does not cause breasts to sag in later years—age and pregnancy alone seem to be enough to cause weakening of the tissue supporting the breast.

HOW CAN A WORKING, BREASTFEEDING MOTHER MANAGE BEST?

You may have to get up earlier to breastfeed prior to leaving for work (but you would also have to get up to fix bottles or make breakfast for your baby). Formula or stored breastmilk can be provided while the baby is at day care or with a sitter. Most likely, you will need to pump your breast while at work. Federal law enacted in March 2010 now requires that work environments provide reasonable time and a private place other than a bathroom so that this can be easily accomplished.[8] You will need a place to store the milk safely (see table 3.1). Then you can return home in the evening and breastfeed once again. And if you can, please try to find some time for yourself to relax (with your significant other, if possible) and recuperate.

AM I ABLE TO DIET WHILE BREASTFEEDING?

Breastfeeding is an excellent way to lose the 10 extra pounds most women retain after their pregnancy. If you consider that 500 to 900 calories are used each day to supply milk to your baby, that is equivalent to running 5½ miles or one hour of constant jump roping (for a 150-pound person to burn 700 calories).[9]

Some of those calories come from the food you eat, but if you maintain your normal eating pattern (drinking only an extra glass or two of milk each day to maintain your calcium supply), you should begin to lose approximately 1 pound per week. You should try to restrict yourself to losing no more than that, since you, the baby, or both may suffer. Note that when drinking fluids, excess sugars in soft drinks, sports drinks, and juices do add extra calories, so you might want to limit these.

To make sure that neither of you have any ill effects from your attention to your own weight, you should have your baby weighed every two weeks initially to ensure an adequate weight gain (of at least a ½ ounce per day or approximately 1 pound per month), and you should have your own doctor monitor your weight as well as your vitamin, iron, and calcium supplements.

Dietary restrictions have changed over the years. Diets for mothers used to seem as limited as their infants'. But only rarely is that necessary. Yes, the breast serves as a conduit from mother to infant, and many of the nutrients and chemicals the mother ingests can cross to and affect the baby. How your baby is affected then dictates what you can eat.

For most infants, garlic and spices in your food will have little effect. And you can eat anything since what you eat and drink stays in your system and does not affect the baby. Yet there are other babies who are sensitive to anything in their mother's diet—including milk. Therefore, if your baby is placid, you needn't worry about what you eat—unless you notice some upset every time you eat a certain food (hopefully, not chocolate or whatever else you love). This is truly different for different mother-baby pairs. Reactions to a particular food can occur from within a few minutes to within 24 hours, with a rash, irritability, vomiting, or a change in behavior showing up whenever the baby has that same food.

If your baby is colicky, and you are breastfeeding, sometimes you can relieve some of the baby's irritability by restricting your diet. Gassy foods, particularly gas-producing vegetables (such as cabbage, broccoli, cauliflower, and mushrooms), and gassy drinks (sodas, beer, and champagne) upset many babies, so consider eliminating those first. If that doesn't make a difference, you can add them back into your diet.

Correlate your baby's behavior with what you eat. If your infant is far fussier than usual just hours after you've eaten onions (for example), you might want to avoid onions for several days. Then try a small amount of onions again. If the baby becomes fussy again, you should avoid them for a while. If your baby is frequently fussy, consider the foods you eat daily, particularly milk and dairy products (not including eggs, only foods made from milk), especially if you drink large quantities of milk. Avoid milk for several days (while keeping calcium levels high with cheese and greens), and see if there is any improvement. If not, eliminate cheese as well, particularly if it has been a significant part of your own intake. But it may not be dairy or gassy foods. Other babies are sensitive to eggs, soy, or wheat in their mother's diets, though admittedly these sensitivities are far rarer.

You can have coffee or other caffeinated drinks, but in limited quantity (two to three cups per day). More of either and the extra sugar or caffeine might cause the baby to be fussy. Alcohol is also best limited and should not be consumed closer than two hours before a feeding or pumping session.

DOES A BREASTFEEDING MOTHER NEED SUPPLEMENTAL VITAMINS?

Even though the baby starts off only taking a walnut-size portion (1 ounce) of breastmilk at a week old, the average breastfeeding mother will be providing her infant with approximately 20 to 30 ounces of milk daily between one and six months of age.[10] The breastmilk will contain protein, fat, carbohydrates, calcium, iron, vitamins, and minerals. Yet the average mother's diet will have very little impact on her breastmilk or the baby (except for vitamins). If her own diet lacks protein or calcium, her infant generally will not suffer—he will receive all he needs as long as the mother is not having a critical shortage. Instead, the mother will deplete her own body's stores to provide for the infant. So unless she wants to become nutritionally deficient, a mother should eat a well-balanced diet with emphasis on protein, calcium, and iron.

Protein needs are easily met, but the calcium requirements (see calcium table 15.8 in chapter 15) are difficult to achieve if a woman is not particularly interested in dairy products—mainly because the calcium in green vegetables is often bound by the fibrous parts of the vegetable. However, a breastfeeding mother can compensate with a calcium supplement if need be. Iron, too, may be a problem in the woman who had a great deal of blood loss during her delivery.

All of these requirements (except perhaps iron) can be met by a nutritious, well-balanced diet. Most vitamin needs can be similarly met (see table 3.2), with the exception of vitamin D (please read this section in chapter 15 and see table 15.6). If they are not, a prenatal multivitamin with adequate iron should protect both the mother and her infant. Additionally, a DHA supplement of 200 milligrams per day has been recommended for mothers who don't eat three servings of fish per week (in order to enhance neurological and immune development, as discussed in chapter 4). The requirements (expressed as DRI, which stands for *Dietary Reference Intakes*) are considered standard. They have been issued since 1997 by the Institute of Medicine, with numerous revisions thereafter, the most recent reflecting a greater understanding of the need for increased vitamin D.[11]

Vegan mothers should also take vitamin B_{12} supplements when breastfeeding, since they might not have sufficient amounts of that vitamin in their diet or routine supplements. And mothers who have chronic illnesses that create nutrient losses or problems with absorption should discuss their desire to breastfeed, in their particular situation, with their physicians in order to discuss their own nutritional needs.

What to Feed Your Baby

Table 3.2. Daily Dietary Requirements for the Breastfeeding Mother[a]

Nutrient (Unit of Measure)	Normal DRI (19–50 Years Old)	Lactating DRI (>19 Years Old)
Energy (cal.)	2,000	2,500
Protein (g)	46	71
Vitamin A (IU)	700	1,300
Vitamin B_1, thiamine (mg)	1.1	1.4
Vitamin B_2, riboflavin (mg)	1.1	1.6
Vitamin B_6, pyridoxine (mg)	1.3	2.0
Vitamin B_{12}, cobalamin (µg)	2.4	2.8
Vitamin C (mg)	75	120
Vitamin D (IU)	600	600
Vitamin E (mg)	15	19
Vitamin K (µg)	90	90
Niacin (mg)	14	17
Pantothenic acid (mg)	5	7
Folate (µg)	400	500
Biotin (µg)	30	35
Choline (mg)	425	550
Calcium (mg)	1,000	1,000
Iodine (mg)	150	290
Iron (mg)	18	9
Magnesium (mg)	310–320	310–320
Phosphorus (mg)	700	700
Zinc (mg)	8	13

DRI = Dietary Reference Intakes; cal. = calorie; g = gram; IU = International Unit; mg = milligram (1/1000g); µg = microgram (1/1,000,000g).

[a]Established by the Institute of Medicine of the National Academies of Science and Health Canada. Please refer to chapter 15 for more information on the individual recommendations (particularly for vitamin D, calcium, and iron).

Source: Adapted from J. J. Otten, J. P. Hellwig, and L. D. Meyers, eds., *Dietary Reference Intakes: The Essential Guide to Nutrient Requirements* (Washington, DC: National Academies Press, 2006), with updated recommendations 2010 incorporated.

DOES THE BABY NEED VITAMIN DROPS?

For a long time, it appeared that human milk was lacking in some essential elements and vitamins. The concentration of iron, zinc, and vitamin D did not appear to meet what had been described as an infant's minimum daily requirement (table 3.3). However, more recent studies have proven nature right regarding the minerals. But science is just beginning to understand the full importance of vitamin D and that we have been underestimating the babies' needs for vitamin D (with all the vitamins and minerals discussed in chapter 15). As a result, the nutritional recommendations for infants have been updated (table 3.3). The concept of a daily requirement is easily understandable. Basically, an individual at a particular age needs to eat a certain amount of some food or nutrient in order to maintain his metabolism and keep a slight bit for storage. Additionally, infants, children, and teens need to include what is necessary for growth, and pregnant and lactating women need to have an amount added for what they are sharing with their babies. If everything that a person eats is absorbed, then 100 percent of the nutrient is available and usable. But if half of what she eats is not digested and passes out in the stool (and is thus not *bioavailable*), then she needs to eat twice the amount recommended in order to absorb an adequate quantity.

Table 3.3. Nutritional Recommendations for the First Year of Life

Nutrient (Unit of Measure)	Infants 0–6 Months Old	Infants 7–12 Months Old
Protein, g	9.1	11.0
Fat, g	31	30
Carbohydrate, g	60	95
Vitamin A, IU	1,350	1,700
Vitamin D, IU	400	400
Vitamin E, IU	6	8
Vitamin K, μg	2	2.5
Vitamin B$_1$ (thiamine), mg	0.2	0.3
Vitamin B$_2$ (riboflavin), mg	0.3	0.4
Vitamin B$_6$ (pyridoxine), mg	0.1	0.3
Vitamin B$_{12}$ (cobalamin), μg	0.7	1.0
Niacin, mg	2	4
Folic acid, mcg	65	80
Pantothenic acid, mg	1.7	1.8
Biotin, μg	5	6
Vitamin C (ascorbic acid), mg	40	50
Calcium, mg	210	270
Phosphorus, mg	100	275
Magnesium, mg	30	75
Iron, mg	0.27	11
Zinc, mg	2	3
Manganese, mcg	0.003	0.6
Copper, μg	200	220
Sodium, g	0.12	0.37
Potassium, g	0.4	0.7
Selenium, μg	15	20

Source: Adapted from J. J. Otten, J. P. Hellwig, and L. D. Meyers, eds., *Dietary Reference Intakes: The Essential Guide to Nutrient Requirements* (Washington, DC: National Academies Press, 2006).

Let us look briefly at the case of iron in the infant, where the iron's availability becomes important. The recommendation currently states that a seven-month-old infant should receive 11 milligrams of iron daily. This is based on the fact that only a small amount is actually absorbed. Only 4 percent of iron in commercial formulas enters the system. Therefore, at the usual concentration of 12 milligrams per quart of formula, 0.5 milligrams of iron is actually absorbed. Human milk contains an even smaller amount of iron, an average of only 1.4 milligrams per quart. If 4 percent of this were absorbed (as was previously assumed), the infant would certainly be deficient in iron, receiving a tenth of what is provided by the formula. However, the iron in breastmilk is more readily available, and roughly half is absorbed, providing an adequate 0.7 milligrams to the baby. Similarly, zinc appears to have a greater availability in human milk than in other sources and is present in adequate quantities.

The situation with vitamin D is different. While the well-nourished mother can provide most vitamins to her infant, little vitamin D is in breastmilk, even when the mother is taking a multivitamin. As a result, the American Academy of Pediatrics Committee on Nutrition suggests 400 IU of vitamin D be given daily.[12] I actually recommend more (as you'll understand from the discussion in chapter 15). We used to get some of that vitamin D from the sun, with the ultraviolet rays converting cholesterol into usable vitamin D. But that had little benefit for young or dark-skinned infants and those living in the northern part of the United States or northern Europe. And now that we use high skin-protection-factor sunscreens to ward off skin cancer, we limit skin-produced vitamin D.

According to the American Academy of Pediatrics, fluoride supplementation is not recommended in babies less than six months old. Babies older than six months only require supplementation if they live in an area where the drinking water contains less than 0.3 parts per million of fluoride.

WHAT ARE TYPICAL BOWEL MOVEMENTS OF BREASTFED INFANTS?

The bowel movements of babies fed human milk vary considerably. Usually they are yellow to brown and slightly watery, but they may contain small "seeds." Occasionally they are green and still normal. Most babies have many bowel movements each day, often one after each feeding (because emptying of food from the stomach causes the rest of the intestine to contract and expel the waste). I actually find it humorous that manufacturers not only want to simulate breastmilk with their formulas but even want their formulas to re-create the soft, seedy, frequent bowel movements that breastmilk typically produces.

An older breastfed infant may rarely have very infrequent bowel movements, even once a week or every 10 days. There is no cause for alarm as long as the stools remain soft and show no blood. Most likely, this is caused by breastmilk that is extremely well absorbed, leaving little residue or breastmilk with a high fat content, which slows the intestine down. The key again is that the stools remain soft and the baby isn't uncomfortable in between evacuations. Suppositories are usually not necessary, since this is a short-term situation that will change when solids are added to the diet because they create more waste material, resulting in more frequent bowel movements. If you have any questions or continued concerns, however, see your pediatrician or the baby's primary care provider, since he or she can evaluate the baby and arrange a test of your breastmilk (a "creamatocrit") for fat content, though this old measurement is not readily available and sometimes hard to interpret.

WHAT IF BLOOD IS PRESENT?

The quantity of blood and texture of the stool are signs your baby's primary care provider will want to understand and correlate with the baby's age and physical examination in order to make an accurate assessment. Firm stools are relatively infrequent for the breastfed infant; when they occur with a few drops or strands of blood, the hard stool may have torn an area in the rectum or anus (that torn area is called a *fissure*), producing a painful bowel movement with blood on the outside of the stool (see chapter 8).

When blood is present and the stool is soft, the provider will have many more possible causes to sort through. Infection, bleeding disorders, and anatomic or intestinal abnormalities have to be considered, but these problems are usually associated with very loose stools, much more blood, or a significant decline in the baby's condition (with the baby less active, irritable, or not eating well)—in which case, you should see your doctor or call to find out if your provider wants you to go to a nearby emergency room.

The far more common situation is that the baby is otherwise healthy or perhaps a little more irritable, passing a few specks of blood in an otherwise normal, seedy stool. Those specks are often indicative of a substance crossing your breastmilk that is not being tolerated by the baby's gastrointestinal tract. This is not a true allergy to your breastmilk or to the offending protein but what is referred to as food-protein-induced enterocolitis syndrome (FPIES). The symptoms can be mild, as described, or much more severe: the baby can become listless with vomiting and severe diarrhea as well, prompting an emergency room visit.

The most frequent offender is cow's milk crossing the mother's breast. Removing all sources of dairy in the mother's diet (milk, cheese, yogurt, butter, and ice cream) usually resolves the situation, though a small amount of blood can be found up to two weeks later. There is an argument about whether foods that have a small amount of milk products cooked in them (pastries and breads, for example) need to be excluded. I will exclude them for a few days until the infant's intestine settles down; then I allow the mother to gradually add these cooked or baked foods back in, though I still recommend that she restrict foods (such as puddings and sauces) with a higher content of cooked milk.

However, cow's milk is not the only food causing an FPIES reaction. Occasionally other foods can be implicated as well. Soy, eggs, wheat, shellfish, and nuts are among the next most common foods to cause problems, though rice and other foods can also irritate the intestine in this manner. The severity of the bleeding and the child's condition will determine how extensive the initial elimination should be. If a single food can be isolated at the start of symptoms, it may be all that is restricted. Occasionally, a wider elimination is required at the onset, and then foods are individually added back to the mother's diet. However, the presence of this condition should signal to the mother that when it's time to introduce solids into the child's diet (see chapters 13 and 14), the foods should be added cautiously and with the pediatrician's or a pediatric gastroenterologist's input.

WHAT IF AN OLDER INFANT HAS POOR SUCTION OR LITTLE INTEREST IN FEEDING?

The first thing to consider is the scheduling. If the infant is not on a demand schedule but is simply being fed on a routine basis, the conversion to periods when he is most actively interested may easily alleviate this problem. If, despite this, the baby still seems disinterested, you should be certain that someone is not giving the baby water or formula prior to your time for breastfeeding. If the baby is still in the hospital for any reason, check whether the baby is getting anything other than breastmilk and why. It may be necessary. But if it isn't, the other feedings may be hampering the baby's interest.

If the baby is not receiving other feedings, it would be advisable to contact your pediatrician in order for him or her to examine the baby to alleviate any concerns about the baby's health or alertness. The baby may be developing reflux or an infection that is interfering with his normal, healthy appetite.

WHAT SHOULD BE DONE IF THE BABY DEVELOPS THRUSH?

Thrush is simply a yeast infection in the baby's mouth, usually seen as a white cake on the tongue and along the insides of the cheeks. It often comes shortly after a baby has been on an antibiotic for an infection, but it may develop on its own in the baby's mouth or with a bright red rash around his bottom. Milk looks somewhat the same, but thrush will not come off when you rub it with your finger or the back of a spoon.

If thrush is present, your pediatrician will prescribe an antifungal solution to be placed in the baby's mouth for several days, and you may need a similar product in the cream or ointment for your breasts after each feeding. This prevents the yeast from transferring back and forth between your breast and your baby's mouth, causing another bout of thrush or diarrhea. Make sure you wash the ointment off with soap before putting the baby to the breast, since the emollients may leave a residue that the baby could ingest.

WHAT IS BREASTMILK JAUNDICE AND WHY DOES IT DEVELOP?

Jaundice is a frequent characteristic of the newborn period. The newborn's liver is not fully developed at birth, particularly for transporting and storing the normal products of red blood cell breakdown. In everyone, the red blood cells age and their proteins and iron break down, with one of the fragments metabolized by the liver into bilirubin, which is then delivered to the gallbladder and into the intestinal tract.

With the delay in the development of the newborn liver, the bilirubin accumulates, causing many babies to become jaundiced, particularly those who have had an excessive amount of red blood cell breakdown due to traumatic birth, blood incompatibility between the infant and the mother, or even from blood that is swallowed during birth. This is generally expected at two to three days of age, gradually disappears in a week or so, and is not considered a problem. For this reason, the jaundice is termed *physiologic.*

Breastfed infants may have additional reasons for jaundice as well. Some mothers' breastmilk contains hormones or fat particles that interfere with the uptake and transportation of the bilirubin that is formed. Moreover, the limited supply of breastmilk available in the first day or two of life decreases bowel movements (the normal elimination route for bilirubin). As a result, more of the bilirubin has a chance to be absorbed again by the intestine and transported back to the liver, so that an excessive load may be present not only from the continued breakdown of red blood cells but from recycled bilirubin as well. This is generally not dangerous. With the use of fluorescent and blue lights, doctors are usually able to prevent any complications from developing. The lights break down the bilirubin that stains the skin, giving it that yellow jaundice color. You, too, can aid the effort by feeding the baby frequently to stimulate better stool elimination of the bilirubin and to prevent dehydration, which the high-intensity lights can contribute to as well.

Breastmilk jaundice is the term for a high bilirubin level that continues for several weeks. It often can be interrupted (though there is still controversy about what bilirubin level justifies concern). After being assured that there is no other cause for the jaundice in your infant, your pediatrician will generally suggest that you supplement the baby's feedings with water or formula in order to stimulate the intestines to move their contents more rapidly, diminishing the bilirubin available for absorption. If this is unsuccessful, your pediatrician may suggest that you discontinue breastfeeding for a day or two in order to stop the cycle and the factors that are interfering with the liver's handling of the bilirubin. While we are not sure why this brief interruption in breastfeeding stops the jaundice from progressing, it is effective and will generally resolve the problem.

Since you will be returning to breastfeeding within a brief day or two, you should express your milk for the period when you are not breastfeeding. Occasionally, your pediatrician will allow you to try to warm your breastmilk for the baby, since this technique can also destroy the factors that interfere with liver function. Once again, this is a transient problem only and rarely a serious one.

You can plan on resuming breastfeeding, and you need not worry that the interruption will interfere with your success.

However, you should not proceed on your own without an evaluation by your baby's doctor. There are serious conditions that must be distinguished from breastmilk jaundice by a simple blood test that looks for *direct bilirubin* and indicates a different set of circumstances.

WHAT SHOULD BE DONE FOR THE BREASTFED INFANT WITH VOMITING OR FREQUENT SPITTING?

The infant who is spitting up as a result of a brief infection can usually do quite well with frequent, smaller breastfeedings during the days when he is vomiting. This usually resolves itself and is not of major concern.

However, many infants have the common problem of reflux (detailed in chapter 6), in which they regurgitate when they are fed. These infants often require very frequent feedings with small amounts in order to maintain hydration and prevent complications. For the breastfed baby with mild reflux, keeping the baby upright for 30 minutes or so after feedings (to let gravity work) and avoiding overfeeding are often sufficient measures. Should that not be successful, particularly if the baby is actively vomiting large amounts or uncomfortable during or after the feedings, your pediatrician should be contacted since special studies, medications, or further treatment may be required.

CAN YOU OVERFEED YOUR BABY?

Healthy breastfed infants often gain substantial weight, but they actually have more than a 30 percent reduction in the risk of becoming overweight.[13] Their diet is even higher in saturated fat (butterfat); yet that does not increase the risk of increased cholesterol later. (Interestingly, this the one feature of breastmilk that manufacturers do not replicate.) So seemingly excessive weight gain is not an indicator that the baby is overfed.

A true indicator is if the baby is gaining well but spitting up frequently or in large amounts. If that's the case, the baby is basically overfilling his tank, consuming more than he needs, and spitting out the excess. The problem is that overfeeding can be a difficult habit to break. The best way is to feed the baby less often, distracting him and/or giving him a pacifier (after at least a month of age). There is debate about whether it would be better to let him stay at the breast longer (getting a little hindmilk at the end) or interrupting by shortening the length of feeding on the first side. If distraction or these alternative techniques don't work, please read the chapter on reflux for additional suggestions.

SO IT'S OKAY TO USE A PACIFIER?

Before a month of age, using a pacifier can lessen a baby's active sucking at the breast and thus decrease breastmilk production. After that time, a pacifier can be used—but judiciously, please. It can help to calm an infant and may possibly help to lessen reflux after meals and promote stomach emptying.[14] However, be aware that many babies swallow excess air when they suck their pacifiers and that air can distend the stomach, giving them more gas and discomfort. In addition, overuse of pacifiers can cause some pressure on the roof of the mouth and problems with teeth alignment. Dentists also warn that pacifiers dipped in honey (or other sugary substances) can contribute to infant tooth decay.

WHAT DO I DO IF MY BABY IS PREMATURE?

As discussed in chapter 11, premature infants (those born more than three weeks before their due date) require increased calories and proteins and higher levels of certain vitamins and minerals in order to grow and develop as they would have if they had remained in the womb longer. Fortunately, the breastfeeding mother of premature infants often can meet most of those needs—but not entirely for the protein and calories. As a result, powdered and liquid fortifiers should be added to your breastmilk (see table 11.1), whether you are feeding the baby with your pumped breastmilk through a bottle or in small increments through a feeding tube that goes into his stomach. Your neonatologist (if your baby is still in the hospital) or your primary care provider will be monitoring those feedings and increasing them or augmenting them as necessary.

DO I HAVE TO STOP BREASTFEEDING IF MY BABY IS NOT GAINING WELL?

Babies need to gain and grow. And internally, their brain and other organs need to be growing as well—and that is more important than whether you breastfeed, add a supplement, or use formula as a substitute. Use a ½ ounce per day of weight gain as a guideline, along with urine and stool output. If the baby is having problems, do not hesitate to speak with your pediatrician. Hopefully, your primary care provider can change the schedule, add a supplement if necessary, and give you the instructions and encouragement you need so that you can continue to breastfeed for most, if not all, of the baby's feeding. Otherwise, your provider should be able to refer you to a pediatric gastroenterologist, a nutritionist, a lactation consultant, or someone else who can help. Chapter 10, which deals with the formula-fed infant who is not gaining, may also have some suggestions for you to consider. Additionally, the growth charts in the appendix and other chapters in *What to Feed Your Baby* and the additional resources we've listed may also offer further reassurance and guidance.

SUMMARY

- Breastfeeding should begin as soon after birth as possible and then continue as frequently as the baby is willing to suckle in order to optimize breastmilk production.

- Once breastfeeding is well established, an "on-demand" schedule usually works well, recognizing that most mothers and babies will do well approximately 2½ to 4 hours after the previous feeding.
- The size or shape of the nipples and breast is usually of no concern.
- Breastfeeding will not distort breast shape, though pregnancy itself can.
- Mastitis, inflammation of the breast, is often caused by increased pressure on the milk ducts, blocking them. This can be treated in several ways to lessen the discomfort and return the breast to normal function and flow. Redness, extreme tenderness, or fever should prompt a phone call or visit to your doctor.
- The risk for breast, ovarian, and uterine cancers can be decreased by breastfeeding.
- Mothers can maintain their nutrition with a healthy diet and vitamins, often losing weight as they do so. If they seek to lose more, they can do so gradually, though this is often best accomplished with a physician's guidance.
- Babies require vitamin D supplementation.
- Babies benefit from an adequate amount of docosahexaenoic acid (DHA) that comes from the mother's diet or supplements the mother can take.
- Breastfed babies usually have several seedy stools daily, though this can vary, and some healthy infants may have infrequent bowel movements.
- The passage of blood in the baby's bowel movement should be investigated by the baby's primary care provider, but the usual cause is from food proteins passing across the mother's breastmilk. This usually does not require that breastfeeding be discontinued.
- Gastroesophageal reflux, fussiness, and other problems can exist even if the baby is breastfed. These can be treated if necessary, but the baby generally does not need to stop breastfeeding.
- The breastfed infant who is not gaining adequate weight may require investigation for the cause and may need supplemental feedings.
- Breastfed babies often appear larger than other infants, but they do not usually become obese from breastfeeding. In fact, breastfeeding decreases the risk of obesity by 30 percent or more.
- While breastfeeding is natural and instinctive, additional knowledge is helpful and often appreciated. Fortunately, numerous supportive organizations and resources are available.

4

⌒⌒

If You Choose to Use a Bottle

All of the emphasis on the advantages of breastfeeding should not demean or in any way cause guilt among mothers who are unable to breastfeed or choose not to. While I am a breastfeeding advocate and my own children and grandchildren were breastfed, they were supplemented with infant formula when necessary. Additionally, I have served as a consultant or speaker for most of the major formula manufacturers, so I do have a sense of what those formulas can offer and what they can't.

The formulas now on the market can certainly provide adequate nutrition for infants. However, their cost varies widely, as you'll see, and some are better suited for your own infant. The focus then of the next five chapters is to define the options based on your baby's health or any medical issues he may have and to provide recommendations for the appropriate formula(s) and any modifications that may be needed for each scenario.

IN THE GARDEN OF EDEN, EVE DIDN'T HAVE A CHOICE

Historically, the perspective was quite different: there was no alternative. The survival of an infant was based largely on the ability of the mother to feed him. Until the 1800s, other sources of milk, including cow's and goat's milk, were tried with little success. The milk obtained, as well as its processing, was so unsanitary that disease and death resulted for those who drank it.

When deprived of breastmilk, infants often died.[1] The only reasonable alternative was for another woman, a wet nurse, who could produce milk to take over the feeding of the infant. As late as 1940, medical and child-care texts commented on desirable attributes—and the dangers:

If a wet nurse is to be employed, she should be selected with care. A careful physical examination and a blood Wasserman test [for syphilis] should be insisted on; an x-ray of the chest [for tuberculosis] is highly desirable. The condition of her own infant is the best evidence of the quality and a quantity of her milk. She should have nursed her infant long enough to demonstrate her milk supply and the infant should always be seen before the nurse is accepted.[2]

A nineteenth-century text is even more explicit:

[The wet-nurse] should be between 20 and 30 years, healthy, not fat, of good habits and character.... Usually the woman comes from an unfavorable class.... The change from poverty and hardship to ease or even luxury is hard for her to bear. She is liable to become lazy, to take insufficient exercise, to eat and drink unreasonably. . . . She realizes the strength of her position, becomes dictatorial and insubordinate, and interferes with the discipline of the household. Commonly, she has vicious habits and vicious associates, and the influence upon the child is not for good.[3]

As a result, substitutes were sought. Various infant foods were tried. The earliest infant formulas were commercialized in the 1860s and 1870s, but it was the discovery of pasteurization (in 1882), homogenization (in 1921), and sterile containers and nipples that truly led babies away from the breast and allowed cow's and goat's milk into adult diets.

For the infant, however, these milks remained inappropriate. The protein in cow's milk is four times that of human milk, making it difficult for the baby's kidneys to filter and often causing diarrhea or intestinal bleeding. The fat is poorly digested. The high phosphorus content and low levels of vitamin D make the baby susceptible to rickets. The absence of folate in goat's milk and its high protein content make it equally unacceptable.

Ways to overcome these disadvantages and create a suitable commercial formula for infants were pursued. Prior to that, infant foods combining grains and liquids were homemade. Merchants like Baron Justus von Leibig and Henri Nestlé are credited with creating the first artificial infant formulas.[4] Soon, pharmaceutical companies became actively involved and altered cow's milk in order to "humanize" it, coming as close to breastmilk as possible. They altered the ratios of the whey and casein that constitute cow's-milk protein to approximate the ratio that an infant would receive from breastmilk. They used additional sugar of the same type (lactose) present in both breast and cow's milk to reduce the protein and phosphorus load and help ensure the absorption of calcium, magnesium, zinc, and iron. They altered the fat to a variety of vegetable oils, which are more easily digested and absorbed than butterfat. They then supplemented these formulas to provide an infant's minimum daily requirements of vitamins and minerals.

The Federal Food and Drug Administration (FDA) now mandates the minimums for a formula to be released in the United States. As with most science, it's a work in progress. When iron was noted to be important (1957), it was added.[5]

In the last decade, it was recognized that infants cannot manufacture sufficient amounts of important, long-chain fatty acids, arachidonic and docosahexaenoic acids (ARA and DHA), that are present in breastmilk, so these have now been added (table 4.1). Since *nucleotides* are present in breastmilk, these building blocks of deoxyribonucleic acid (DNA) and ribonucleic acid (RNA) are present to support energy metabolism and enzymatic reactions. And just recently, prebiotics and probiotics have been added to some formulas (and some baby foods) to try to replicate the improved immune function that breastmilk provides (more about those later, too).

In the United States, formulas such as Similac (the name derives from "similar to lactation") and Enfamil (from "infant milk") were developed to replace human milk when breastfeeding was unsuccessful or inappropriate. They were modeled to deliver what breastmilk does, with the manufacturers trying to match almost every detail possible and with each decade or two bringing a new discovery of another element of breastmilk that was then added in order to possibly improve the baby's immediate or eventual health and development.

Now they are tinkering with the protein again. The amount of protein has been higher in formula because more cow's-milk protein is needed to supply all the essential amino acids that breastmilk provides. Fine, except that these greater amino acid loads have been thought to contribute to a greater weight gain.[6] And increased weight gain as early as six months of age is a risk factor for being overweight later in life.[7, 8] So you might expect to see more alpha-lactalbumin providing more of those essential amino acids for infant and toddler formulas, allowing the total protein concentration and the potential for increased weight to decrease.[9]

And while such advancement is good (typified by this latest possible change), another connotation has come across in marketing these formulas: not only are these products as good as breastfeeding, they are better! At least this was sometimes inferred from the products' advertising in some areas of the world.

Women who were themselves breastfed began to use these "modern" formulas to feed their young. The percentage of infants who were breastfed declined rapidly. In the United States, for example, 65 percent of infants born in 1940 were given human milk. The other babies at the time usually received a homemade concoction of evaporated milk, water, and salts. But as commercialized formulas became more successful, less than half that number were being breastfed two decades later, and by 1970, only 20 percent of the babies born that year were breastfed.[10]

The dependence on human milk was no longer absolute. Nutritious substitutes were readily available, acceptable, and convenient. The idea of human milk began to sound strange and even repulsive. When many thought of milk, they thought of a glass or pitcher of cold cow's milk with water droplets condensed around the rim. As far as feeding an infant, a bottle angled at a baby's mouth, with the mother coaxing him to finish every drop, was the prevailing image.

Mothers in less economically developed countries began to get the same impression, and they, too, adopted formula feeding—but with dire implications. The

hygienic methods and implements used in the United States and more economically mature environments were not possible, and often the mothers overdiluted
the formulas (wanting to use them but trying to make them go further). Babies died
from malnutrition and infection at alarming rates. As a result, the World Health
Organization, as well as national and a number of international health agencies,
recommend exclusive breastfeeding for the first six months of life.[11, 12, 13] Boycotts of
formula companies, particularly Nestlé, evolved since they were manufacturing
their products in Europe but promoting them worldwide. The boycotts reached
their height in the 1970s, citing marketing practices in Third World countries,
with ongoing protests and continued resentment to this day, because of the pro-
testers' continued concerns regarding marketing practices and labeling issues in
the Asia-Pacific region.[14]

But please don't let the World Health Organization or anyone else dissuade
you. Commercial infant formula that is fortified with iron and increased amounts
of DHA is an adequate and complete food for infants. It may not be appropriate
for Third World countries, where cost and contamination make breastfeeding
much safer and more sensible. But if you cannot breastfeed or choose not to, you
can be assured that if you follow the label's directions, you are providing your
baby with all of the nutrients he needs.

WHICH FORMULA IS BEST?

The formula companies today are competing very actively for your business.
They are all going to try to give you what they consider to be the best possible
product. Of course, this is not for your benefit alone. Your purchases represent
a portion of the $3.5 billion US formula market.[15] But you benefit: the principal
formulas are similar and widely available.

I used to joke that Similac and Enfamil, the two main formulas in the US
market, were so nearly identical that you couldn't tell them apart if you took off
their labels. They were both made from cow's milk that was modified to match
breastmilk's protein content; then all the extra sugars, fats, vitamins, and minerals that the baby needs were added. Now the formula companies recognize that
mimicking breastmilk's component parts is impossible. For example, breastmilk
contains hundreds of oligosaccharides (sugar chains) that feed the intestinal bacteria (or *microflora*),[16] whereas only four are commercially available and generally
regarded as safe by the FDA.[17]

Additionally, the mix of the various proteins and nutrients in each of the
formulas affects the absorption of the nutrients (for example, calcium absorption is affected by the protein, phosphorus, and lactose present). So formulas
now try to mimic not only what is in breastmilk but how breastmilk affects
the baby (they even try to have their formulas produce the soft, creamy bowel
movements that breastfed babies have). The way they do this has created differences in the formulas that are noteworthy and will help you understand my
recommendations.

The protein content becomes important in sorting through the routine formulas on the market. All animal milk contains a combination of casein and whey. Think of Little Miss Muffet eating her curds and whey (before homogenization). The curds are casein, the predominant protein in cow's milk (but it represents only 40 percent of breastmilk protein by the time a baby is one to three months old and an even smaller fraction when a baby is younger). Most of the rest of milk protein is whey. Whey actually contains a combination of several proteins that make up approximately 60 percent of breastmilk protein (and an even higher proportion in the first weeks of life), so the two main American formula companies in the 1970s began using an elaborate filtering process to match mature breastmilk protein ratios. And the two formulas remain similar, both using intact cow's-milk protein to match the primary protein composition of breastmilk.

I say "primary protein component" because the individual proteins in breast and cow's milk are not identical (and because new research now identifies a small fraction of mucins in breastmilk). The ratios and actual proteins that make up the whey group are somewhat different (for example, lactoferrin, one of the main whey proteins, is 70 percent identical in human and cow's milk),[18] but in all the years that cow's-milk-based infant formulas have been used, those differences do not seem to have affected any baby's growth or development.

What's interesting is that Nestlé, whose founder developed one of the first commercially successful formulas, now promotes a "routine" formula that totally leaves out the casein and is entirely whey based. The whey is partially digested, or *hydrolyzed*, so that the formula contains 80 percent chopped-up proteins that are short chains of amino acids. They leave 20 percent of the proteins intact to produce a more flavorful formula than if the entire protein fraction were digested.

Although Nestlé Good Start, now called Gerber Good Start (because Nestlé now owns Gerber Baby Foods as well), is promoted as a routine formula, it is the least like breastmilk, which is still the gold standard for feeding infants. I, therefore, do not usually recommend Good Start as a routine formula. Instead, I recognize the formula for what it is—a partial whey hydrolysate that has an important use, lessening potential allergies for babies whose parents or siblings have significant allergies. (Therefore, we will discuss it in chapter 9. As you will see, I do recommend the Gerber formula in several other instances.)

That brings us back to the two main formulas, now named Enfamil Lipil and Similac Advance. I often refer to their attempt to gain market share as the Coke and Pepsi wars. Both are made by quality companies, and both have their advocates, sometimes generated by how well they promote their entire product lines, which include various formulas for problem patients (which we will discuss later).

Subtle but significant differences distinguish these routine, cow's-milk-based formulas. The biggest difference, the one that drives my recommendation, is the DHA levels in the two product lines, extending not only to the routine formula but also to their soy and hydrolysate formulas. The Enfamil products all contain nearly twice the amount of this important oil that stimulates brain development, and that seems to have an important impact on immune function, helping to lessen an infant's respiratory illnesses and doctor's visits in the first year and possibly decreasing allergies, and particularly eczema, as the child ages.[19] To me, the improvement in neurological function is most important, though some analyses still question whether that claim is valid.[20]

WHY DO THE TWO BRANDS ADD DIFFERENT AMOUNTS OF DHA?

The difference in the amount that the two manufacturers add is actually interesting. Ross Labs, a subsidiary of Abbott Pharmaceuticals and now known as Abbott Nutrition, commissioned a study that examined the amount of DHA in the breastmilk of American women. They found very low levels—not unexpectedly, considering the small amount of fish in many American diets (since DHA is one of the long-chain fatty acids derived from omega-3 fish oil). They therefore added that level of DHA (complemented by a balance of ARA, the omega-6 oil that, together with DHA, ensures sufficient growth) to their products. Importantly, they looked at IQ and visual function in the babies of the mothers whose milk they tested and didn't see any real increase compared to babies who were fed their regular formula or their DHA/ARA-enhanced formula.[21]

Almost simultaneously, a study sponsored by the National Institutes of Health (NIH) that addressed the same issues found much higher levels of DHA in the mothers they tested, levels that were more in line with DHA levels found internationally, with the highest levels found in coastal countries like Japan and Norway (table 4.1). Interestingly, when Mead Johnson added an amount of DHA matching the levels found in the NIH study, the researchers found earlier eye development and improved mental development, though some of the babies only breastfed exclusively to four or six months.[22] This parallels the breastfeeding data discussed in chapter 2, or at least the initial data, since these formula-fed children aren't yet old enough to give us the decades of information available on individuals who were breastfed and tested later in life.

There is still a dispute over whether DHA or other factors in breastmilk raise IQ and whether the studies really show that DHA supplementation increases mental development. But the data are enough that many international societies, though not the American Academy of Pediatrics, have recommended that formulas be supplemented with DHA in the range that Mead Johnson provides (table 4.1). In fact, all formula manufacturers other than Abbott Nutrition now add these higher levels of DHA to their formulas, and even Abbott adds the higher level to the formula they produce for Costco (more about that later). Hence, my recommendation, if you are buying formula, is to use one with higher DHA levels.

However, if you are enrolled as a WIC recipient and your state provides one of the other major formulas to you at minimal or no cost, the equation changes (the substantial cost savings outweighing the difference in the formulas), and I would recommend that you use the formula WIC supplies (whether it's the Enfamil, Similac, or Gerber product). Your child will gain and grow just as well.

The states make individual decisions about WIC formula contracts every several years. In Georgia, Mead Johnson had the contract for six years, then Ross had it for three, and Nestlé won it in the last round. The contract makes Nestlé's milk-based and soy formulas the sole source for the state's WIC standard formulas. Mothers receive vouchers and exchange them at the store for formula. In turn, the stores receive payment from the state, and the state then receives a hefty rebate from the company, with the company deriving some indirect marketing benefits during the years the company holds the contract. (There may be other aspects to the contract that I do not know.)

At least in Georgia, the process repeats itself every three years, with new bids tendered, comments solicited from the community, and a company winning the bid. FDA minimum standards are met, and healthy formulas are provided, with taxpayers subsidizing the cost not covered by the rebates.

So, it is in all our best interests as taxpayers to make sure the least expensive formula is used for the appropriate indication. Usually that's one of the formulas provided under the WIC contract, because the rebates drop the price by as much as 80 percent. That does change the cost-benefit ratio substantially. Even when an infant's problem dictates the use of another formula, the choice should be to use the least expensive formula that will work effectively, which is precisely the premise of *What to Feed Your Baby*.

Table 4.1. Mean (Average) DHA in Breastmilk, Formulas, and Recommendations

	DHA as a Percentage of Breastmilk Fatty Acids
Arctic Canada	1.40
Japan	1.10
Sweden	0.53
British Nutrition Foundation	0.4
Food and Agricultural Organization/ World Health Organization	0.35
Italy	0.35
Nigeria, Spain	0.34
Enfamil, Gerber, Most Store Brands	0.32
France	0.32
United States (Birch NIH Study)	0.29
Beijing, China	0.28
Australia	0.21–0.6
Germany	0.21
Children's Health Foundation, Germany	≥ 0.20
Netherlands	0.19
United States (Carlson, 1986)	0.19
Similac	0.15
Israel	0.15–0.38

Source: Adapted from J. T. Brenna et al., "Docosahexaenoic and Arachidonic Acid Concentrations in Human Breast Milk Worldwide," *American Journal of Clinical Nutrition* 85 (2007): 1–8.

If you feel your baby will not be getting sufficient DHA by using one of the formulas that provides less, you can supplement with DHA drops, use one of the cereals or foods that now have DHA added, or provide fish in your family's diet (with the fish oil including DHA) when your child is willing to accept it (generally after 8 to 10 months of age; see chapter 14).

WHY WOULD MY PEDIATRICIAN RECOMMEND THE ABBOTT OR GERBER PRODUCTS?

I also recommend some of the Abbott and Nestlé Gerber products, as you will see, because I am not loyal to a particular brand but looking for the best for your baby in each product class (routine formula, soy, hydrolysate). However, your pediatrician might think that some feature of the Abbott or Gerber routine formulas is more important than the reasons that prompt my recommendation.

Abbott's routine formula has a higher level of nucleotides in its patented blend, which it claims will enhance immune function (though, to my knowledge, no studies have yet demonstrated this effect). Abbott adds different fats, claiming that it's formula does a better job with mineral absorption and that its prebiotic produces less gas. Okay. And some primary care providers may like the Gerber whey protein. That's fine, too. Some might argue that the DHA data is not solid enough for them or that they have always trusted one brand or another. Your baby likely will grow and thrive on whichever you and your pediatrician choose, provided that a routine formula is right for your baby.

Thus, there is no absolute right or wrong, just different choices (for different reasons). These products are promoted like Coke and Pepsi, with millions of dollars at stake for the company and jobs on the line in their marketing and sales departments, so each is going to tout its formulas. I have stated the reasons for my recommendation with the current product composition. But to be clear, I have done more consulting and speaking for Mead Johnson than for the other companies, because currently I agree with the studies that support their DHA levels and Mead's protein blend and find the other factors of less importance. So ask your doctor for his or her recommendation and the rationale behind it; then use all of the information to help you decide.

WHAT ABOUT THE LESS EXPENSIVE STORE BRANDS?

Cost-conscious nutrition focuses in part on cost savings, but my greatest concern is your baby's health. In these times of economic constraint, with the number of cheaper, look-alike formulas on the shelves at your favorite grocery or discount store, this question needs to be answered—especially since the US Food and Drug Administration mandates the minimum requirements for the formulas. In many ways the formulas are alike, carefully matching most of the various components of the major formulas and the DHA and ARA levels of the Mead Johnson products, which are the two criteria I cited for my recommendations. So I'll explain my hesitation.

Wyeth used to be another company that made infant formula, but its brand, SMA (which stood for "simulated milk adapted"), had little of the market and was discontinued. Instead, it began making store brands that were distributed by PBM Products, which eventually bought their plants and continued manufacturing. PBM Products, now known as Perrigo Nutritionals, is manufacturing the generic formulas sold by Target, Walmart, Sam's Club, and many other retail outlets in the United States and overseas. They comply with all of the FDA requirements and recently won a lawsuit against Mead Johnson, which was advertising that its formulas were superior to generic formulas.

Perrigo submitted to the FDA growth studies done on 357 infants with its milk-based formulas and on 260 infants with its soy formulas (both of which are marketed under numerous store brands), as well as noninferiority studies against Mead Johnson's products and limited studies on DHA, calcium, and phosphorus, claiming its research proves that the nutrients provided in its formulas are absorbed as well as those in formulas provided by the major manufacturers. As of this writing, these studies have not been published.[23]

Interestingly, these studies are similar to some of those done by the major formula manufacturers. The difference is that the major manufacturers, Abbott, Mead Johnson, and Nestlé, funded many of the studies that originally explored the components of breastmilk that could be added to their formulas to make them healthier, and they then did the research that determined the safety and effectiveness of these nutrients. DHA and ARA are excellent examples of that kind of research. Perrigo, to my knowledge, has not done any of that difficult and expensive work.

I do understand the cost savings. The company hasn't had to spend money on nutritional research and doesn't have to spend much money on promotion since having the product on the shelf in discount stores and identifying it as similar to one of the major brands is often enough of a recommendation for some parents. Therefore Perrigo can charge less (with, I suppose, a higher profit margin). But it is probably not going to invest in advancing nutrition and developing best practices the way the other formula manufacturers are. And so, the cost savings are important, but to me, as a physician, the incremental cost for those who can afford it makes a real difference in the long run, though I would certainly like to see some of the promotional costs for the major brands decrease so that their products are more affordable.

What's interesting is that Abbott actually makes the lower-priced formula for Costco, adding DHA at higher levels (that match the Enfamil and Gerber products) at Costco's request but leaving out Abbott's patented blend of nucleotides and substituting its prior blend (from the version before Similac Advance). I don't know if you have any difficulty accepting the two different makes, as if they were different car models by the same manufacturer. Since we are talking about optimizing infant nutrition, it seems awkward to have two different routine formulas, a full-price product that has nucleotides that the company claims helps babies and a lower-price Costco label that doesn't have the nucleotides but has higher levels of DHA, which it claims are unnecessary in the full-price brand. For me, however, the Costco-labeled product seems to be almost exactly what some parents should want—a less expensive, well-tested formula with high DHA levels.

So, bottom line: For routine formula, I recommend Enfamil Lipil. For those who want a less expensive, similar, generic version, I recommend Kirkland Signature Infant Formula or the Perrigo products, which have passed FDA muster.

THE PRODUCTS ARE CONFUSING WITH SO MANY VARIETIES, EVEN OF THE SAME BRAND

The companies have fallen in love with branding, so the formula labels now all start with their primary (routine) product's name (e.g., Enfamil, Similac, or Gerber Good Start), and then they tell you the actual name of the product, expecting you to differentiate by the second name or the color of the label. But mothers come in all the time, telling me only that they are using Similac, Enfamil, or Good Start, not knowing what they are actually giving their infants, since the manufacturers make a variety of formulas for the various infants who have particular problems and require specialty products designed for them (table 5.1 in the next chapter). For example, Isomil, which is a very good soy formula made by Abbott, is now confusingly rebranded Similac Soy Advance (similar to Similac Advance); the lactose-free formula, previously called Lactofree, which had few advocates, reports that it is now selling quite well because its name was changed to Similac Sensitive, while Abbott's very good formula for reflux is now Similac Sensitive for Spit Up. I do not want to imply this confusion is caused by Abbott alone. Mead Johnson does the same with its product line (Enfamil Lipil, Enfamil AR, Enfamil Gentle Ease, etc.), and then, of course, there are two different Gerber Good Start routine formulas, Protect and Gentle, that come with or without their probiotic, and Soothe, with a different probiotic and lower lactose, so that it can compete for some of Similac Sensitive's market share, it seems.

This naming craze may help the marketing, but it is detrimental to parents and primary care providers. The worst case was one mother who told me her baby had problems with gas, irritability, and reflux; additionally, the mother had multiple food allergies, and of course she wanted her child to get the maximum amount of DHA. She read every label carefully, and as a result she was mixing the various formulas into a cocktail every morning and giving her child that combination through the day. And there are dozens of other mothers who are uncertain why their infants are on a particular formula or why they have switched through several, finding that none actually help.

My intention in the next several chapters is to help you sort through the common problems that often afflict infants and determine the best, least expensive specialty formula to combat the problems that your baby may have. Often the symptoms overlap. A baby with reflux or allergies is often irritable (because of the underlying condition). And yes, the formula names further confound the situation. But you can use *What to Feed Your Baby* to guide you, and because it seems

like a new development or formula is being announced on a regular basis, www
.what2feedyourbaby.com will attempt to keep you updated.

WHICH SHOULD I USE: CONCENTRATE, POWDER, OR READY TO FEED?

These different formulations of the same product add to the confusion, but at
least this issue is easier to understand and justify. "Ready-to-feed" formulas are
exactly that: prepackaged, convenience formulas. Open the can and pour the contents into the bottle. But you pay for that convenience. The ready-to-feed versions
are more expensive (you pay for the water added and for the company to ship that
water in the can). However, they may make sense when you are camping or in
situations when you cannot easily prepare your own formula.

The concentrated variety needs to be mixed with water in equal volume (one
can of formula to one can of water—or bottle by bottle, 4 ounces of formula and
the same amount of water). The advantage: it's cheaper than the ready-to-feed
version but still more expensive than the powdered form (see table 4.2).

The ready-to-feed version comes in a 1-quart can (32 ounces), and the concentrate comes in a 13-ounce can that makes 26 ounces—if it is diluted to the
same 20 calories per ounce (more about this in chapter 10 on the underweight
infant). Quart-size bottles of the concentrate are also available, potentially confusing parents who could offer it without dilution, which would be dangerous for
the baby—so please be extra cautious when purchasing either the ready-to-feed
or the concentrate version. Both the concentrate and the ready-to-feed formulas
remain fresh in the refrigerator for 48 hours (24 hours if the formula was poured
into a bottle that the baby has actually had his mouth on). Your baby needs to be
taking about 24 ounces a day or more to make the purchase worthwhile or you
will be wasting a lot.

The powders are considerably less expensive and equally easy to prepare. They
are especially practical for the baby in early and late infancy (and the breastfed
baby) who is taking so little formula each day that the open cans of formula in the
refrigerator must be discarded before they are finished.

The formula content is exactly the same, with one small but notable exception.
That exception is Alimentum, a formula we will discuss in chapter 5, which has
corn maltodextrin (a derivative of corn syrup solids) in its powder, while the

Table 4.2. Cost Comparison of Available Formulations

Formula Formulations	Cost per Ounce (cents)
Powder formulations	
Major brands	15–17
Store brand	8
Liquid concentrate	20–29
Ready to feed	20–22

ready-to-feed product has sucrose and tapioca starch because they are soluble in the fluid form but less able to convert into a powder. The change in carbohydrate makes the ready-to-feed variety sweeter, but this has no consequence for infants who are corn sensitive, since the powdered version does not have any corn protein. The simplest formulas to digest, the amino acid formulas that we will discuss later, also have these same sugars, and the corn makes no difference there either.

Powder has several benefits: not only is it cheaper, but it is more portable (and lighter in the baby's diaper bag), assuming a ready source of water is available to mix with it when the baby is ready to be fed. The powder remains stable, and for underweight babies who need to gain more weight, it can be concentrated easily (by using less water, as will be described in chapter 10).

Again, we need to note exceptions. Powdered formulas are not safe for severely premature infants who still require in-hospital care and for infants who are immune compromised (such as those infants whose mothers have AIDS). Those fragile infants are particularly susceptible to a rare bacteria, *Enterobacter* (or *Cronobacter*) *sakazakii*, that has been found in the powdered versions, and so formulas for those premature infants are only available as sterile liquids. The potential for infection from that exceedingly rare bacteria (affecting 1 in 100,000 infants) can be lessened by only making the amount of formula you need for that feeding and by following the instructions for formula storage and safety, which will also help you prevent other infections for your infant, whether full-term or premature. Use hot water (158°F, 70°C) that's been cooled to reconstitute powdered formula when possible, do not leave formula out on the counter for more than two hours, and throw away refrigerated prepared formula if it's unused in 24 hours. Note, too, that there was a recent tragedy when several full-term babies died from an infection from this bacteria, but it was not found in the original formula, and the suspicion is that contamination occurred later, since this bacteria is also common in the environment.

The cost difference for the various forms is substantial (table 5.3), so my recommendation is to use powdered formulas whenever possible, with cost and safety as the prime determinants. It is much more likely that an infant will be harmed by spoiled liquid that sat too long in a refrigerator or baby bag, rather than by the potential exposure to a rare bacteria.

Please note that when you are making a bottle using the powder, room temperature water should be placed in the bottle first and then the appropriate amount of powder should be added. You do not want to add water to the powder to make up a total of 4 ounces, for example, because the powder will displace some of the water that needs to be added, making the formula and nutrients more concentrated than intended.

WHAT ABOUT ORGANIC FORMULAS?

Organic infant formulas and infant foods are a logical outgrowth of the desire of parents who maintain an organic diet for themselves to provide similar nutrition for their infants. In order to qualify as organic under the US Department of Agriculture's (USDA) National Organic Program and to be certified by one of the organic certification boards, the products have to be grown without harmful pesticides, contain no artificial flavors, colors, or preservatives, and have no modified starches, refined sugars, or genetically engineered ingredients.

Abbott and Perrigo both have produced organic formulas under those guidelines. Similac Organic and a number of Perrigo dairy and soy products, Earth's Best formulas marketed by the Hain Celestial Group, Vermont Organic, Bright Beginnings, and Parents' Choice are all certified by Quality Assurance International at the time of this writing. Nature's One organic formulas, which are actually toddler formulas that somehow are still able to be called Baby's Only Organic Formulas, are also on the market, certified by a different agency.

The problem is that there's a dispute as to whether the infant formulas are truly organic, since, for example, the DHA is extracted using hexane, and then preservatives are used to maintain the DHA. So complaints have been lodged with the certification boards and the USDA.[24] Thus it is unclear at this time whether truly nutritious infant formulas can be manufactured as organic under current guidelines.

ARE VITAMINS NECESSARY FOR INFANTS ON FORMULA?

Commercial formulas contain vitamins sufficient for most infants (the exception being infants with very rare, specialized needs, such as those with liver or kidney disease and premature babies) until they are four to six months of age, when solids are introduced to meet their additional needs (see chapter 13). Fluoride may need to be supplemented after six months of age depending on the fluoride content of the water supply.

Again, there is an exception. The American Academy of Pediatrics Committee on Nutrition has recently advised that all babies receive 400 IU of vitamin D daily in order to prevent rickets.[25] As a result, newborn formulas (described in chapter 5) are now being produced with increased vitamin D, since newborns drink less and need higher concentrations to provide sufficiency.

The infant who is primarily breastfed and only occasionally supplemented should receive the recommended daily supplement of vitamin D and therefore does not need one of the higher vitamin D formulas. On the other hand, newborns who are solely formula-fed may benefit from the new products for the first month or two. An alternative is to give your newborn vitamin D or other liquid vitamins, since your baby can then receive the higher levels that I recommend (chapter 13), though the drops add a small expense.

IS WELL WATER SAFE FOR INFANTS?

The best way to make sure is to ask your health department to take a sample of your well water while you are still pregnant. They can test for bacteria and other bugs and for mineral content. If they charge, it's well worth the price to be sure that your baby is receiving safe, pure water. In any case, water should be brought to a rolling boil for one minute and then cooled before it is mixed with formula. Bottled water may be a better alternative now that it is widely available, and the cost is relatively reasonable for the margin of safety it provides.

HOW DO YOU START THE BABY ON FORMULA?

You will actually start the baby on formula in the hospital, shortly after delivery. When the baby is awake and somewhat alert (usually four to six hours later), he should receive his first bottle of formula. Babies are not immediate experts at their first feeding. They occasionally cough or sputter, though they usually get a small amount into their stomachs (remember, they only need 1 teaspoonful in those first feedings). Occasionally, sugar water is given earlier if the baby is at risk for low blood sugar (if the baby is small, exceptionally large, or jittery).

Check the tightness of the bottle's nipple and lid. Then turn the bottle upside down. A drop or two may drip out, but it shouldn't be a constant flow. Next, squeeze the nipple aiming the stream at the palm side of your wrist. If the formula is lukewarm (roughly room temperature), you may begin. If it's too hot, you can often cool it with a flow of cold water on the bottle; if it's too cold, warm water around the bottle should quickly raise the temperature, but remember to check again before offering it to your baby.

Get yourselves comfortable so that you can both be calm and relaxed. Your baby should be warm, dry, and held comfortably close. Enjoy each other. Eye contact and talking to your baby will make this one of your baby's first pleasant experiences and one of your favorites as well.

Your baby will go after the bottle himself if you stroke his cheek with your finger or the nipple. If he is awake at all, his mouth will open slightly and he will search for the nipple. Gently insert the bottle at a slight angle (keeping the air bubble away from the nipple). Easy. If bubbles are coming up, you know your baby is getting the formula. If they are slow in coming, you might try loosening the lid slightly. If your baby is choking a bit, check to see that the lid is not too loose or that the nipple hole is not too large. Once these corrections are made, your baby will tend to settle down.

You may note that the baby will pause occasionally and then begin to suck again. This is normal and to be expected. You needn't jiggle the bottle; he will start again on his own.

Some healthy babies spit up or vomit after their first feeding(s), often bringing up clear secretions or mucus along with the formula. If the vomiting is forceful, notify your nurse or doctor, so he or she can check if the baby was born with a significant problem. If the vomiting is milder, know that this is a common situation, with the baby needing to clear what's in his stomach. Try again with the next feeding, but do let the nursery personnel know. They will track the amount and frequency. This does not imply a formula intolerance and does not require a change in the formula or a need for testing unless it recurs repeatedly.

WHEN DO I STOP THE FEEDING?

While you can now be assured of the quality of the formula that your infant receives, the guidelines for the quantity of formula have long been one of the major drawbacks of bottle feeding. The healthy breastfed infant takes what he wants (and presumably needs), and there are no standards to judge by except weight gain and urine output. What about the bottle-fed infant? A 4-, 6-, or 8-ounce bottle is filled, and the infant is fed. Somehow, though, our clean-your-plate attitude to nutrition pervades, and we try every possible trick to get the infant to finish the bottle. If the infant doesn't finish, we almost blame ourselves because the baby hasn't met some preconceived notion on our part about how much the infant should take—whether he wants it or needs it. This philosophy and practice has led many infants either to become obese or to spit up the overfed excess.

The best protection is to follow the excellent advice of Dr. Samuel Fomon during his long career: Infants should be permitted to stop eating at the earliest sign of willingness to stop—not at a point of maximum consumption. No attempt should be made to get the infant to drain the last drop from a bottle or, later on, to finish the last spoonful in the dish.[26]

My suggestion is to know your infant and what he truly needs. Most infants will open their mouths when hungry and instead scan the room or play with their food when they've had enough. An approximate guideline is that for every pound your baby weighs, he should take about 2 to 2½ ounces of formula each day. If your infant weighs 8 pounds, 16 to 20 ounces will be what the baby takes in a day. If he weighs 12 pounds, 24 to 30 ounces will be enough. But the amount taken at each feeding may vary—and that is entirely normal. Often babies do best taking smaller, more frequent feedings, similar to breastfed infants who sometimes cluster-feed, wanting nourishment or nurturing every hour or two for several feedings after or before a time period when they may not have taken much for a while.

HOW LONG SHOULD THE BABY GO BETWEEN FEEDINGS?

Your baby can tell you far better than I can. He will set his own schedule (usually between 2½ to 4 hours). Each child is different, so be flexible. A precise schedule is not necessary. This is "demand" feeding.

Once the baby begins to sleep through the night (often at about 10 to 16 weeks), it is not necessary to wake him. If this occurs in the first week or so that you are home, you may be a sound sleeper or you have an exceptional baby. If the baby is gaining weight well (averaging ½ to 1 ounce a day), then there is no need to wake him. If weight gain is less, consult your doctor.

WHEN DO I BURP HIM?

Burping your baby helps remove swallowed air. Burp or bubble him by holding him upright over your shoulder and patting or rubbing his back gently. You may also place him down over your lap and gently rub his back. Also, you can burb your baby by holding him in a sitting position (with the baby leaning slightly forward) on your lap, with your hand supporting his chest. Don't be alarmed if he spits up a few teaspoons of milk. These wet burps help to expel the extra air and even extra formula he has consumed.

Burping should be done at the end of each feeding (and occasionally during a feeding if the baby appears to be uncomfortable). Your baby may not belch every time you go through this. If he doesn't, you can still let him go to sleep—just lay him on his side. If he becomes fussy later, you can always try to burp him again.

ARE THERE ANY ADVANTAGES TO BOTTLE FEEDING?

Yes. Formula and water feedings can be given by both parents. You may be surprised at how much your husband or partner wants to participate (and not just get stuck changing diapers). Encourage and welcome his participation—it will be gratifying for all of you.

And if you have older children, they can also be included. Help them help you, but do not force the issue if your child balks. Jealousy may be expected. Extra attention for the older one(s) will gradually defuse this normal emotion.

HOW AND WHEN DO I WEAN FROM BREAST
TO BOTTLE AND FROM BOTTLE TO CUP?

The how is easy. In the first instance, breast to bottle, I usually recommend that the process take place over several days for the mother's comfort and the baby's ease, with a new bottle feeding replacing a breastfeeding every day or two. This is particularly easy if the baby has occasionally received a bottle of breastmilk or formula as a substitute feeding when the mother has been out. Often it is easiest when the father or grandparent caregiver introduces the initial bottles so the infant is not confused and expecting to be breastfed. If the baby is old enough, generally eight or nine months, he can be weaned directly to a cup.

When breastfeeding mothers ask that when question, I sometimes joke that it should usually be done before kindergarten, or college at the latest, since it can be embarrassing in the classroom. In reality, it's often more a matter of the mother's milk supply diminishing, her own needs, or the baby biting and the feedings becoming uncomfortable. All of those situations can be dealt with by a good lactation consultant if the mother prefers, but the mother can certainly elect to wean and be proud of whatever time she breastfed.

When possible, though, I usually suggest that mothers breastfeed for at least six months. By then, the baby's intestinal cells are well knit together (allowing less potential for allergy), and the baby's own immune status has improved significantly. If a mother is willing to go longer, my next goal would be eight or nine months so that the baby can be weaned directly to a cup rather than from breast to bottle to cup.

A number of mothers wait until their infants are toddlers to wean. Sometimes those toddlers are more difficult to wean, however, and that can become a problem when they are using their mothers as pacifiers, taking little calorically from solids, and failing to gain sufficient weight. But as long as the toddlers are maintaining adequate growth, there is no real problem nutritionally with continuing breastfeeding.

Please do remember that breastfeeding is not an adequate contraceptive. That is a myth. Mothers can get pregnant while breastfeeding.

As far as weaning from bottle to cup, there's no real rule. I usually suggest that parents introduce a sippy cup at around nine months and use it for the formula or water. Babies seem to be able to hold the cup then, and they are becoming interested in feeding themselves. The alternative time is when they transition to regular milk, putting the new milk in the cup and offering it gradually (one cup feeding replacing a bottle each day). If your baby is having little interest in the cup or its contents, you can persist with the introduction extending over a longer period to get the baby used to the difference. However, if your baby is having difficulty gaining weight or having a significant decrease in his wet diapers, you should discuss the matter with your pediatrician.

HOW LONG SHOULD I USE FORMULA INSTEAD OF REGULAR MILK?

As we will discuss in chapter 13, breastmilk or iron-fortified formula is all that is needed until your baby doubles his birth weight. And most breastfeeding experts advocate exclusive breastfeeding until six months of age. At that point, solid foods can and should be added to the diet of the term infant.

Feeding with breastmilk or formula should be continued until the latter part of the first year, possibly preventing intestinal blood loss and allergies. When cow's milk is introduced at around one year, regular homogenized and pasteurized whole milk should generally be used. There are exceptions for the allergic child and the very picky toddler (as will be discussed in chapters 9 and 14).

These days it seems that "baby" yogurt is often introduced as the first dairy product, and often cheese is next, with both often in the baby's diet by 8 to 10 months of age. Babies who tolerate those dairy products usually do quite well with cow's milk itself. But don't rush. Yogurt and cheese are only a small fraction of the baby's diet, while formula represents a third to a half of his calories and nutrients. So I usually recommend that the baby be taking three good meals of finger/table foods before he is transitioned to whole milk (more about this process and the timing in chapter 14).

ARE ANY PARTICULAR NIPPLES OR BOTTLES PREFERRED?

The bottle does not seem as important as the nipple that is used. Collapsible containers (such as the Playtex Nurser), Playtex's Ventaire angled bottles with small holes to release air, and Dr. Brown's bottles with an internal venting system are intended to prevent air swallowing, but they really offer no advantage over a parent's careful feeding. With the baby in a semi-upright position (leaning back in your arms), the bottle tipped at a reasonable angle, and feeding stopped as the formula enters the nipple, the baby should not have problems with swallowing air. Even babies who are breastfed swallow some air around the nipple. With all that said, these various systems do seem to sell well, and parents often prefer to know that they are doing everything possible to lessen their babies' gas and irritability.

Similarly, I am not sure that one particular shape of nipple is better than any other. Most work quite well for the average infant. The hole size is of greater significance and must be sufficient to allow a reasonable flow. This can be partially controlled by the tightness of the cap. The tightness determines the suction pressure that the infant must exert to obtain the formula without a struggle. (Therefore, be careful with the cap and never completely tighten it.) Nipples that have a "Y" or an "X" (crosscut) often provide a more reliable flow. The hole simply opens wider when the baby is sucking more vigorously and limits the flow when less suction is required. For those infants who must have cereal or other nutrients added to their formula because of recurring vomiting or reflux (chapter 6), the Y or cross-cut nipples are already adapted to let the thicker formula through.

SHOULD I BE CONCERNED ABOUT THE SAFETY OF THE BOTTLES OR NIPPLES?

You may also be familiar with the "baby bottle scare" that made headlines in April 2008. Subsequently, Canada and the European Commission banned Bisphenol-A (BPA) as toxic.[27] BPA is a synthetic chemical that mimics the hormone estrogen and is used in clear plastic containers, including polycarbonate baby bottles and sippy cups. The claim was that polycarbonate baby bottles could leach detectable amounts of BPA into the bottle contents.

This is not a recent issue, however. There have been thousands of scientific studies throughout the years concluding that the amounts of BPA released from polycarbonate bottles are minimal and far below the safety standard for babies. The US National Toxicology Program states that there is "some concern for neural and behavioral effects in fetuses, infants, and children" and "some concern [about] effects in the prostate gland, mammary gland, and an earlier age for puberty in females." Scientists state that "some concern" is considered a minimal risk and, again, is far below the safety standard for babies.[28]

IS STERILIZING NECESSARY?

Sterilization of nipples and bottles is not necessary. "Kitchen clean" is adequate. A good, thorough washing with hot water and soap and a final hot-water rinse (by hand or in the dishwasher) are all that is required to prevent infection.

SUMMARY

- Infant formula provides a safe and reasonable method of feeding for mothers who are unable to breastfeed, choose not to, or want to supplement.
- The major manufacturers have done extensive research that has produced safe routine formulas that are modeled on breastmilk, which is logically considered the gold standard for infant feeding.
- The recommended formula for the healthy infant is Enfamil Premium because, like Similac Advance, it provides a close match to breastmilk, but the Enfamil products have a higher content of DHA, which should contribute to better immune and neurodevelopmental outcomes, though the research is not thoroughly established and may not be for another generation. For parents wanting a generic brand, the Costco brand, Kirkland Signature Infant Formula, or the Perrigo brands are reasonable and less expensive, FDA-approved options.
- The cost-benefit ratio changes if your baby receives a WIC subsidy, and the ample rationale for all the major formulas leads to the recommendation to use the formula WIC provides.
- The powdered versions are easy to mix, the most portable, and the least expensive. The water should be put in the bottle first, and then powder should be added to bring the total volume up to the specific number of ounces.
- All the nutrients the baby needs for the first four to six months are present in the formula, including the vitamins and minerals, though newborns consuming smaller amounts may need more vitamin D initially to meet the recommendations established by the American Academy of Pediatrics. This is provided by using a newborn formula. However, my recommendations are to consider even higher amounts of vitamin D in infancy (explained in chapter 15), and in order to receive that, infants need vitamin drops.
- Bottle feeding is easily begun while the baby is in the hospital or most anytime thereafter. Demand-feeding schedules are easy to accomplish and can often incorporate fathers and other family members so that they, too, feel part of the baby's care team.
- The baby does not need to take a certain number of ounces per feeding just because that amount was placed in the bottle.
- Burping can be done in a number of positions to release extra air the baby may have swallowed.

- When the baby is weaned from breastfeeding, the bottle can be introduced easily, particularly if bottles were occasionally used for supplemental feedings.
- Bottles and nipples need not be sterilized, but they should be thoroughly washed and rinsed.
- Plastic bottles and nipples are not hazardous, a suitable combination can be found, and adjustments will allow an appropriate flow for the baby.

5

⌒

Specialty Formulas for Babies
with Problems

Not every baby does well on breastmilk or routine formula. Perhaps the best story to illustrate this was when Jack Keats licked his hand after he touched an area where someone else's formula had spilled in my office. Within 20 minutes, he was vomiting profusely.

The formula manufacturers have recognized this need and developed alternative specialty formulas. But because these have proliferated, sorting through them and determining the best (and most cost-conscious) choice for your infant is often difficult.

To help, I constructed a tiered algorithm, a logical stepwise approach, that health providers in Georgia are now using.[1] And here, in *What to Feed Your Baby*, I've converted the algorithm into individual chapters that explain the points fully so that you can use the same rationale to understand the options when you speak with your physician and to guide those decisions, bringing affordability into the equation as well. In doing so, I want to convert the process from one in which it seems like your doctor is just saying, "Well, just go home and try this one," or "Here are a few that might work for Sally. See what she handles the best," into a well-informed choice.

The chapters provide a mechanism to break the components of what might seem like a daunting decision process into individual steps, for which I can provide the further details that pertain to particular situations. The reason for the tiers is that each one represents a significant decision for that particular problem, and the further tiers represent the next decision to be made if the previous one doesn't solve the problem. As you'll see, the tiers also represent a difference in formula composition and often a price jump as well. Of course, you are welcome and encouraged to read the entire book, since the later chapters also address introducing solids and more information on important nutritional issues. But you can also read just those sections that reflect the problems your baby seems to be having, and you can refer back to the tables, figures, and summaries for a quick reference. I have tried to cross-reference sections in the chapters so that, for example, the mother of a fussy infant will be directed to parts of the chapters on reflux and allergies, since these problems can overlap or be mistaken for each other. But remember, the idea is to come away with a better understanding and a single formula to try, as well as options to consider if that isn't working. Also remember to follow the full instructions for a complete trial, because it's rare that you'll see complete resolution of a particular problem after a single feeding.

We already addressed the Tier 1 decision: breast versus bottle. Assuming that a mother is unable to breastfeed, chooses not to, or is going to supplement, the choice for her infant will usually be routine cow's-milk-based formula. That's true for almost all infants.

The next step, Tier 2, then defines a baby's specific problem and determines the appropriate and cost-effective choice for that infant. If that initial strategy doesn't work, the infant progresses to the next logical formula, often requiring a formula on Tier 3.

As might be expected, the majority of infants do well with routine formula, and a majority of the ones who don't then thrive on the formulas on Tier 2. Perhaps 8 to 10 percent will require the Tier 3 formulas, and very few will require the expensive Tier 4 formulas, which are in the simplest absorptive state possible. All of these formulas and their uses are summarized in table 5.1.

Just recently, however, there's been enough evidence to suggest that children who are born into families with significant allergies might lessen their own risks of developing allergies by avoiding routine and soy formula and going directly to one of the Tier 3 hydrolysates (as discussed chapter 9).

Some doctors and providers will automatically jump to the third tier for their difficult patients because those formulas are tolerated by almost all infants. Or they will rapidly move to the fourth tier because those are so well tolerated in almost every circumstance. Yes, there are reasons to do so (for example, in a hospitalized infant who has just had intestinal surgery). However, that's also the most costly approach and often unnecessary.

If your baby's formula is provided within the WIC program, your state agencies, with the input of the state's health-care providers, determine what formulas are allowed to be used and when. They are required to provide acceptable formulas for each of the problems babies can have. But because they provide the formula for so many infants, they are able to lower the cost of doing so by providing a specific routine formula. Some states also have a contract for the specialty formulas, again, to lower the cost. These formulas are all acceptable and will work for the majority of infants. And it is rare for infants to benefit from switching to a similar product in the same class (you'll read more about that shortly, but it's the equivalent of a child being changed from the Similac routine formula to the Enfamil routine formula, or vice versa), though the formula representatives are

Table 5.1. Formulas and Their Intended Use

Type	Indications for Use	Names of Proprietary Formulas[a]
Routine cow's milk based Similar to nutrient composition of breastmilk	Term babies who are not breastfed.	Similac Advance Enfamil Lipil Premium, Newborn Organic (Earth's Best, Similac Organic) Store brands[b]
Soy Similar to nutrient composition of breastmilk but with soy-protein source	Babies with milk-protein allergy or intolerance. Babies of vegan families. Lactose-intolerant babies.	Similac Isomil Advance Enfamil Prosobee Lipil Gerber Good Start Soy Organic (Earth's Best) Store brands[b]
Rice-starch formula	Babies with gastroesophageal reflux.	Enfamil AR Similac Sensitive for Spit Up
Intact protein with low lactose	Babies with lactose intolerance.	Similac Sensitive
Partial protein hydrolysates	Fussy babies.	Gerber Good Start[c] Enfamil Gentlease
Protein hydrolysate Partially broken-down proteins	Babies with cow's-milk and soy-protein allergy or malabsorption.	Similac Alimentum Advance Enfamil Pregestamil Enfamil Nutramigen Lipil
Elemental Completely broken-down proteins	Babies with severe allergies or malabsorption.	EleCare Neocate Puramino
Preterm Highest in calories, protein, vitamins, and minerals	Babies born under thirty-four weeks gestational age or under 5½ lbs. These are hospital-based formulas and are not available at retail stores.	Similac Special Care, High Protein Enfamil Premature Gerber Good Start Premature 24[d]
Transitional High in calories, protein, vitamins, and minerals	Babies born preterm who are ready to be discharged from the NICU. Babies with slow growth on standard term formula or who are fluid restricted.	Similac Neosure Enfamil EnfaCare Gerber Good Start Nourish[d]

[a]All formula names are registered trademarks.

[b]Various store brands are available; most indicate they are comparable to a brand in this chart.

[c]Gerber Good Start varieties within this category include Gentle, Protect, and Soothe (please see text for further information).

[d]These formulas are 100 percent whey protein; the others are whey predominant with casein (please see table A.1 in the appendix for more information).

Source: B. Koch and S. Cohen, www.nutrition4kids.com.

often in physicians' offices trying to make sure that providers have a clear sense of the differences between the formulas and the advantages of the products they are representing.

Also know that some insurance companies, and possibly some state agencies, will reimburse you for some of the more expensive formulas if you can prove the formula is medically necessary and is the child's sole source of nutrition—for example, if the infant is fed by a tube or is unable to tolerate solids.

MAKING THE SWITCH

All too often, parents and sometimes their primary care providers will quickly change formulas because they think the formula they're currently using isn't being well tolerated. The parents may have seen some advertising, or one mother will share her experience with another, suggesting a different formula for a baby who still has a problem. But that change can be premature. The adequacy of a formula trial depends on the baby's underlying symptoms. For vomiting or diarrhea, it can take up to 3 days to see symptoms improve; for reflux, 7 days; for irritability, 7 days; for constipation, 14 days; and for allergic rashes, up to 30 days. So, unless the baby worsens, the formula needs to be tried for at least that long.

The speed with which the change should be made also depends on the symptoms. Generally, it's best to introduce a new formula gradually, substituting one new bottle in the middle of the first day, then adding one more new bottle each day until the new formula has replaced the old. That way a parent can see how the formula is tolerated, and this method may actually improve that tolerance. If the baby is doing exceptionally well with the new formula, you can speed up the introduction. If the baby is fussier or vomiting more, the introduction can be stopped and discussed with the provider who recommended it.

That slow introduction, however, is not appropriate for infants with profound diarrhea or vomiting. In that case, a bottle or two (or occasionally a day's worth) of Pedialyte may be needed to rehydrate a baby before the new formula is substituted.

This chapter is intended to help you understand the differences among the various specialty formulas and the basic rationale for using them. We will also discuss the prebiotics and probiotics that are now in many of these products. The following chapters will then explore the individual problems your baby may be experiencing and the best feeding choice in each particular situation.

LACTOSE-FREE AND LACTOSE-REDUCED FORMULA

Lactose-free formula is essentially routine cow's-milk-based formula with the sugar changed from lactose to sucrose. The protein, fat, vitamins, and minerals are the same, except that calcium is increased by a third because calcium is less well absorbed with sucrose than with lactose. The major difference is the switch in carbohydrate. Mead Johnson pulled its product from the market because lactose sensitivity is rare, rare, rare in infants (occurring primarily during and briefly after an intestinal infection), and instead the company developed a partially digested protein product with lower levels of lactose (discussed below). On the other hand, Abbott, in a shrewd marketing move, renamed its formula, originally called Lactofree, to Similac Sensitive, and that labeling has convinced an enormous number of mothers that this formula makes a difference. To compete for that business, Nestlé has released a formula, Good Start Soothe, that is 30 percent lactose reduced. Maltodextrin is substituted and *Lactobacillus reuteri* is added (which is a different probiotic than in the company's Protect formula), though all of the other features of its routine formulas remain the same. And Perrigo Nutritionals is now pursuing efforts to launch competing store-brand formulas as well.[2]

These formulas essentially cost the same as routine formula, and it is usually acceptable if a mother chooses to use one. However, it is a poor choice for a child whose routine formula is subsidized by the state's WIC program, because the program's contracts substantially reduce the cost to the state for the subsidized reduced formulas, while it generally pays full price for these very similar products.

As discussed in the previous chapter, the WIC program in each state contracts with one of the formula manufacturers to provide routine and soy-based formulas to families at a reduced price, which the federal government subsidizes. That discount is substantial but worth it to the formula companies, because it usually helps them sell more of their products to other parents as well through increased shelf space and other marketing measures.

If an infant goes onto another formula, the WIC program (with tax dollars) pays full price for that formula. Most of the time, the need is justified, but the need for a lactose-free formula is far exceeded by Abbott's sales of this product. I understand that the company has marketed it enough that it now captures more than 10 percent of the total formula market. No harm done to the babies. Smart marketing. But it's taken a considerable amount of money from my pocket and yours, when the discounted soy formula could be used instead. To rectify the problem, WIC in Georgia now (at the time of this writing) allows infants to switch to Nestlé's lactose-reduced brand within its rebate policies, returning money to the program while lessening parental concern about their infant's possible lactose intolerance.

RICE-STARCH FORMULAS

Both Abbott and Mead Johnson make formulas that contain a rice derivative that thickens in the stomach in order to lessen gastroesophageal reflux. The rationale for and best way to use the formula and control the constipation that can accompany it will be discussed in chapters 6 and 8. In these, rice starch has been exchanged for the lactose in the routine formula, keeping the number of calories and all the nutrients the same otherwise.

SOY FORMULAS

In the 1920s, the formula companies sought an inexpensive way to provide a nutritional alternative for babies who were milk sensitive. (We will discuss milk allergy, milk sensitivity, and lactose intolerance in chapter 9.) Soy was used and gradually improved, refining the protein put in the formulas. They provided the same vitamins and minerals as they did with their cow's-milk formulas. They found that methionine, one of the amino acids, and carnitine, a molecule important in fat metabolism, were deficient, so both were added. They also recognized that one of the elements from the soy husk, phytates, interfered with mineral absorption (the bioavailabilty of the mineral), so more of the minerals were added to compensate.

The sugar sucrose is the carbohydrate in all three brands (Abbott, Mead Johnson, and Nestlé). Because calcium is less well absorbed with sucrose, more calcium has been added. The fat blends are similar to the fats in the cow's-milk formulas (replacing buttermilk fats in normal cow's milk). Abbott claims its fat provides better calcium than the Mead Johnson variety, though the bioavailability of both is sufficient, as is Nestlé's calcium bioavailability.

The biggest controversy has been that soy formulas contain isoflavones, which are estrogen like in their structure but with little estrogenic potency, though apparently at high doses, they have an impact on experimental rat hormones. However, the issue has largely been dismissed since a human study done at the University of Iowa compared adults (20 to 34 years of age) who had been fed soy or cow's-milk formula as infants and found no significant differences in their growth, pubertal development, and reproductive outcomes.[3]

So, bottom line: The soy formulas from the three major manufacturers are safe, healthful, and considerably cheaper than most of the other substitutes for cow's-milk formula. The problem is that I am not sure about the mineral bioavailability and protein content of the soy formulas from the me-too store brands. They may be fine; I just don't know, since I can't find publications to support their claim.

So which to recommend? Abbott claims it has better calcium absorption than Mead Johnson; Mead Johnson claims its calcium bioavailability is sufficient. But Mead Johnson and Nestlé have higher docosahexaenoic acid (DHA) in their products (Enfamil Prosobee and Gerber Good Start Soy), so I recommend theirs (or whichever one is provided by your state's WIC program).

PREDIGESTED FORMULAS (HYDROLYSATES)

These are the Tier 3 formulas. They are intended for fewer babies than the ones we have discussed so far but come in more variations (and flavors) than the others. The proteins are digested (*hydrolyzed*) into amino acids and smaller peptide chains (of up to eight amino acids that are still linked together). Because food allergies are triggered by the protein fraction of foods, these predigested formulas lessen the potential for allergies and improve formula tolerance for some infants.

Two of the formulas have proteins that are partially digested (or hydrolyzed), leaving some of the protein intact. We have already discussed the Nestlé variety known as Gerber Good Start, which has approximately 80 percent of its all-whey protein digested by trypsin, a pancreatic enzyme, while the other 20 percent of the protein is left intact. The Mead Johnson partially digested product is Enfamil Gentlease, which has a combination of both casein and nonfat milk as its protein source, with the proteins mostly digested by the enzymes from pork pancreas. Mead Johnson claims that Gentlease is digested even more than Good Start. The small bit of intact protein improves the taste in both formulas. The fats, minerals, and vitamins for each of these products are similar to the routine formulas for each brand. The sugar for Nestlé is lactose (except in Soothe, as already discussed), because the company markets this formula as its routine formula with the additional benefit that it can help to prevent atopic dermatitis, a common form of allergy (more about this in chapter 9). Enfamil's sugar is 80 percent sucrose and 20 percent lactose, being intended for infants who are colicky and possibly sensitive to lactose, though that is a relatively uncommon situation, as already discussed.

Thus, the marketing and uses for the two formulas are quite different, but one thing is true for both. They should not be confused with the extensively hydrolyzed formulas and used for already existing food allergies, because that small fraction of intact protein can still cause problems for the infant with cow's-milk allergy. The advantage of the Gerber products is they are being sold at near the same price as routine cow's-milk-based formulas.

Extensively hydrolyzed formulas are more complex (and more expensive) varieties made by Abbott and Mead Johnson as hypoallergenic formulas, which means they have little chance of causing any allergy. Here, the proteins are entirely casein that is digested into peptide chains of amino acids (six to eight or fewer) by pork pancreatic enzymes for the Mead Johnson products and for Alimentum, which is the Abbott variety. But, as indicated above, extensive hydrolysis alters the taste as well (Alimentum is supposedly better flavored and more accepted by most infants, especially in its ready-to-feed version). Because these formulas are intended for infants with significant digestive problems (discussed in chapters 9 and 10), and because those problems can be accompanied by secondary lactose intolerance, the sugar in both is a corn syrup derivative, which can be absorbed when lactose can't be digested. The vitamins and minerals again follow the same dictates as the routine formulas, with the exception that calcium is increased because of lactose's absence.

The difference is primarily in the fat content. Now, don't let that term scare you. Babies need their fat from formula as an energy source and for the building blocks it provides the baby's metabolism and cell structure. Enfamil Nutramigen has a routine, long-chain fat that most babies can easily digest and absorb, positioning it as the company's formula for babies who have allergies to both cow's milk and soy. However, babies with specific problems of poor digestion and malabsorption require Enfamil Pregestamil, with 55 percent as easily absorbed medium-chain fats. Alimentum is actually most like Pregestamil, with 33 percent medium-chain fats, and the sugars are a combination of sucrose (table sugar) and modified tapioca starch, which is perhaps what gives it a better taste. For that reason, it is often compared to both Nutramigen and Pregestamil—and though it has lower levels of DHA than the other two, it would receive my recommendation because babies often accept it better than the Mead Johnson products. The slight difference between the sugars in Alimentum's ready-to-feed and powdered forms has already been discussed in chapter 4. That change makes no real clinical difference, but some babies seem to like the sweeter, ready-to-feed form more (table 5.2).

Table 5.2. Carbohydrates in Alimentum

Powder	Ready to Feed
70 percent maltodextrin	70 percent sucrose
30 percent sucrose	30 percent modified tapioca starch

Source: Larry Williams, MD, medical director, Abbott Nutrition.

ELEMENTAL OR AMINO ACID FORMULAS

The protein source in these very expensive formulas is really not protein at all but the smaller amino acid building blocks for the very rare infant who cannot tolerate the easily absorbed and much less expensive hypoallergenic hydrolysate formulas. The composition of fats (with easily absorbed medium-chain fats providing one-third of the fat content in EleCare and Neocate) and sucrose parallels the extensively hydrolyzed formulas and makes these formulas as simply absorbed as possible.

These bank breakers (which cost as much as a monthly Porsche payment) are usually for infants who have required extensive intestinal surgery or who have such severe allergies that they do not respond to the predigested hydrolysates.

PREMATURE FORMULAS

Premature infants require more protein, calories, calcium, phosphorus, and various trace minerals (which they would have received if they were carried to a term delivery). In order to meet their increased nutritional requirements for growth and development (as detailed in chapter 11), specific premature formulas were designed for smaller, hospitalized infants and for infants who were born closer to their due dates or who are ready to be discharged from hospital neonatal units.

The formulas for very small infants (who are often months early) have 20 percent higher calories and more protein, sodium, potassium, calcium, and phosphorus than routine formulas. Their carbohydrate and fat blends are adapted to assist easy absorption, and because of the infant's greater susceptibility to infection, the formulas are only available as preprepared, sterile liquids that are not available outside hospital nurseries.

Infants who are almost ready to go home from the hospital (or babies who are only mildly premature) are transitioned to discharge formulas that still have higher nutrient levels (10 percent more calories and increased nutrients compared to routine formulas) with more readily absorbed fats and carbohydrates to assist their growth. Infants are intended to remain on these formulas until they are six months past their original due date. So an infant who was six weeks premature, for example, would continue on a premature formula until he was seven and a half months old.

The premature formulas from Similac and Enfamil are both protein balanced in terms of whey and casein, whereas the Gerber premature formulas, which are newly released in the United States (though similar products have been available in other parts of the world for years), have partially hydrolyzed whey as their protein, similar to Gerber's term-infant products.

EARLY-INFANT FORMULAS

Some of the newest infant formulas being marketed are those intended for full-term babies in their first three months of life. They have higher whey content relative to casein, though the total protein content is the same as for routine infant formula because breastmilk for babies in the first weeks of life has similar ratios and content of protein. This may or may not be clinically significant, since the composition of breastmilk is constantly changing depending on the mother's diet and her stage of breastfeeding, with the fat content changing in the fore- and hindmilk of a single feeding. The more important feature seems to be that these formulas have higher vitamin D levels, because the American Academy of Pediatrics now recommends 400 IU of that vitamin for all babies.

Because young infants don't drink as much as older infants, this formula compensates for that potential deficiency by increasing the concentration of vitamin D by 25 percent from 12 to 15 IU per ounce. Instead of drinking the 33 ounces that most three-month-olds consume in a day, babies get their entire 400 IU of vitamin D in just 27 ounces.

GOAT'S-MILK FORMULA

This formula was popular for a while as an alternative to cow's milk for babies who were cow's-milk intolerant, because there's less lactose and the protein was supposedly less allergenic (allergy producing) than cow's milk. The products have been taken off the market. There are now far more formula choices than when goat's-milk formulas were available.

Some parents have tried to make goat's milk into a drink for infants, but that is dangerous. The protein content is over three times higher than in cow's milk, and diluting goat's milk by half or even a third to lessen the protein content and the load that the kidneys must filter also dilutes and reduces the other nutrients by the same amount. Additionally, goat's milk is deficient in folate and vitamin

B_6, so there are substantial reasons why it should not be used for infants. The various alternatives that are now on the market have become less costly and more appealing to most parents.

METABOLIC FORMULAS

Babies who have specific metabolic and kidney problems have benefited greatly from formulas tailored to these conditions by Abbott and Mead Johnson, both providing carefully engineered formulas for infants who would not thrive or even survive without them. Because there are so many separate genetic and metabolic conditions that require these special formulas, we will only mention their availability here and indicate that there are numerous resources where caregivers and interested others can go for further information.

PRE- AND PROBIOTICS

A baby in the uterus has almost no intestinal bacteria, but passage down the birth canal exposes the baby to his mother's flora. A baby born by C-section, therefore, has a very different population of bacteria (thought to be acquired from the hospital environment).[4] The bacteria and organisms acquired rapidly proliferate in the baby's lower intestine and develop into what's called the baby's microflora or microbiota. That intestinal population remains remarkably stable throughout the baby's entire lifetime. So researchers are now looking at whether giving pregnant women probiotics can enhance the intestinal flora of their infants in the same way that giving mothers DHA during pregnancy improves their infants' blood levels.

Yes, the population is partially eradicated and may change when a person gets antibiotics for an infection, but usually the same organisms come back. The problem is that sometimes some of the bacteria or yeast resistant to that antibiotic gain a foothold and can cause a secondary infection.

Probiotics, as you're probably aware, are live microorganisms that can be taken to help populate the intestine. In order to be effective, probiotics must survive the defenses of gastrointestinal transit, including the gastric acid, bile, mucin, and immune system of the gut itself.

Once they establish themselves in the large intestine, probiotics reduce the diarrhea that can accompany antibiotics or viral infections, and they can lessen the potential for recurrence of certain infections. But these benefits are often strain specific, with some probiotics more effective in certain conditions. In other words, not all probiotics do the same thing (otherwise, it would be like saying, "You have pneumonia—just take any old antibiotic," without specifying which one would work best for your infection).

Their benefit is usually temporary because a probiotic only colonizes the intestine briefly. Eventually, the bacteria that remain colonized in the infant's lower intestine reemerge as a much larger, adherent bacterial population, making long-term changes to intestinal flora unlikely unless the probiotic's growth is encouraged by prebiotics (which will also be discussed).

Three formulas, Enfamil Nutramigen, Gerber Good Start Protect, and Gerber Good Start Soothe, each contain a probiotic in their powdered forms, presumably to help in managing allergic manifestations of cow's-milk protein allergy and in supporting a healthy immune response. The Gerber variety provides a minimum of 100 million colony-forming units (CFU) of *Bifidobacter lactis* in 16 ounces of Protect and approximately the same number of *Lactobacillus reuteri* in Soothe. The *L. reuteri* in Soothe is Biogaia, another popular probiotic. Nutramigen has approximately the same amount of *Lactobacillus GG* (which is better known as Culturelle and is available to help ameliorate diarrhea).

To put that 100 million CFU in perspective, most probiotics for adults provide approximately a billion CFU per dose. And to put that into perspective, you and I have 100 trillion cells in our bodies and ten times that number of organisms (a quadrillion) making up the microflora in our intestinal tracts. So even a dose of a billion represents a millionth of the number of organisms already in place. (But please also remember that most intestinal infections begin with relatively few organisms entering the intestinal tract. Shigella requires only ten organisms to start a severe case of dysentery. And a case of salmonella can come from as few as 15 to 20 bacteria.)

The idea is that the colony-forming units of the probiotics preferentially adhere to and protect the intestinal surface and begin to form a formidable bacterial population that can balance the flora that's already there and protect against any disease-causing pathogens and any allergy-causing offenders while they are present.

The term *prebiotics* describes food components, typically carbohydrates, that resist digestion in the upper gastrointestinal tract to reach the colon (large intestine) intact, where they feed the intestine's beneficial bacteria. In doing so, they selectively stimulate the growth and activity of those bacteria in the colon that are thought to have positive effects on the development of the infant immune system, since an estimated 70 percent of the immune system is located in the gastrointestinal tract, which then establishes a first line of defense against environmental infections.

Prebiotics exert their effect on the metabolism and immune system by supporting the growth of healthy bacteria groups, including *Bifidobacterium* and *Lactobacillus* species. They can also hamper the growth of disease-producing bacteria directly by binding to them, thereby inactivating the "bad" bacteria themselves by blocking their ability to attach to the intestine and by supporting the growth of the intestinal lining, allowing it to become a more effective barrier.

The beneficial bacteria also produce absorbable nutrients, including vitamin K and folate, and help metabolize certain medications. Additionally, the healthy bacteria break down dietary substances (antigens) that might otherwise cause sensitivity reactions, thus helping the body to develop a tolerance for foods that might produce an allergy.

Current research indicates that breastmilk prebiotics play a key role in supporting the colonization of the infant gastrointestinal tract by feeding and thus supporting the beneficial bacteria after birth, influencing the composition of intestinal flora. Research has identified at least 200, and possibly as many as 900, different, naturally occurring prebiotic varieties in breastmilk (the breastmilk prebiotics seem to vary in different parts of the world and in different stages of lactation).

Commercially, four prebiotics are now available as supplements and have been added globally to a wide range of food products, including all the routine infant formulas, in order to approximate the benefits of naturally occurring prebiotics. However, these pre- and probiotics are not mandated by the FDA, and apparently probiotics are technically difficult to incorporate, so some of the store-brand products may not contain them.

SUMMARY

Rather than abbreviated summaries for the various formulas, a series of tables is provided, reviewing the uses for each of the formulas, the components of each of the formulas (table 5.1), and a comparison of their costs (table 5.3). This comparison was performed in Atlanta supermarkets. While costs may vary in different locales and types of stores, the relative costs are similar for these different products, which will be discussed further in the chapters where their primary use is detailed. A more extensive table (table A.1) is available in the appendix.

Table 5.3. Comparative Costs of Infant Formula

Average Monthly Cost of Georgia's WIC-Approved Infant Formulas[a]		
Breastmilk with vitamin D 400 IU daily supplement	Vitamin D 50 ml container = $8.33 (1 ml per day = $0.16 per ml × 30 days) = $4.80 $4.80	
Tier 1 Formula	**Powdered (12 oz.)**	**RTF (1 qt.)**
"Routine" cow's milk based (partially hydrolyzed, 100 percent whey)	Yield 85 oz./32 oz. = 2.65 30 days/2.65 = 11.32 cans a month 12 cans × price $12.49 = $149.88 **$149.88**[b]	Price $6.38 × 30 days = $191.40 **$191.40**[b]
Tier 2 Formulas	**Powdered (12.3–12.9 oz.)**	**RTF (1 qt.)**
Soy protein	Yield 90 oz./32 oz. = 2.81 30 days/2.81 = 10.67 cans a month 11 cans × price $13.96 = $153.56 **$153.56**	Price $6.55 × 30 days = $196.50 **$196.50**
Cow's milk based with rice starch	Avg. yield 91.5 oz./32 oz. = 2.85 30 days/2.85 = 10.52 cans a month 11 cans × price $14.49 = $159.39 **$159.39**	Price $6.16 × 30 days = $184.80 **$184.80**
Partially hydrolyzed casein and whey (60 percent whey, 40 percent casein)	Avg. yield 87 oz./32 oz. = 2.71 30 days /2.71 = 11.07 cans a month 12 cans × price $14.99 = $179.88 **$179.88**	Price $6.99 × 30 days = $209.70 **$209.70**
Tier 3 Formulas	**Powdered (16 oz.)**	**RTF (1 qt.)**
Extensively hydrolyzed casein (100 percent casein)	Avg. yield 114 oz./32 oz. = 3.56 30 days/3.56 = 8.42 cans a month 9 cans × price $24.84 = $223.56 **$223.56**	Price $9.17 × 30 days = $275.10 **$275.10**
Extensively hydrolyzed casein containing MCT oil (100 percent casein)	Avg. yield 112 oz./32 oz. = 3.50 30 days/3.50 = 8.57 cans a month 9 cans × price $28.71 = $258.39 **$258.39**	—
Tier 4 Formula	**Powdered (14.1 oz.)**	**RTF (1 qt.)**
Amino acid elemental	Avg. yield 90 oz./32 oz. = 2.81 30 days/2.81 = 10.67 cans a month 11 cans × price $46.53 = $511.83 **$511.83**	—

[a]Amount of formula is based on an infant consuming 32 ounces (1 quart) per day for a month (30 days). Based on average retail grocery store price as of November 2010 through January 2011.

[b]This price does not reflect the rebate to the Georgia WIC program.

Source: S. A. Cohen and K. Crane, "An Evidence-Based, Cost-Sensitive Infant Formula Algorithm for the Infant on Georgia's WIC" (in press).

6

~~

Gastroesophageal Reflux

What Goes Down May Come Up

Babies spit up. Mothers know that and have known that forever. In fact, Shakespeare wrote about "the infant mewling and puking in the nurse's arms" as the first of the seven stages of man in *As You Like It*.[1] But the question is this: What can be done?

Probably the best advice is to remind yourself that it will get better—and then lay in a good stock of bibs, always carry an extra outfit for the baby when you go out, and bring along one for yourself, too. Your baby will probably make several attempts to redecorate your dress or the nursery carpet in those first few months of life. This does not arise from an early desire to become a designer (interior or fashion, as the case may be). Nor is it an early attempt to communicate an underlying Freudian emotion.

Spitting up is simply the result of a number of differences between your baby's developing anatomy and yours. You may have heard it said that babies have a weak stomach. Actually, that is not true. Babies have a smaller stomach that is less compliant (i.e., stretchable) than those of older children and adults. In addition, babies are fed more frequently and thus have a relatively full stomach most of a 24-hour day. The angle of the esophagus (the tube that carries food from the mouth to the stomach—and in this situation, back up again) as it enters the stomach is greater than 90 degrees (figure 6.1), making it easier for stomach contents to come up into the esophagus, especially since babies spend a good deal of time lying down on their tummies or on their backs. Taken together, all of these factors contribute to babies spitting up more, or, as it is termed, having more reflux—that is, having stomach contents come back up the esophagus.[2]

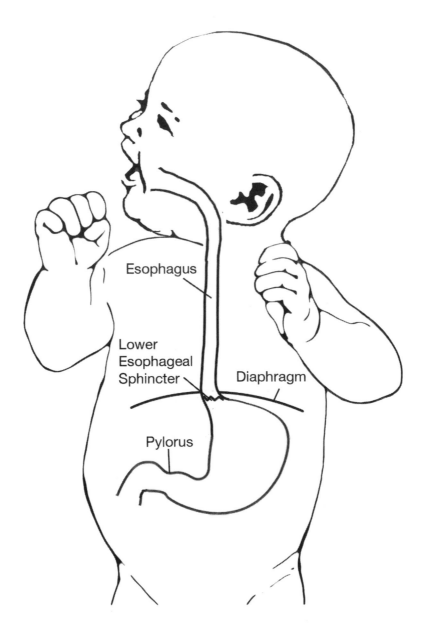

Figure 6.1. Infant's esophagus and stomach.

The result is that the baby will have harmless "wet burps" about the size of a tablespoon or even an ounce of formula. These wet burps occur after many, if not most, feedings. Most babies will do this occasionally, and formula will harmlessly dribble down their chins. This is the reason parents should remember not to lay infants on their backs after feeding, particularly if they spit up often. It is important to keep their heads elevated for 30 to 60 minutes. And understand that many babies will worsen at around three months of age, when they become more active, putting more pressure on their stomachs as they jubilantly kick and move about. They'll begin to improve at approximately five to six months, when they are sitting upright more often, are on thicker infant foods, and are fed less frequently. At that time also, the stomach becomes more stretchable, or compliant. In fact, the babies who keep most of their spoon-fed foods down at that age seem to be the ones who outgrow their reflux sooner, with most babies outgrowing the problem by 8–18 months of age.

Mark was different, however. His spitting up started in the same way as for most other babies. In the first several weeks of life, he returned small puddles of formula after each feeding, with one or two repeat performances over the next several minutes. His mother, Mrs. Aurelius, was not excessively worried, having been cautioned about this earlier. But she became appropriately frightened when the formula filled his nose as well as his mouth and caused him to sputter. He never turned blue (which would have been worrisome), but he did seem to choke, turning red during and shortly after feeds.

Mrs. Aurelius tried sitting Mark up in an infant chair for an hour after each feeding. She even prevented him from slumping in the chair by putting towels on each side. Placing him in the chair decreased the number of times that he would spit up the formula, as it does for most babies, but the problem persisted. At least once a day, he brought the formula back more forcefully, showering everyone and everything for two feet in front of him. To be sure that nothing was blocking the passage of the food, a barium X-ray was performed and was normal.

I heard little else about Mark until he was three months old. Mark's problem had become worse, as expected. He was more active, and that seemed to force the food back up more frequently. Mark appeared no worse for all this vomiting. In fact, he was gaining weight and growing in length regularly. But his mother complained. "It's not just Mark that's getting to me. It's the smell of his curdled milk on my dress. It's the laundry that I do for both of us each day. The spit-up and vomit escapes his bib and ends up all over the place."

Her words and concerns, as well as the potential for developing problems, made me want to do more for them. I took a careful history. Mark's mother wasn't overfeeding, with Mark bringing up what his stomach couldn't handle, but his spitting varied in character considerably. Sometimes he'd bring up his entire four-ounce feeding (or so it seemed), and at other times he wouldn't bring up anything. To get a better estimate of the volume of regurgitation or vomiting, I filled a syringe with formula and shot a small amount onto the paper that covered my exam table. "Is that how much he spits?" I asked, repeating the question and the spray until the mother thought it looked like the puddle he produced. It was somewhere between a teaspoon and a tablespoon, though it looked like a larger amount when it spread across the table.

That was reassuring to both of us. As a result, I had his mother feed him more frequently with a slightly smaller amount each time. The intent was to lessen the stomach contents, since an overfilled stomach might provoke more vomiting. But Mark continued to spit up, though in decreased amounts.

Since I wondered whether Mark was having difficulty in emptying his stomach, I had his mother tilt him slightly toward the right side to enhance the drainage from his stomach, but that also made little difference in his spitting up.

Finally we had some measure of success when we thickened Mark's formula with cereal. The rationale is simple: it's harder for a thick solution to exit from a large container through a smaller one (you may remember this as Bernoulli's principle). Dr. John Herbst, a well-known pediatric gastroenterologist, compared this thickening to a bottle of ketchup. The illustration makes sense. Thicker ketchups are much harder to pour than thinner brands. Note that all of the glass bottles have narrow necks (like the esophagus) and larger bodies that look like a stomach (at least to a pediatric gastroenterologist).

For Mark, this change helped considerably. He didn't stop vomiting entirely, but once again he had the smaller wet burps, as in his earlier months.

Fortunately, he stopped regurgitating entirely before his 15-month checkup, and his bib was removed except at mealtime. Mark's case points out much of what you should know about a spitting baby: this condition, which doctors call gastroesophageal reflux (GER), usually starts early in life and improves when the compliance of the stomach improves, the stomach becomes less full over the 24-hour period, the baby's overall muscle tone improves, more time is spent sitting or in a walker or seat (thus less time is spent lying down), and the angle that the esophagus makes with the stomach shifts to less than 90 degrees. For many babies, it clears by several months of age, and almost all infants stop vomiting (or refluxing) by 1 to 1½ years of age. The few babies who don't improve will often have a condition similar to a hiatal hernia in an adult, which weakens the action of the sphincter or pulls it into the chest.

WHEN SHOULD I BECOME CONCERNED?

For most, this pattern is common, without problem, and generally goes away by itself, with the babies often smiling even while spitting or shortly afterward. Unfortunately, a small percentage of babies do not fit into this category of "happy spitters." Their symptoms persist and are troublesome. They are considered to have not just GER but gastroesophageal reflux disease (GERD). In these cases, just like in adults with GERD, the lower esophageal sphincter muscle opens inappropriately and frequently during the day, and the esophagus fails to constrict (squeeze) and push the stomach contents back into the stomach before the acid, digestive enzymes, and other stomach juices can do harm.

I become concerned when the vomiting does not improve as it should or when babies do not do as well as they should. Had Mark lost so many calories with throwing up that he lost instead of gained weight, I would have been concerned, and I am sure his mother would have been as well. If he were crying or irritable during or after his feedings or throughout the day, exhibiting behavior like arching his head back and throwing his arms over his head or tilting his head to the side during the feedings, I would have wanted to test his stools for blood to see if stomach acid was causing inflammation or ulcers in his esophagus that could be contributing to the feeding problems. If he or some other child had had repeated pneumonias or bronchial infections from the formula rising into his throat and then going down into his windpipe and lungs, I would have been even more concerned. When these symptoms and complications occur, with or without spitting up, and are perceived as troublesome by the parent, they are red flags that the child has GERD.

When these symptoms occur without any actual spitting up, the condition is described as *silent reflux*. When the reflux is obvious to everyone, often dietary and positional changes can be tried, and perhaps a trial of medication might be warranted. But to diagnose silent reflux, and sometimes to determine whether reflux is underlying the symptoms, it is often necessary to perform tests, such as a pH esophagram, which documents how often acid or formula comes up into the esophagus, and how long it stays, even when not regurgitating all the way out of the mouth. I might have pursued additional tests to rule out other conditions that can either masquerade as reflux or begin with regurgitation as one of the first symptoms (table 6.1). Knowing these results would determine whether I should use medication as well as dietary changes (e.g., thickening of formula or a trial of hypoallergenic formula) to treat the problem, or whether, as in the most severe cases, particularly those in which dietary and positional changes and medical therapy have failed, I might have to refer Mark to my surgical colleagues in order for them to try to tighten the sphincter in the operating room.

Mark, as I noted, did not have any of these red flags or complications (table 6.2). He was one of those happy spitters, for whom dietary and positional changes are all that is necessary.

Table 6.1. Signs and Symptoms Suggesting Diagnosis Other Than Reflux

Forceful vomiting
Blood in the vomit or stool
Diarrhea or constipation
Poor weight gain
Fever or lethargy accompanying the vomiting
Abdominal tenderness or distention
Onset of vomiting after six months of life
Large or small head, bulging soft spot, or seizures
Large liver or spleen or persistent jaundice

Source: www.nutrition4kids.com.

Table 6.2. Significant Concerns in GERD

Red Flags for Reflux during Infancy
Poor weight gain
Excessive crying or irritability
Head usually tilted to one side
Feeding problems
Respiratory problems, including
• wheezing, difficulty with or noisy breathing, apnea
• recurrent pneumonia, bronchitis, or sinus problems, ear infections
Symptoms that continue beyond infancy

Source: www.nutrition4kids.com.

Yet there were several simple things I still wanted to do in order to prevent weight loss, excessive irritability, or respiratory infections. Unfortunately, not every one of these measures works for every baby, and seeing what will work is often a matter of trial and error, guided by knowledge and experience.

WHAT CAN I DO TO DECREASE THE SPITTING?

The first and simplest treatment is to sit your baby in an infant seat or in the infant "bouncer" after feedings. The idea behind this is to allow gravity to help bring formula or human milk toward the bottom of the stomach, allowing the stomach to empty its contents into the intestine more easily. For this to be effective, the chair should be at a 45- to 60-degree angle (approximately one-half to two-thirds of the way up), and the baby should be upright in the chair. You may need to place some rolled up towels on each side of the baby to help you accomplish this. You may also want to cushion the bottom of the chair so the legs aren't folded onto the stomach, increasing pressure on the abdomen.

Because babies can slump down in spite of your efforts, parents instead can purchase wedges that elevate the head 45 to 60 degrees. Some parents have made their own inclines for their babies to lie on. The simplest way is to place a pillow under the mattress or bricks under the legs of the bed near the baby's head. But because babies can roll easily, some parents fashion an incline with a padded peg between the baby's legs that holds him in position, whether he is lying on his back or stomach. An additional sheet is often needed to hold the baby on the board. While this apparatus looks like something designed for torture during the Spanish Inquisition, it may work when the infant seat doesn't, particularly for the young infant with little muscle tone to keep him up or the squirming one-year-old who will no longer sit in an infant seat. Babies who require this incline are usually on it around the clock rather than just for an hour after meals. Note that the American Academy of Pediatrics recommends that babies be put on their backs to sleep.[3] This is not necessarily advisable in my mind if a baby has significant reflux with the potential for the formula to reflux and be aspirated into the lungs. So I often recommend the elevation and that the babies be positioned on the their right side so that gravity will help move the stomach contents to the intestine and so any regurgitated material will empty out of the mouth.

Another simple concept is to try small, frequent feedings. This also helps to keep the stomach empty, so little is left to be burped up accidentally. This is particularly useful for babies who seem to be hungry around the clock. They spit and seem hungry afterward.

While these techniques work for most newborns, some babies may have difficulty emptying their stomachs. The valve at the outlet (the pyloric sphincter) is positioned slightly higher (figure 6.1). The upright position will not help, since a puddle of formula lays in the bottom of the stomach, unable to exit. These babies can be helped by lowering the infant chair slightly (still keeping the bottom of the esophagus higher than the rest of the stomach) and turning the baby over toward the right side so that drainage is once again enhanced.

Some babies with a high pylorus, as well as others with normal placement of this valve, will also have some thickening of the muscle around the valve. In the extreme (a complete blockage of the stomach outlet), where vomiting, and often forceful vomiting, is the norm, this is called pyloric stenosis. The valve at the end of the stomach and entry into the small intestine (called the duodenum) is thickened, and almost nothing except perhaps a dribble of formula can enter into the intestine. The result is that the baby vomits large volumes almost every meal, with enough force to literally shoot the formula back across the room. The baby can become dehydrated and quite sick, but appropriate surgery readily relieves all problems. When the muscles of the pylorus have swollen only slightly, surgery is not indicated. The valve still works. Food passes, but at a slower rate than usual. The stomach stays full longer, and with each stomach contraction, the remaining food can exit up the esophagus more easily than through the tightened pylorus

Two things may help: keeping the feeding small as before and having an ultrasound or X-ray to ensure that pyloric stenosis is not the underlying problem.

If your baby does not improve on smaller feedings (and pyloric stenosis is not the cause), then you must take additional steps. The problem is not that the stomach is retaining food but the original problem alone: a wide-open and easily passed lower esophageal sphincter.

If your pediatrician has any doubts about this, he can do a number of fancy tests to prove that esophageal reflux is the cause. But tests are usually not necessary. The repeated wet burps almost make the diagnosis of reflux alone. He may need the tests, however, if your child has other, more troublesome symptoms, such as wheezing, irritability, or poor growth. This is the child with silent reflux that we previously described. The formula is either swallowed or rises part of the way in the esophagus, causing irritation and respiratory difficulties but not vomiting.

Esophageal reflux that has not responded to the previous tactics may yet improve with careful dietary manipulation. As in Mark's case, I would thicken the formula, based on the ketchup-bottle theory.

As indicated in the previous chapter, two different formulas have rice starch as their principal carbohydrate: Similac Sensitive for Spit Up and Enfamil AR. These are used in place of routine formula, but they are most effective when no acid blockers (Zantac, Prilosec, Prevacid, or Nexium) are prescribed, since the rice starch requires the normal acidic environment of the stomach to convert from a thin liquid, as it was consumed, into the denser material that has less chance of being regurgitated. Even then, it is important to limit the feeding volume and to try to make sure the baby takes it slowly. The rice starch won't have time to form into a thicker substance if the baby spits up right after gulping down 4 to 6 ounces.

The alternative is to add cereal to the formula or breastmilk. This may be the first choice if the baby is already on a different specialty formula (one of the premature or hydrolysate formulas because of other needs). Rice cereal is the usual choice unless the baby has constipation, and then oatmeal can be substituted. Begin by adding 1 teaspoon to each ounce of formula you use. If the baby does not improve, continue to add more rice cereal (going up slowly, adding up to an extra ½ teaspoon per ounce every day or two). Try to see if the baby keeps the thickened formula down after each additional addition. Some babies require the formula to have the consistency of honey or thick ketchup before they are able to retain it without problems. The maximum is 3 teaspoons (or 1 tablespoon) per ounce, which is the thickness that the rice-starch cereals provide.

The thickened formula will be more difficult for a baby to suck out, too. You will need to make sure that the nipple hole is large enough to permit the formula to come through easily. Any cross-cut or "Y" nipple should work. Or you can take a hot sewing needle or small blade and carefully enlarge the hole in a regular nipple. Either technique should be fine. A coffee grinder can decrease the particle size of the cereal and help the flow.

No matter what tactic is being tried, your physician will need to keep close tabs on your baby's weight and hydration. With the baby spitting up some of his formula, he will be losing calories that he would normally be using. With smaller, frequent feedings, you must make sure the baby is receiving enough as well. If you give 2 to 2½ ounces of regular formula each day for each pound the baby weighs, that should be enough for the baby to gain weight and thrive happily. If the baby is on thickened formula, you might find that he is taking less but still gaining because of the calories (and protein) the cereal adds. That is expected and not a problem as long as the baby remains well hydrated, which can be judged better by checking that the urine remains frequent and light in color than by trying to calculate the amount he theoretically should be taking.

Weight loss is not the problem for the child on thicker feedings. He will have a tendency to gain too much weight—since each teaspoon of cereal adds another 5 calories. While that doesn't seem like much, 4 teaspoons is the equivalent of another ounce of formula. Multiply that times six feedings per day, and that's the equivalent of an extra 120 calories, which can add an extra pound a month to the baby's weight. This is fine for a baby who is having difficulty gaining. But for the otherwise healthy infant, you may need to cut down how much the baby eats (helping to prevent obesity and regurgitation).

But the only way to be sure is to weigh him. You do not need to buy an infant scale. Just stop by your physician's office at least once a week until the baby's symptoms improve so that you can use the scale there and obtain any additional advice if you need it.

WHAT IF THE SPITTING UP DOESN'T STOP?

These are the babies we usually see in our office. The pediatrician has done all he can, and the baby needs the kind of further evaluation that the pediatric gastroenterologist can provide. We have briefly discussed some of the tests: a pH esophagram to evaluate the extent of the reflux; an upper gastrointestinal series and/or a pyloric ultrasound to evaluate the anatomy. Other possible tests include an endoscopy to view and biopsy the esophagus and stomach to ensure that nothing else in the gastrointestinal tract is contributing to the problem; a gastric scan to see whether the stomach is emptying appropriately and/or to make sure the infant is not aspirating any of the formula; and blood work or further tests to rule out other causes. Often none of these tests is necessary, especially when the mother or even her next door neighbor can make the diagnosis.

Occasionally, reflux can be confused with milk allergy. Then a trial of a soy- or other non-milk-based formula is indicated. We suggest soy, because fewer than 14 percent of infants with milk allergy will have an allergy to soy, and even those who don't have a true allergy will only have a 30 to 40 percent chance of being soy intolerant, meaning that 60 to 86 percent of infants should do well on that substitute.[4] A more expensive choice would be one of the partially or fully hydrolyzed formulas, the partially hydrolyzed formulas being cheaper and likely to work if there is not a true milk allergy. (The distinction between a true allergy and an intolerance or sensitivity will be discussed in chapter 9.)

WHY ARE SO MANY BABIES ON MEDICATION?

Many infants with persistent reflux end up on acid blockers, like Zantac (ranitidine), Prilosec (omeprazole), or Prevacid (lanzoperazole). Zantac and the other medications in its class (Tagamet, Pepcid, and Axid), known as H2 blockers, prevent certain (histamine) signals from stimulating the acid-producing cells to secrete acid. When the infant is on one of the H2 blockers, the acid-producing cells will then produce less gastric or stomach acid. The Prilosec medication is in a class known as proton pump inhibitors (PPIs). This class of medications includes compounds that are appropriate for infants and children: Nexium and Zegerid, which come as powders; Prevacid, which comes as a dissolving tablet; and Protonix, Aciphex, and Dexilent, which come as pills more appropriate to adults and older children. These compounds, while they are active, totally block the pumps from producing acid.

Stomach acid has several effects: first, it contributes to damage to the esophagus when acid refluxes into that area; second, it can lessen the overall tone of the valve-like area (called the lower esophageal sphincter, or LES) separating the esophagus and stomach and impair its function, thereby weakening the valve's effectiveness. Over time, exposure to the acid and the enzymes that accompany it can cause a narrowing of the esophagus (called a stricture) or, later in life, a tendency toward cancer.[5] Lastly, acid has an important role in protecting the stomach and intestinal tract from infections, as well as in facilitating digestion of certain proteins, vitamins, and minerals.

So if you lower the acid with these medicines, the reflux causes less irritation to the esophagus and thus lessens an infant's irritability, if that is being caused by reflux. However, studies haven't shown that it consistently lessens the actual reflux. Reflux can still occur, but without the acid, so your baby can still spit up just as much.

For the child with severe reflux, the medicine is warranted and actually important. For the child with milder symptoms, the PPIs may not be particularly useful, and there is the potential for increased infections with long-term use (in adult studies, though; there have been no infant studies to prove this is true for babies). Adult studies also show some calcium derangements, but we drink less milk and are less active than children who are running and playing and remodeling their bones as they do so. So the calcium concerns in adults are less of an issue for infants and children.

WHAT ELSE CAN I DO TO HELP MY BABY?

Relax. That's not a glib statement, but actually a recommendation. My office practice is full of infants with reflux who have reflux-induced feeding problems that worsen when their mothers become anxious. It's a logical cycle. The babies have feeding problems as a result of the reflux, but stress can add to them. Mothers worry that their babies are spitting up so much that the babies will lose weight, so they tend to feed more (and often too much), so the babies spit up and shy away from the feeding, making the mother all the more anxious. And some babies get "spoiled" and feeding averse (they push their food away). Mothers carry their infants constantly or pick them up immediately if they even threaten to regurgitate—a tense, difficult situation, certainly. And worse, long-term feeding or behavioral problems can develop. So, please really do try to relax and follow the suggestions here.

For some babies, medication and further testing may be needed. But this is rare. Most infants can be managed with the guidelines provided. And know that 95 percent of babies outgrow the condition by 14 months of age.[6] They may get worse from three to five months of age, but then most begin to improve. Those that spit up minimally with thick formula and solids outgrow their reflux issues the soonest. But still, most babies do outgrow reflux when they advance to table food and are walking. I hope your baby is one of them.

SUMMARY

- Spitting up is caused by a number of factors in infants and is usually normal.
- Most babies simply have wet burps and can be termed "happy spitters," with the reflux causing no significant problem.
- Most infants respond to simple dietary modifications and to changes in position, and most reflux usually improves noticeably or is gone by the child's first birthday.
- Children who vomit everything forcefully, have repeated pneumonias, or are constantly irritable or fail to gain weight, as well as those who do not improve, require further medical or surgical attention.
- Figure 6.2 brings together all of the recommendations into a stepwise approach or algorithm.

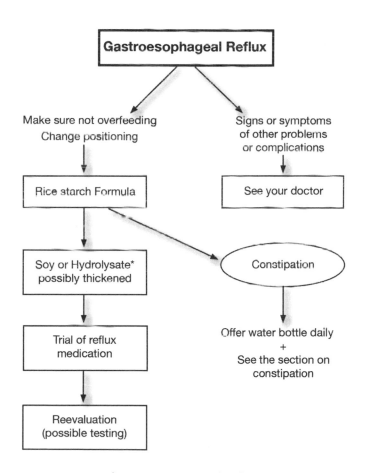

Figure 6.2. Coping with reflux.

7

⌒

Colic and Fussiness
Or "Let's Rock around the Clock Tonight"

Mrs. Arnold was in my office waiting for me to wash my hands and enter the room. She was not sitting quietly—she was actively pacing the room, bouncing Matt, her inconsolable infant. The five-week-old infant was kicking his legs and screaming with distress that was mirrored on his frantic mother's face. She smiled weakly as I entered and then burst into tears: "Doctor, I don't know what to do! I'm scared to death."

A sharp contrast could be drawn between Mrs. Arnold on that day and when I had seen the well-experienced mother in the hospital after Matt's uneventful delivery. She had been relaxed and nudging Matt's mouth patiently to her breast. He was so quiet but disinterested in feeding during those first days of his life. Even at Matt's two-week checkup in the office, all was well.

Shortly thereafter, however, life had deteriorated in the Arnold household. Matt began to cry and fuss, particularly in the late afternoon, just when Mrs. Arnold was preparing dinner and trying to settle her other children after soccer practice.

At first, the fussing had been limited to some agitated squirming of his entire body in his bassinet. Matt would draw his legs up and would often become red-faced as he expelled gas from his rectum. But the crying that occasionally accompanied or preceded this activity increased rapidly. What had been a whimper and whine became full-fledged shrieks of discomfort. Matt now slept less, and his periods of wakefulness, especially in the evening, were punctuated by hours of unrelieved tension.

Trying to feed him was even more frustrating than trying to console him. Matt would suck voraciously just as soon as he could get his mouth around his mother's nipple, but within a few minutes he would once again pull away crying and rejecting further efforts to be fed—that is, until an hour or so later, when the scene would be replayed. Mrs. Arnold had become convinced that her milk was insufficient and had begun to offer a commercial formula after feeding, but that was regarded with equal disdain. His nipple confusion and her frustration had led her to switch him entirely to the formula, but he was still uncomfortable.

Mrs. Arnold was seeking help for two very obvious reasons: she wanted to know what was wrong with her infant and what could be done about it. She had lost confidence in her own ability to care for Matt and started to question herself and her abilities as a mother, though she had successfully nursed her other sons: "Is it my milk? Am I doing something wrong?"

She held Matt on her lap as I completed my examination. She seemed to be praying that I would find some easily treatable explanation for his behavior. Fortunately, the only problem that my examination revealed was a full abdomen, with very active, high-pitched rumblings throughout the intestine. The remainder of the exam was normal, including the rectal exam to determine whether the anal outlet was too tight or whether there might be blood inside.

Once Matt was changed, the first thing that I did was simply let Mrs. Arnold know that, despite the enormous frustrations in taking care of her son, she was not to blame and that usually these heart-wrenching cries dissipate on their own over time. But she was nearly in tears, so my reassurance was of little benefit. I let her know I was there to help her. I couldn't perform miracles, but I could review the problem with her and provide a rational and effective approach for her. "Matt has colic," I said and began to explain.

A good definition for "infantile colic" is a fretful infant with consistent periods of intense irritability that extend for approximately two to four hours per day between three weeks and four months of age, after which they almost magically improve. When irritability is more prolonged or occurs outside those time parameters, the fussiness does not fit into the standard definition and generally means that there is a different explanation.

WHAT CAUSES THE FRETTING FUSSINESS?

Fussiness is a symptom; compare it to fever. Saying that a child has a fever tells both the parent and the pediatrician that the child's body temperature is too high. It does not say what is wrong with the child (a virus, ear infection, pneumonia, or other cause), only that something is. This same principle holds true for the inconsolable infant. Irritability tells us something is wrong, but what's causing it still has to be determined.

A pediatrician can be helpful in sorting through what has become the family's problem. Extracting a complete history of the situation and examining the baby will help make certain that the baby is indeed "healthy." Your pediatrician can weigh the baby to make sure that he is gaining and getting enough at each feeding. That reassurance alone is important, because it relieves any worry that something severe, like a twisted or obstructed intestine, has occurred. But that reassurance must be coupled with an understanding of what is causing the colicky symptoms and what can be done about them.

The best way to understand colic is by reconsidering the most prominent symptoms: the passing of rectal gas and the swelling (distention) of the abdomen. Both appear during the periods of irritability, and both appear to begin or worsen after eating. And you can certainly reason that a baby's belly, bulging with gas, could make him irritable enough to announce his discomfort to the world by his only means—his cry.

As a new parent, you may remember how you attempted to interpret those first irritated cries. Both you and the baby survived those early months because you learned your baby's schedule. A cry at feeding time usually suggested that a hungry mouth and stomach were awaiting nourishment. You fed the baby, and the crying stopped. But between feedings, you might wonder, is the baby hungry or just wet? A sensitive nose can help, but countless diapers have been changed when the baby and diaper were dry, and when the baby's crying continued unabated anyway.

Should a clean diaper and a warm breast or bottle not be successful, the crying from a fussy infant often gets progressively worse. The initial cry of irritation increases to violent shrieks so constant and riveting that one can only picture the worst of all horrors (whatever they are) going on inside the baby to cause such a scream. The baby appears to be in agony, and parents become frightened and frustrated. Within an hour or two, mothers become as distraught and as irritable as their infants, wearing nerves and floorboards thin trying to calm and console the baby.

It then becomes hard to remember that every baby does not just sleep or eat all the time, and each may be expected to have fussy periods during the day. Babies are burped to expel extra gas, hopefully decreasing discomfort in the process. Yet studies show that six-week-old infants have unexplained periods of crying that may add up to three hours a day, despite the burping. This is considered normal (and may represent nervous energy that babies relieve by crying).[1]

What differentiates that baby with three hours of fussing from an infant with colic? Often it's that normally fussy infants don't cry straight through, although their irritability may extend longer at each stretch. Some self-reliant mothers can tolerate those hours without any problems of concern (especially if that crying is spread through small periods during the day). Yet others would be thoroughly challenged by those same infants. Some infants with more severe colic—those who would challenge any of us—seem to have more gas, more distension, and more irritability than babies who do not have this problem.

The distinction then is not that colicky infants have different symptoms. They have the same problems, but with greater intensity and often for longer periods each day—and generally in the late afternoon or evening. We must therefore look for other explanations that can account for these symptoms in various degrees.

If we link these symptoms together, we may see a parallel: the more gas a child has, the greater his irritability. Somehow it seems logical—gaseous distension causing discomfort and that discomfort reflected as irritability. Many babies with colic have enormous abdomens—so enormous that the abdomen looks as if it will burst. It won't, but that distention certainly could make an infant as uncomfortable as I am just seeing it. Moreover, many colicky infants seem temporarily improved after they pass the gas. That observation supports this relationship further.

WHERE DOES GAS COME FROM
AND WHAT CAN BE DONE ABOUT IT?

Gas can enter the intestinal tract in only two ways: it can be introduced or produced. What's introduced comes from the baby swallowing air when sucking or crying.

Internal gas production usually occurs in the large intestine. The bacterial flora that reside there digest unabsorbed foods to form various gaseous (and odorous) products. It is no more complicated than eating a bowl of beans. Most sugars are absorbed in the upper portion of the small bowel (the jejunum) after enzymes break down starches and complex sugars into smaller, more easily digestible sugars. Humans, however, lack the enzyme to cleanse the sugar (raffinose) in beans, and so that sugar passes to the large intestine, where it is available for bacteria to digest it into acid and gas.

Your colicky infant could have a similar problem. He could be swallowing air when sucking at the breast or a pacifier. If he consumes more sugar than his small intestine can absorb, gas is going to be formed. There are multiple reasons that could happen, but no matter the cause, the significance (and solution) is clear.

If you are breastfeeding, most of what you eat is metabolized and remains within your own body. But it is possible that if your diet contains large amounts of certain sugars and starches, you could transport some of the sugars in your milk and unwittingly overwhelm your infant's capacity to absorb those carbohydrates. If you avoid these indulgences, you may ease your infant's colic. Conventional wisdom has taught many pediatricians to recommend that you avoid the more complex carbohydrates that give you gas as well: beans, beer, broccoli, brussels sprouts, cabbage, carbonated beverages, champagne, lentils, and mushrooms, as well as any spices that seem to cause irritability in your infant.

If you have your baby on a bottle, the way to avoid excess carbohydrates is to avoid excess formula. Of all of the causes of colic, this is generally the easiest to correct. Often the baby is anxious to feed and will chug down several ounces of formula before he has satisfied his need to suck. He wants a nipple, but unfortunately that gets interpreted as hunger all too often, and quickly another bottle with more formula is given.

Worse, some mothers will begin cereal or other solids. These foods contain starch that requires pancreatic enzymes. These enzymes are not fully active in those early months of life. Even if digestive enzymes could degrade all the carbohydrate, a stomach stretched with formula is just as distended and equally uncomfortable for the infant.

Overfeeding is less of a problem with breastfeeding. Less milk is left for the infant toward the end of feeding at each breast. If an infant wants to continue to suck, he can continue to nurse, but less milk will enter his stomach.

Where both the breast- and the bottle-feeding mother can get trapped is two hours later, if the infant begins to get fussy again. When you feed your apparently hungry infant once more, you may be doing two things: you will refill a stomach that may not even be emptied yet, increasing the potential for reflux and regurgitation; equally important, you are going to tire yourself out. If you care to devote your entire life to feeding your infant, that's fine—temporarily. But by tiring yourself excessively, you may also deplete your own reserves and make less milk. Then you really will have a hungry infant to feed. And you may drain your own emotional reserves as well—to the point that it feels you only have a single, already overstretched nerve left to contend with a crying infant.

CAN MY BABY JUST BE SWALLOWING TOO MUCH AIR?

Absolutely. As your infant is gulping down his milk, he is getting air in his stomach as well. You know that, because it's for that reason you burp your baby after, and sometimes during, the feeding. As long as your baby is relieved by burping, the amount of air that the baby swallows is unimportant. Some babies, however, swallow excessive air, especially in their first voracious gulps. You can control that somewhat by expressing some of your first milk, which may otherwise let down quickly into the baby's mouth; or for the bottle-fed infant, by checking the flow from the nipple (which depends on the size of the holes and how tightly the nipple is attached to the bottle).

Air swallowing that occurs inadvertently with feeding or even with sucking on a pacifier can usually be controlled, as I have said, by burping or, when necessary, by a medication (simethicone) that breaks down the gas into smaller air bubbles that pass more readily through the intestine. However, the air that is swallowed when the baby cries may compound the problem even further. Once colic begins and the baby's fussing leads to crying, any swallowed air may distend the baby's abdomen further, which then causes him to cry more. An uncomfortable cycle develops (figure 7.1). The baby may become increasingly irritable the more that he cries and, again, he could swallow more air.

The seemingly simple solution is to use a pacifier. The problem is that some babies will not seal completely around the pacifier, whether it is round or flat. The result is that they swallow more air, and the cycle repeats itself. A better technique is to invert a clean finger (turn it upside down) with the nail trimmed so it won't gouge the baby's mouth. Place the soft part of your finger up against the roof of his mouth, being careful not to go too far back (that could gag him), and let him suck on that for a few minutes until he's comfortable. Alternatively, use the pacifier for a few minutes (but then remove it).

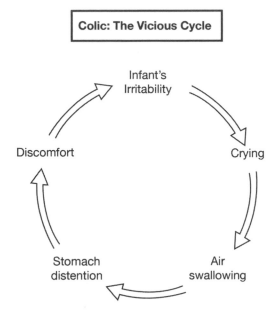

Figure 7.1. The vicious cycle of colic.

One other possibility is that the distention may not be caused by an excessive amount of gas alone. Certain infants may not be able to handle their normal gas and feedings. Their intestinal contractions run out of sync and retain everything (causing distention) instead of passing the contents on through the intestine.

There are several alternatives to help the baby, as shown in figure 7.2. The first is to use a probiotic to populate the baby's intestine with *Lactobacillus* and *Bifidobacterium*, which are prevalent in breastmilk. These favorable flora feed on the excess sugar and metabolize it. A number of studies sponsored by the company that makes Biogaia show that their drops (*Lactobacillus reuteri*) improve bowel evacuations and decrease crying time.[2, 3] A second choice is to use Gerber Good Start Soothe, which contains *L. reuteri*. While Soothe is a whey hydrolysate, the formula is priced like a routine formula and may relieve the discomfort.

A third choice is to use simethicone to break down the excess gas, though in the patients I see, that has already been tried with limited effectiveness. A small amount of an antacid (1 to 2 milliliters) before feedings can coat the stomach, though the benefits have not been proven in that situation, to my knowledge.

Additionally, medicines have been used to relax the intestine and decrease the cramping. Gripe water, originating in England in the 1800s, supposedly containing alcohol, fennel, and dill, now can be found as different blends of various herbs, depending on whether it is homemade or a commercially available remedy. Some mothers swear that it helps, but variability in the products makes them difficult to test accurately.

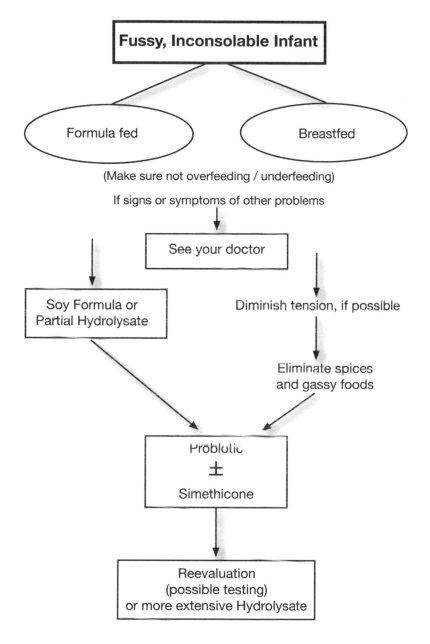

Figure 7.2. Helping your fussy baby.

Prescribed medicines have also been used to lessen intestinal spasms; however, dicyclomine is no longer available for that purpose after two deaths occurred with its use. Hyoscamine is still prescribed as infant drops in some instances, but the medicine has to be used carefully since overdosage can result in increased irritability, a high heart rate, and a flushed appearance. Another medicine that blocks the chemical responsible for stimulating intestinal contractions is being tested in the United States and Europe at the time of this writing. While it can only be used before six months of age, because enzymes develop that metabolize it rapidly in older infants, it has been effective in lessening discomfort in the few babies who have used it in clinical trials.

ARE THERE OTHER CAUSES AND CONSIDERATIONS?

Colic-like symptoms can develop with milk allergy. The milk protein in commercial formula can set up a reaction in the intestine with inflammation and, occasionally, with bloody diarrhea (from food-protein-induced enterocolitis syndrome, or FPIES, as already discussed). An eczema-like rash or a runny nose may be an early indication of milk allergy, but these manifestations may not occur at all. Colic may be the only symptom. Although the diagnosis of allergy may be difficult to prove, the treatment is simple: the cow's-milk formula can be changed to another kind of formula, most often to one that is soy based or that has been designed for fussy infants. As discussed in chapter 5, Abbott makes a lactose-free formula, called Similac Sensitive, for the rare child with lactase deficiency. Mead Johnson has a formula, Gentlease, that maintains 20 percent of the carbohydrate as lactose in order to assist calcium absorption. That formula also has a partial hydrolysis of milk proteins, as does Gerber Good Start, which can be purchased with *Bifidobacterium* added (Good Start Protect) or with *Lactobacillus reuteri* (Soothe), with the second also having 30 percent of the lactose replaced by maltodextrin. At this point, the Nestlé variety is the least expensive, being priced the same as a routine formula, and the most cost-sensitive choice. If the *Bifidobacterium* variety is selected, there is no need to combine that with an additional probiotic. Should that formula not work, then consideration should be given to Gentlease or the medications discussed.

Of course, should the previous measures not suffice, your baby should have a thorough reevaluation by your physician. Numerous other causes of colic-like fussiness exist because irritability is such a nonspecific symptom. That is why different infants require different therapies. Your pediatrician will help you find what is appropriate for your infant. This may include some testing for other rare conditions that can cause irritability or a trial of a more extensive hydrolysate.

If you recall the analogy of fever to colic that we used earlier, you will see that treatment of colic is the point at which that parallel between these symptoms no longer holds. If you reduce the fever without knowing its cause, the fever will often return. On the other hand, if the infant's irritability can be controlled, his colicky symptoms will often abate (unless some underlying intestinal problem is the cause, and that is relatively rare).

The reason is that the infant's irritability is due to that vicious cycle (in figure 7.1) subject to his distention and crying. He is irritable and cries, swallowing air, becoming distended. Yet that cycle can be broken.

WHAT CAN I DO?

You can do a great deal even without resorting to Asafetida bags, which once were used to ward off colic in the Georgia backwoods. First, you can take heart that these symptoms usually get better even without your doing anything, although you should at least have a physician examine the baby and ensure that nothing else needs attending to.

There are also several things you can do actively. If you are breastfeeding, you can remove carbohydrates and gaseous foods from your own diet. Vitamins may be withheld temporarily as a trial to see if the carbohydrates or chemicals in these products could be problems. If the baby is bottle-fed, a milk-based formula can be replaced with a soy or simplified formula to rule out milk allergy or low intestinal lactase (discussed above and in chapter 4). The baby's diet should be streamlined, eliminating any solids that may be contributing, until the cause of his irritability is understood. These trials should last a minimum of three days in order to give the baby a chance to clear his system of any of the substances from his previous formula.

Most importantly, the baby should not be overfed. In between feedings, an upside down finger, a mother's knuckle, or a pacifier can be used to satisfy the baby's need to suck. If the baby demands something else, you can try plain water. If the baby refuses the water, add 1 teaspoon of apple juice to entice the infant to take the bottle. After feeding, keep the baby upright or on his right side. The baby may then be able to empty his stomach better.

Once you have thought about the causes of your infant's fussiness (and have tried to alleviate them), you may begin to see your own contribution to the problem. Just as you are sensitive to your infant, your infant is sensitive to you. Your tenseness will show in the way you hold and rock the baby and in the way you feed him. He can feel the extra pressure on the bottle in his mouth and the tightness in your muscles. It only gets worse. Once the infant picks up your tension, he becomes further distressed, which you will rapidly see and communicate back to him, beginning another round of both of you being upset.

You have reason to be anxious; your baby is not well, and you are still worried. The doctor has reassured you that he finds nothing wrong (but you may be afraid that he has missed something). Yet it can be absolutely devastating to have an irritable but otherwise healthy infant, especially in the early evening as you are preparing dinner, tired from the day. The telephone is ringing, your older kids are seeking your attention, and the baby is crying ceaselessly through it all. Then your husband walks in, wanting to know what's wrong so he can help.

You end up frustrated, because you don't feel as if you are in control. You may even feel guilty because you think that, as the mother, you should be able to make your infant feel better—yet he cries anyway. You may even feel angry at your husband for not supporting you enough, at your pediatrician for not having the answer, and even at the baby for all that he is putting you through.

Those feelings are very real and very hard to live with. However, once you recognize that you have some of these feelings, and that they can interfere with your infant's care, you need to get out from under them and take care of yourself as well as your baby.

One of the best ways is by taking a hint from baseball. Call in a "relief pitcher." Colic taxes and tires a mother at least as much as her infant. You need and deserve the opportunity to find some sanity. Find a relative or babysitter to take over while you and your husband have an evening out. If you can't find a sitter, ask your husband to demonstrate his understanding and support—not only verbally, but also by taking care of the infant himself, even if it's just long enough for you to take a walk or a bath.

Once you return, try to renew your soothing relationship with your infant. A warm bath for the baby or a gentle back rub while the infant is lying on a warm surface is pleasurable for both mother and child. Many physicians recommend a number of different infant carriers. The baby can then relax on your chest (even when you are engaged in your normal activities), and he will become quiet in response to the familiar and gentle body rhythms of your movements, heartbeat, and breathing. The only potential disadvantage is that an infant's head could get trapped in a shirt or sweater—so please be careful.

When you are ready to feed the baby, make the experience as pleasant as possible—not only for your baby but for you as well. If you enjoy music, turn it on. A cup of tea, a small glass of wine, or another beverage (for you, not the infant) seems to add a measure of tranquility to those tension-filled feedings. I don't know if the alcoholic content works as much as the relaxed mood transmitted just by the glass being there. Then make yourself comfortable in a rocker or your favorite chair. And once again, enjoy your baby.

The simple steps outlined in this chapter (figure 7.2) are available to every mother to help her infant with colic before any medication needs to be tried. Far too often in the past, these methods were ignored, and sedatives (such as paregoric, a tincture of opium) were used automatically to relax the infants. While these may have been needed for some infants who responded to nothing else, they were used far too frequently. More often, they resulted in a drowsy infant who admittedly cried less, but may also have fed less easily and could not indicate his hunger. Fortunately, those remedies are now used less often, particularly since most pediatricians now prefer a probiotic, simethicone for excessive gas, or hyoscamine, if simply switching to soy or one of the inexpensive hydrolysates doesn't work.

Unfortunately, there are no guarantees in treating colic. Knowing that most babies get over it by three or four months of age doesn't help. However, making active efforts to relieve the cycle of tension and irritability, while attempting to find and remove the cause, represents a sound, practical approach.

SUMMARY

- Colic is inconsolable crying during a specific time period between three weeks and four months of age, often associated with abdominal distention and excess gas.
- Colic-like irritability can be a baby's response to a number of causes, such as overfeeding, underfeeding, milk allergy, infection, and intestinal complaints, or you might just have a very fussy baby.
- Your pediatrician should examine the baby to find out if a specific problem exists.
- If you are breastfeeding, you may be overfeeding or underfeeding the baby, or your diet may be contributing to the gas.
- Probiotics may be helpful, particularly Biogaia drops (*Lactobacillus reuteri*).
- If you are using formula, you may need to try a different formula or cut down the amount you are feeding.
- The most cost-sensitive partial hydrolysates are Gerber Good Start or Gentlease, depending on pricing (Good Start Soothe also includes *Lactobacillus reuteri*).
- Soy formula or complete hydrolysates become a real alternative if milk allergy is suspected and the partial hydrolysates do not reduce symptoms.
- Medications may be necessary—but beyond gripe water, simethicone to diminish gas, or an antacid, they may merely create a drowsy baby instead of a well one.
- Learn how to take care of yourself. You need to relax. Guard your health, energy, and emotions so that you can be at your best in order to take care of your baby during this frustrating period.

8

~~

Pooping Problems

Red, White, and Blue (and Sometimes Loose)

Whenever mothers bring in a diaper that they want me to examine, I thank them for the gift and tell them it's what I've always wanted. I note the color, the texture, the amount, and any accompanying substances. Sometimes I will test for blood, pH (acid), or fat content; sometimes I will send the specimens off for further testing; and we always talk about the stool, sometimes in quite a bit of detail. Great job I have (actually, it is a fantastically interesting profession, though not necessarily at that moment). But as gastroenterologists often joke, one person's evacuations are another's research project—not entirely funny, but then it's our bread and butter (equally disgusting humor).

The topic may seem hardly humorous, and perhaps nauseating, but I'm actually making a point. In polite company (and I consider you polite company), we may joke about bowel habits tentatively, not in the way preschoolers laugh openly at their potty jokes, and we couch our remarks in inoffensive terms, which even then aren't quite comfortable. But in my office, parents and I speak directly about what our bodies produce, while any children or teens in the room make faces or giggle uncomfortably when I point to a chart on the wall so parents can match their child's bowel movements with the pictures there. The subject is at least a little serious, and nobody wants to talk about it more than a parent who perceives that her infant has a bowel problem (unless, of course, we're in a nursing home, where the topic is a common one).

Often, I restate the obvious: the output is largely determined by the input and the processing it goes through inside. In children and adults who don't get much in the way of fluids, fiber, fruits, and vegetables, evacuations are compacted, infrequent, and often difficult to pass. We expect the opposite from infants.

Infants who are breastfed produce stools that are creamy to seedy and mustard yellow in the early weeks, darkening to a greenish brown. They will often have an average of three bowel movements daily (and about twice that number of wet diapers, though some of these may be mixed together). As the baby gets older, the number of bowel movements may diminish. But there is considerable variability, probably because there is tremendous variability in breastmilk. Cows predominantly graze on grass all day, every day, but mothers have a much wider selection in their diets, even when they are restricting what they eat to some degree while they are pregnant and breastfeeding. Similarly, babies are variable in the way they breastfeed. Babies who are feeding longer and get more hindmilk tend to have creamier, yellower stools than babies who are getting relatively more foremilk. Those babies have thinner, often greener stools. And as stated previously, some breastfed babies don't follow the usual pattern of frequent stools at all. They seem to absorb the nutrients so thoroughly that there is little residue, and thus they can have bowel movements as infrequently as once a week or every 10 days. Even adding water doesn't increase the number of bowel movements because these infants absorb that, too.

This is not constipation, which we'll discuss in a while, where the stools are firmer. This is a normal variance in pattern. You can be reassured that these babies with infrequent bowel movements are healthy if they are gaining and growing well, normally comfortable, and passing the same creamy stools, just less often. If there is any question, discuss the situation with your primary care provider, who will probably want to examine the baby, evaluate a specimen, and consider testing if there is any uncertainty, especially if the baby is distressed and trying to expel stool more often.

Formula-fed infants generally have less frequent, tan-colored stools that darken as the transit time through the intestine lengthens. With the addition of probiotics to formulas, and with commercial manufacturers trying to mimic the effects as well as the content of breastmilk, the stools of formula-fed infants are becoming more frequent and thinner. Hydrolysates create looser, greener, more frequent, sometimes mucoid stools that parents sometimes mistake for diarrhea.

WHAT DO WHITE STOOLS SIGNIFY?

White bowel movements are rare. They can be a cause for concern if they are actually white, grey, or very pale yellow because those underpigmented stools can indicate that not enough bile is entering the intestinal tract from the liver and gallbladder. Normally, the stomach contents stimulate the bile enzymes' release and intestinal entry. However, that entry cannot occur when the ducts that normally drain the bile within the liver or from the gallbladder are blocked. Differentiating the location of the blockage is essential, since the first, poor drainage from the liver, requires medication and patience, while the second, a physical blockage in the ducts that exit the gallbladder, indicates a surgical condition that needs prompt intervention. In both situations, the babies are usually jaundiced, with a yellow tint to their eyes and skin, and they often have noticeably enlarged livers on careful examination. Very thorough, prompt testing is required to distinguish between the two conditions and to pursue the appropriate course.

Occasionally (in older infants), the stools are completely white (and often firm) in otherwise healthy babies who are consuming massive amounts of cow's milk—not cow's-milk-based formula, but milk itself with little else in their diets. The milk is undigested in part, and nothing else is there to color the stools. Since most babies don't start on actual cow's milk until around a year of age, this situation is rarely seen before then. Often a series of blood tests will be obtained to check how the liver is functioning, and the urine and/or stools may be checked as well, with all of these tests hopefully showing that the liver and gallbladder are entirely normal.

WHAT IS CONSTIPATION? WHY DOES IT OCCUR?

Constipation is more about the texture of bowel movements rather than their frequency. Babies (and children and even adults) can have daily bowel action but still be considered constipated if they are struggling to pass hard, dry stools. Usually the stools are like hard rabbit pellets (scybala) that are sometimes clumped and passed together. They can be passed every few days or even several times a day with the baby just releasing one or two, then retracting the pelvic floor and passing a few more scybala later, when the urge inevitably returns (with the baby again holding far more that are still pressing down on the rectum but that the baby is still unwilling or unable to pass).

Think of it as a reflex similar to what happens when you touch a hot stove. You pull your hand away before the overwhelming sensation reaches your brain and suggests you should move your hand away from the danger. In the same way, the natural instinct is to prevent the painful passage of that hard, rough stool, which is going to hurt coming out. So the baby is caught between two urges, one to evacuate the stool and the other to withhold it, not thinking about it in any logical way but rather following two counterpoised natural instincts. Often you can see the infant in obvious discomfort, crying and turning red or blue, trying to push the stool out or hold it in (hence the chapter title).

Constipation often begins as the baby is transitioned from breastmilk to formula, switched to another formula, or is introduced to solid foods, particularly cereals. The alteration provides a more constipating substance the baby must contend with. Occasionally, it can occur when the baby has a cold and doesn't eat well or drink all the fluids he needs for a few days, so the stools get hard, and he begins to resist their passage, beginning the cycle of withholding. A similar cycle can begin after the baby acquires a gastrointestinal virus and can't keep up with his hydration needs. The diarrhea and vomiting stop and are quickly replaced by constipation, which steadily worsens as the baby holds back more and more.

When a baby has constipation from birth on, your pediatrician should be consulted to rule out a rare condition known as Hirschprung's disease, which

represents an absence of nerve cells in the rectum and lengths of the large intestine. Normal babies have their first *meconium* stool within the first 48 hours after
birth—most have one within 24 hours—and most will again pass all their thick,
green meconium by the third day. If that does not occur and the baby doesn't
transition to those yellow or tan stools by the third day, do let your primary care
physician know so that he or she can examine the baby and order any necessary
tests (often an X-ray, possibly a biopsy of the rectum, and/or blood tests). Cystic
fibrosis can cause similar complaints, but now babies with that condition are usually identified by the metabolic screening that's done shortly after birth.

WHAT SHOULD I DO WHEN MY BABY GETS CONSTIPATED?

Taking care of the baby with constipation does not necessitate a change in formula or require that you stop breastfeeding. Often the condition can be treated by
increasing the frequency with which you offer the breast (increasing your production and the baby's intake) or by adding a bottle of water for the formula-fed infant. If the baby will not take the water or giving him water does not work, you can
add prune or pear juice to the water. Some pediatricians recommend Karo syrup,
but in my clinical practice, that seems to produce far more gas and distension than
stool. If your baby has already been started on infant foods, minimize the cereal
temporarily and increase the "p" fruits, particularly pears, prunes, and papaya.

You can also try a probiotic, particularly a *Bifidobacterium* or *Lactobacillus*,
to help the stooling pattern mimic the healthful effects of breastmilk. Be careful,
though. Use probiotics that are early in their shelf life (they usually have a higher
count of colony-forming units), and stay away from those that advertise that they
mainly help when your baby has diarrhea.

Your doctor's office might suggest an occasional glycerin suppository or a
lubricated cotton swab to stimulate a bowel movement until the dietary factors
have a chance to work, particularly if your baby is passing large or firm stools or
is uncomfortable until that passage occurs. They might also consider a mild stool
softener, similar to what you might have taken during your pregnancy. Most
of the time, even these mild medications are unneeded. If the problem persists,
however, do discuss it with your physician. He or she might want to evaluate the
baby's hydration and consider other medications or suppositories.

WHAT IF I SEE BLOOD?

Red blood in the stool will raise your level of concern, no doubt. It should, but it's
not a reason to panic. Often this indicates that a hard, larger movement has torn
a small fissure in the baby's tender rectum. It will hurt, but it will heal and need
no treatment other than aggressive management of the constipation as described
in the last section.

If the constipation clears and the stools soften and thin, but the blood remains,
then there probably is another source of the bleeding. Track the amount of blood

and the character and frequency of the bowel movements. Also note the baby's general condition (happy and playful, irritable, or lethargic). These will be important symptoms to relay to your physician.

If the baby is healthy and active, passing just a few specks or small mucoid streaks of blood in otherwise normal-appearing stool, the baby most likely has a mild condition, such as lymphoid hyperplasia, where the intestinal lymph tissue is slightly enlarged and particularly vulnerable to the stool passing it. The lymphoid enlargement appears to arise from an allergic-type reaction to one or a number of foods (dairy being the most common) and eventually improves with elimination of dairy or other foods your doctor will help you sort through. This is not dissimilar to how the lymph glands in your neck swell and become tender with throat or upper respiratory infections, since the lymph system is protective and reactive to offending infections and proteins.

Of the more common conditions that can cause rectal bleeding, food allergies and related diagnoses represent a broad spectrum of food-related illnesses. We will discuss them in more detail in chapter 9. Most are mild, like lymphoid hyperplasia, but even the most severe, like food-protein-induced enterocolitis syndrome (FPIES), improve dramatically with elimination of the offending food. And all warrant extra caution as new foods are introduced into the baby's diet.

At times, the bleeding can come from an intestinal infection, but most significant infections will cause diarrhea as well. Clotting problems and intestinal conditions can also cause bleeding, but these are rare and will be investigated by your primary care doctor or by a specialist he or she may refer you to. Obviously, the urgency of the situation depends on the amount of blood present, the looseness and frequency of the stools, and whether there are any associated problems. The baby who is passing a large volume of blood (not just a few specks) or who is having profuse diarrhea, fever, vomiting, or other symptoms deserves at least a call to the doctor.

WHAT IF MY BABY DEVELOPS DIARRHEA?

The real question isn't if, unfortunately, but when. Common, run-of-the-mill intestinal infections with diarrhea are a curse to us all. During their brief presence, these intestinal illnesses, *gastroenteritis* in medical parlance, are devastating in their effect, but most of us get over them without difficulty. At those times, we can appreciate how important our intestines are to our everyday existence.

The infant or child with gastroenteritis is at far greater risk, especially if vomiting or fever accompany the diarrhea. His smaller reserve of nutrients and water lessen his ability to withstand the wasting of precious bodily fluids. For that reason, parents and physicians alike become concerned about the child with gastroenteritis, and particular attention should be paid to maintaining an infant's hydration. That cannot be emphasized strongly enough. The diarrhea (and vomiting) can continue for days (and often do), but as long as children continue to drink plenty of liquids, urinate normally, have moisture in their mouths, and have tears when they cry, they will generally do quite well.

Medications are often sought to stop the diarrhea, particularly in toddlers and older children. One hundred years ago, the president of the New York State Medical Society recommended plugging the rectum with bee's wax and oilcloth; little has changed.[1] Most of the chemical "plugs" do slow the intestinal tract down and stop the diarrhea from leaving the system, but they probably do not stop the diarrheal fluid from accumulating in the intestine. We are thus treating ourselves and not the children with these medicines. Medications can present great danger, in fact. The child still loses water and salts from his bloodstream and his body's cells into the intestinal tract, but we cannot detect it. When it remains there, we must wait until the child becomes truly dehydrated to know that he is in trouble. In stopping the diarrhea, these medications also stop the body's elimination of the bacteria or virus causing the infection. For some bacteria, these medications, which also slow intestinal passage, prolong and perpetuate the illness. The one advantage that these medications, such as Lomotil and Donnatal, do have is that by diminishing the rapid intestinal contractions, they also diminish the cramping one feels. These medicines can be used, but they should be reserved for older children with severe abdominal cramping.

The infant doesn't need medicine, but fluid—to replace the salt and water that he is losing in his stool and to keep up his normal maintenance requirements. An infant's fluid requirements are compounded by fever. For every two degrees Fahrenheit that the temperature rises, he needs a fluid increase of 10 percent. But these infants need more than water alone. Sodium, potassium, and bicarbonate are lost in the diarrheal stool and must be replaced meticulously to avoid problems of salt imbalances and dehydration.

Breastfeeding babies can usually continue with their usual feedings, and you might increase them if the baby is having frequent diarrhea that is not being caused by some food substance crossing the breast. If you have similar symptoms, you can continue to feed, as long as you remain adequately hydrated yourself. You may transfer the infection to the baby, but you may have done so even before you developed the actual symptoms.

Formula companies have realized the potential market in providing a consistent solution that can be administered to infants with diarrhea. As a result, already-mixed solutions, Pedialyte and Lytren (by Abbott and Mead Johnson, respectively), are available at grocery stores and pharmaceutical counters, with Pedialyte, which dominates the market, also available as freezer pops. These salt, sugar, and water mixtures have truly done wonders for ensuring that infants survive gastroenteritis without hazard. There are, however, limitations. A maximum of 1 quart of these solutions should be given per day. Some babies want to drink more of these solutions than their regular formulas. If your baby remains hungry, you can offer cereal and fruits (particularly bananas for potassium) if he has already begun infant foods. For the child with vomiting, these fluids should be given frequently but in very small quantities. Often, that will mean feeding the infant as little as a tablespoon every 15 minutes and advancing that volume as tolerated by the individual infant.

Gatorade and Jell-O water (appropriately diluted as recommended on the package) can serve as acceptable substitutes for the toddler or older child (who does not react to artificial food coloring and flavoring). However, for the young infant, these should be avoided or used only temporarily (in the middle of the night, until you can get to the store). Both have adequate amounts of sodium but are low in potassium and have a large amount of sugar. The sugar itself may stimulate further diarrhea, which will be difficult to differentiate from an infection. If you do use the Jell-O water, please remember (particularly if cherry Jell-O is used) that with little else in the child's intestine, the coloring may come through unchanged, and you should not be frightened by this "bloody" diarrhea.

Please stay away from boiled skim milk and the like. This popular remedy of the 1940s and 1950s concentrates the protein and salts. It has led to real problems, but Grandma may not know of the complications when she suggests that you use it. And while there are less expensive, online recipes for rehydration solutions that replicate the World Health Organization's recommendations, these salt and sugar versions are generally tasteless (though they can be adapted by adding bananas or chased with a small amount of juice). They are also potentially harmful if an error is made, because the ratio of sugar to salt is crucial—so I recommend using the commercially available products, which are still relatively inexpensive, during the short course of an intestinal infection.

Also, a probiotic can shorten the duration of the diarrhea. Several have proven helpful, but, again, be careful in your selection. The usual *Lactobacillus* in the store may not have enough active cultures to resist breakdown by the gastric acid, and they have to adhere to the surface of the intestine. Yogurts with live active cultures (the label should say that) can be used for older infants (at least eight months of age) and children. However, even those with the live active cultures only have to have 100 million colony forming units per gram at the time of their manufacture, and the number of units tends to decrease over time.

Among the commercially available probiotics, Culturelle is the most tested for various types of diarrhea. Culturelle contains 1 billion cells per packet of *Lactobacillus GG*, a bacteria that is highly acid resistant; it also has a high affinity for the intestinal lining and is able to block other organisms from attaching to the surface. You may not need it if the diarrhea only lasts a day or two, but if it becomes more prolonged, this relatively expensive brand may be worth the investment.

ON THE ROAD TO RECOVERY

Once your child is over the acute stages of his diarrhea and is beginning to feel well enough to eat, you may begin a simple feeding regimen. The breastfeeding child may continue on the breast or generally return to it without problem, since breastmilk is a very low-salt food with little ash content. For the infant who is taking formula, you are generally safest to dilute several feedings by half before returning the child to his normal full-strength formula. This is most important for the child who has been using milk-based formulas because of the lactose and salts in the formula.

The older infant appears to benefit from a very brief period on a relatively bland diet that consists chiefly of bananas, rice cereal, applesauce, and toast, and hence called the BRAT diet. Crackers and similar bland foods can also be added on a progressive basis. These foods avoid lactose and fats, both of which are difficult for the child overcoming diarrhea to handle. Moreover, the BRAT diet has also been praised because of the kaolin in the bananas and pectin in the apples. These foods can generally be expanded to return the child to a normal diet within several days.

WHAT HAPPENS IF MY BABY CONTINUES TO HAVE DIARRHEA?

Some infants will continue to have diarrhea after their fever breaks and the vomiting subsides. A temporary lactose intolerance is frequently the cause. The virus or other infective agent often will briefly destroy the intestine's ability to digest and absorb lactose, or milk sugar. Unabsorbed, the lactose can stimulate a continued diarrhea. In this situation you should switch from a milk-based formula to a soy-based or lactose-reduced formula for up to two to four weeks, which is the time the intestine needs to regrow the tips of the intestinal surface (the villi) that house the lactase enzyme. If the baby is on any other formula, you needn't concern yourself with this, since the only formulas that are lactose predominant are the milk-based formulas.

Although most infants will improve, a few will persist with diarrhea despite, and in fact because of, their lactose restriction. These babies are remaining on a restricted diet for too long. For infants, formula serves as the primary source of fat and calcium. Although feeding milk and fat may worsen the early stages of diarrhea, fat may be helpful if the diarrhea continues. Fat slows down the emptying of the stomach and therefore slows the rate at which nutrients enter the intestine, thereby aiding in their absorption. A second factor is also at work. When formula is removed from the diet, most children are given electrolyte solutions, juices, and other liquids that are high in sugar. In contrast to fat, which slows the intestine, these sugary drinks may speed the intestinal contents through and cause more diarrhea.

If your child has not responded to the measures suggested for acute infectious diarrhea, lactose intolerance, or this latter condition, called chronic nonspecific diarrhea, you are probably going to need the aid and counsel of your pediatrician, if you haven't already sought it. Once you have gotten beyond the more common maladies we have already discussed, your doctor will begin to consider the less frequent causes of diarrhea. They can be far more difficult to identify. Perhaps the first and most important step is to have a thorough evaluation by your pediatrician. Your pediatrician should examine your child and the child's bowel movements as well. While you may be embarrassed to bring in your child's stool specimen, your doctor (who may not be particularly thrilled with receiving it either) will consider it exhibit A. And remember, it's what I do all day.

SUMMARY

- An infant's bowel action is determined by what goes in as well as by how his intestine is functioning.
- Constipation, which can arise from a number of causes, is often worsened by the infant's straining to withhold his stool.
- Constipation can usually be reversed by increasing breastmilk or water intake.
- Certain probiotics can help lessen constipation, while others are better at reducing diarrhea.
- Blood in the stool is reason for concern but not panic; in all cases, it deserves evaluation for the cause so that appropriate treatment can be instituted.
- An intestinal virus is the most common cause of diarrhea in a child as well as an adult. Food-based reactions can cause either diarrhea or blood in the stool.
- In infants, medications to stop diarrhea are usually either ineffective or somewhat dangerous.
- During the first several days of a virus causing diarrhea or vomiting, large amounts of fluids containing balanced sugar and salt are needed to keep a child well hydrated.
- Breastfeeding can usually continue during an intestinal infection.
- Cow's-milk formula may need to be restricted temporarily during, and sometimes after, an intestinal infection because the intestinal lining loses the ability to break down the milk sugar. Soy-based or lactose-free formulas may be substituted.
- The infant should be returned to his regular diet within two to five days to avoid a prolongation of his diarrhea.

9

‿‿

Are Allergies Everywhere?

How do you know if your baby's runny nose is just a runny nose or if it's an allergy? And if it's an allergy, how do you know if he's allergic to a food or to something in the environment? What if he has a red rash? Could that be an allergy, too?

Parents, particularly those who have allergies themselves, commonly puzzle over these questions. Understand that physicians wonder and worry about these same questions, too —because it is often difficult to tell. Allergies can show up in a number of different ways—as a simple runny nose or repeated ear infections, which are typical of environmental allergies, or as the difficult-to-treat skin rashes or life-threatening emergencies that can be seen with food allergies. And other reactions can sometimes mimic allergies, making it hard to tell the difference, but that difference very much matters.

To make the situation even more confusing, specific tests for the various reactions to food only help some of the time because true allergies are only one of the many reactions that you or your baby can have. Though the baby might have real and reproducible reactions to a particular food, these may not reflect actual allergies but another kind of intolerance or sensitivity instead.

ALLERGY OR INTOLERANCE?

The distinction between allergy and intolerance may sound arbitrary or superficial, but it's quite important in understanding what your doctor means and determining the course of action that should be followed. We've touched on this before in talking about food-protein-induced enterocolitis syndrome (FPIES) and lactose intolerance. Both nonallergic conditions develop as a reaction to

111

milk-based formula; however, they are very different in their underlying cause, the symptoms that occur, and how they are treated. And these milk reactions help to illustrate these important distinctions, especially when we consider a couple of composites.

The first is the case of eight-month-old Bobby Frost. Mrs. Frost had brought her son to me and announced, "He's allergic to milk, I'm sure of it." Admittedly, Mrs. Frost had allergies herself, and that gave her some insight. Her allergies also gave Bobby an increased chance (approximately 25 to 35 percent) of developing allergies as well. If one of Bobby's brothers or sisters had allergies instead, his chances would have dropped to 5 to 15 percent, and had both parents had allergies, Bobby would have been more likely to have had allergies than not, with an estimated 40 to 80 percent chance of developing an allergy,[1] with milk allergy being the most common in infancy, though it is also true that genetic factors only account for approximately 50 percent of allergies.[2]

But still I was suspicious. I remembered all the other mothers who had mistakenly diagnosed allergies in their children. I asked how she had reached that conclusion. She explained that she was primarily breastfeeding Bobby, and only once or twice had she offered him a supplemental bottle of formula. Within an hour of his most recent bottle, he vomited and had diarrhea. He never developed a rash or fever.

While Bobby's symptoms could have been related to an allergy, they also could have been caused by a transient virus. I told her so and indicated that if it happened again, we should consider testing Bobby, because we would want to know before he was weaned.

Bobby was not about to be deprived of his allergy testing, and, in fact, he proceeded on his own. Within several weeks, Bobby had another gastrointestinal upset. This time it came after he drank some of his sister's milk. He had blood in the stool and sufficient vomiting that he needed an emergency room visit for intravenous (IV) fluids and several hours of observation.

We took a careful history for other reactions to the baby foods he had tried, but there had been none, other than that he often refused his green vegetables when they were introduced. An allergist performed skin and blood tests for several foods Bobby had tried, but neither set showed an actual allergy (which we'll discuss shortly). Had any of the tests been positive, that would have been doubly helpful, since it would have suggested the presence of an allergy and would have meant the tests were meaningful. Without a positive reaction, it could mean that he had no allergies, but he could just be too young to mount a response, a situation that often occurs in children under 18 months of age (and even more common in infants under three months of age).[3]

I had a choice. We could challenge him when he was wonderfully well, giving him a small amount of milk under close observation, so that we could administer emergency medications or IV fluids if he had a reaction, or we could eliminate milk from his diet all together, waiting to challenge him until he was older. I chose the latter, since, as I informed the mother, he was probably sensitized by the formula he had received, and possibly milk in her diet, reacting then to his sister's milk. This was most consistent with food-protein-induced enterocolitis syndrome, or FPIES, and even a controlled challenge could put him at risk.

We restricted even the most minute amount of milk from his (and her) diet, and he did well. His mother breastfed him a little longer, and when he was weaned, he was placed on soy milk instead. Mrs. Frost learned CPR resuscitation techniques as a precaution, though she fortunately never needed to use them. I indicated that most children outgrow this problem by three years of age, and there is currently no evidence that FPIES will lead to any other allergy. But, I explained, we would have to be careful introducing new foods into his diet, though we would wait until two or three years of age to reintroduce any milk protein.

Let me share two quicker cases: Will Carlos was a robust two-month-old who came to see me for reflux. This seemingly healthy infant was vomiting, not merely spitting up, after each feeding. He also had a slight runny nose and the thick red rash of eczema on his legs and elbows. I suspected a milk allergy and changed the routine formula he was taking to a soy product, and his symptoms disappeared within a week. Had they not improved, I was prepared to try a protein hydrolysate (see chapter 5), though most, but not all, infants with cow's-milk allergy respond to the initial change.

The last case is that of a four-month-old, Emmy Dickinson, who replicated the diarrhea and fever that her sister brought home from preschool. Their parents hadn't wanted to vaccinate them against rotavirus, and they both tested positive. The problem was that Emmy continued to have diarrhea even two weeks later. Lactose intolerance that developed as a result of the virus seemed the obvious cause, since (as you learned in the last chapter) intestinal viruses can temporarily damage the intestine's absorptive surface, and in doing so, they destroy the enzymes that make lactose absorbable until the intestinal cells are replaced (which can take a month). I placed the infant on soy formula since it does not have lactose. Emmy improved within days and returned to routine formula a month later without any difficulty.

There are obviously several points to be garnered from these illustrations:

- Allergies in the family increase the likelihood that other family members will also develop allergies. And these odds increase if multiple family members are involved. But another interesting point is that 50 percent of babies who have allergic rashes do not have anyone in the family with documented allergies.[4]
- Allergies affect individuals differently: some will have rashes (usually on the face or along either side of bends of the knees or elbows), while others will have a runny nose, which can lead to repeated ear infections and can be mistaken for upper respiratory infections.
- Individuals who have food allergies may have them to more than one food.
- A host of food-related reactions are not classical allergies, in the carefully defined way that allergists speak about them. If Emmy had vomiting along with her diarrhea in the way that Bobby did, I would have dismissed lactose

intolerance as a possible cause. Lactose intolerance can create bloating, gas, discomfort, and diarrhea, but not vomiting.
- Symptoms improve when the cause is removed, whether it's a true allergy or another type of food reaction.
- Reflux is not usually part of the allergy symptom complex, though vomiting often is. At the same time, reflux can be worsened by allergies and/or mistaken for them.

I'm sure these points aren't entirely new to you. Numerous people have reactions to food. You probably have reacted to some food at some time, since most people have. If that occurred only once, you shrugged it off, figuring that the food was badly prepared. If others with you had similar problems after that same meal, you possibly worried that the food had been spoiled or contaminated. But if that same food repeatedly caused the same symptoms, you may have presumed you have a food allergy.

Nonallergic reactions are actually far more common than true allergies. The most common cause of that wonderful experience of feeling sick or having an intestinal upset after a meal isn't even caused by the food itself but comes from some *pathogen* or *toxin* in the food we ate or the water we drank. This is appropriately called a "food-borne illness" caused by something contaminating the food.

Some people routinely react to the spices used in food preparation with an upset stomach or *flatulence*; others become nervous drinking caffeinated coffee or get throbbing headaches from monosodium glutamate (MSG). Many of us seem to be more sensitive as we get older, often getting reflux from eating too much of certain foods too late at night.

You wouldn't call these allergies. Neither would your doctor. Your physician might call these sensitivities or intolerances, reserving the label "allergy" for a very specific type of immunological reaction that can be triggered by a very small exposure. The term *intolerance* is used for a gastrointestinal reaction to a food that is often dose related. A person with lactose intolerance might not have symptoms with a small amount of cream in his coffee, but a pizza or a milkshake might make him (and others in the room) quite uncomfortable within an hour or two.

Celiac disease is another type of food reaction (actually an autoimmune disease) often confused with wheat allergy because of the body's reaction to a protein in various grains. This will be briefly mentioned in chapter 14, where we talk about introducing solids.

Our psychological responses have to be included in any list of reactions to a food. Try to force some children to eat their vegetables or some texture they don't tolerate, and you will have an immediate reaction of stomach pain, nausea, or vomiting—even before they've put the food on their tongue. That is an aversion, but certainly not an allergy.

Lastly, a group of eosinophilic conditions are allergy-like in that certain white blood cells, eosinophils, which are associated with allergy, are abundant in the gastrointestinal system (they can show up in the esophagus, stomach, or intestine, where they are rarely present). In some cases, a food reaction can be identified by blood tests or traditional allergy skin-prick tests or by putting patches of the food on the skin (patch testing). These conditions can result in difficulty swallowing (eosinophilic esophagitis) or vomiting, abdominal pain, and low proteins (eosinophilic gastroenteritis). They are rarely seen in infants but are increasingly frequent in older children. When these conditions do appear in infancy, complete hydrolysates or the very expensive (in the Porsche-payment category) amino acid formulas are often required for treatment.

WHAT'S A TRUE ALLERGY?

An allergy is a particular overreaction your body develops whenever you are exposed to an offending substance, or *allergen*. With food allergies, an infant's intestinal development and the foods fed during this vulnerable period may have a significant role. Throughout life, the intestine acts as a selective sieve. A single layer of cells protects us, letting some nutrients penetrate, while all the others are kept within the intestine and eventually passed as waste.[5] In early infancy, and perhaps after infections, that selectivity is lessened, and the proteins that cause allergies can penetrate through the intestinal barrier. Large proteins that would ordinarily not pass penetrate with ease. But the intestine matures, and by four to five months of age, only proteins one-tenth the size are admitted. Our normal defense against these dietary proteins (of any size) is their digestion by enzymes from the pancreas and an antibody response within the intestine that further blocks the protein's penetration. These defenses are diminished in the first months of life, but breastmilk has antibodies and other factors that take over the function of the absent intestinal antibodies for the young infant.

Take the example of Will Carlos and his reaction to milk. The first time Will drank that milk, one of the proteins in the absorbed milk stimulated the immune system to create an antibody against the milk, in roughly the same way that your body forms antibodies against blood cells from people with a different blood type than you. The next time Will drank milk, the antibody was already there, ready and waiting if he consumed it again. As soon as the milk was absorbed, the antibody reacted with the milk protein with an overwhelming response, immediately releasing chemicals, resulting in intestinal inflammation, which disrupts the barrier function of the intestine, allowing more allergen absorption (which logically intensifies the reaction).

The released chemicals created both sets of Will's allergic symptoms: his vomiting (an immediate response) and his runny nose and rash, which remained because of the repeated exposure and also went away, but more slowly. The chemical release of *histamine*, in particular, causes the immediate reactions (which is why antihistamines were developed), with a host of other chemicals (prostaglandins and leukotrienes) mediating the delayed or slower reactions, like the rash.

Remember that Bobby also reacted to milk protein, but in a different way: he had blood in his bowel movement and a life-threatening event because a different cell type was involved; as a result, other chemicals were released, and his lower intestine responded.

To make this a bit more confusing, different antibodies can develop and react. As far as we know, all are formed by our immune globulins. Classic allergy antibodies are those created by immune globulin E (IgE). These are usually reflected by positive skin tests and/or positive blood tests, with the response often (but not always) paralleling the clinical response. The higher the blood test level or the bigger the welt raised on the skin test, the more the baby, child, or adult is likely to react with physical symptoms. And this is true for food as well as environmental allergens, such as dust mites and cat fur.

Patients can also have a different immune globulin, IgG (gamma globulin), response to foods on blood tests or in stool. Most allergists feel that these IgG results do not represent allergies but simply reflect the child's exposure to various foods in his diet or to related foods (for example, he can have a reaction to grapefruit, though he's never eaten it, because he often eats oranges).

WHAT SHOULD BE DONE FOR THE INFANT WITH A POSSIBLE MILK ALLERGY?

The concepts I've explained will help you understand the rationale for our algorithm and the problems and solutions that are entailed. First, laboratory testing may not be helpful. So your doctor will probably have to work from his perception of your child's symptoms and make a tentative diagnosis based on his suspicions. The clearer the symptoms, the more accurate his or her diagnosis is likely to be. If your infant has a rash on his trunk but not on his face, if your older daughter has a cold, or if you don't have a family history of allergies, your physician is going to be less certain. Second, it could take a while for a formula switch to have an impact. You might see a difference with the first bottle of the new formula, or you might have to wait weeks if your child merely has a rash or nasal drainage. So have patience, and give the change a chance to work. Also know that the initial formula change should work, but it does not always. Studies demonstrate that 10 to 14 percent of infants with cow's-milk allergy also have reactions to soy. Those who have non-IgE reactions to milk may have a 40 percent chance of cross-reactivity to soy.[6] In other words, there is a substantial chance (60 to 86 percent) that soy formula will work. Thus, a large number of infants are likely to tolerate soy, and this allows most infants to use soy formulas safely.

It makes no sense to switch between different brands of routine or cow's-milk formula. The proteins in the Enfamil and Similac products are similar. The proteins in Gerber routine formulas and Enfamil Gentlease are partially hydrolyzed (partially broken down), so they still contain some beta-lactoglobulin, which is responsible for many food allergies.

The other choice would be to jump to an extensively hydrolyzed casein formula. But this is an expensive first step, should the infant be able to tolerate soy (soy costs $14 per can of powder versus $25 per can for the hydrolysate, a difference of at least $70 per month). Some physicians are still concerned about the isoflavones contained in soy formulas, although the possible adverse effects (discussed in chapter 5) and any potential benefits of isoflavones are yet to be clearly established. If the soy formula does not relieve the symptoms, the extensively hydrolyzed formulas (Nutramigen or Alimentum) are the next logical choice (figure 9.1). Nutramigen is slightly less expensive (by approximately $4 per can) and contains a probiotic. Of note, one small study of 26 infants with blood in their stool attributed to cow's-milk allergy showed that when *Lactobacillus* was added to that formula (which is the only way Nutramigen is available now), the blood cleared in all the babies on the probiotic-containing formula, and an inflammatory protein was lower in the babies on that formula compared to the former version that did not contain the probiotic. Still, it must be said that some infants refuse to take Nutramigen initially and accommodate quicker to the sweeter taste of Alimentum.

Do recognize that soy formulas often produce a thicker, less frequent stool (if it's difficult to pass, you can offer additional water during the day or speak with your provider about a stool softener). On the other hand, the hydrolysates normally produce a looser bowel movement, sometimes with considerable mucus.

If the hydrolysates do not work, reevaluation is necessary, since fewer than 5 percent of infants do not respond to these products. This is because the hydrolysates have amino acids in small chains, called *peptides*, instead of intact proteins that cause allergies. Thus, a lack of response calls the original diagnosis of allergy into question and may mean that a referral and even a brief colonoscopy are needed before you launch into using one of the extremely costly amino acid formulas.

WHEN SHOULD THE PROBLEM RESOLVE?

If the baby had mild symptoms at the outset and is doing well, a return to routine formula can be tried at six months. The reason is that the cells of the intestinal tract knit together at approximately that age, lessening allergen penetration. On the other hand, if the baby had more significant symptoms or failed the trial at six months and the previous symptoms recurred, the formula should be continued until 12 months of age, when a full discussion should occur about whether a transition to whole milk is conceivable and, if not, what the baby should drink instead. (Table A.2, the Milk Alternative Comparison Chart, in the appendix reviews these options.)

When the milk-based formula is tried at six months, a slow introduction is in order. I agree with the European Society for Paediatric Gastroenterology, Hepatology and Nutrition's recommendations that you start with just 1 milliliter (¼ teaspoon = 1.25 milliliters), then progressively move up to 3 milliliters, then 10 milliliters (2 teaspoons), 30 milliliters (1 ounce), and lastly 100 milliliters (roughly 3½ ounces). These small amounts are progressively given at intervals approximately half an hour apart under medical supervision. It's best to begin the introduction several hours after a prior meal (so nothing in the previous meal will interfere). The infant is then watched for any reaction over several additional hours—all under medical supervision in case there is a reaction that needs to be treated immediately. For those with severe reactions or eczema, or those who have never had a cow's-milk formula or have not had one for a long time, the recommendations start at even lower amounts, which are not given until 12 to 18 months of age.[7]

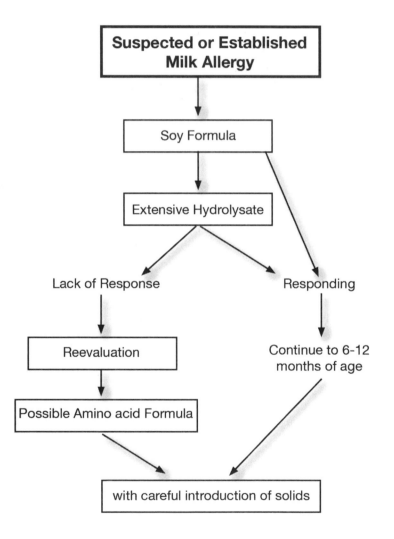

Figure 9.1. When milk allergy has been diagnosed.

CAN I PREVENT MY BABY FROM DEVELOPING ALLERGIES?

Maybe you can. If your family has allergies, breastfeed for at least four to six months and avoid the most common allergens—milk, eggs, and peanuts—in your own diet. The American Academy of Pediatrics in 2012 reaffirmed its support for breastfeeding, showing that in two separate studies, breastfeeding reduced the risk of asthma and atopic dermatitis (eczema) by 26 to 27 percent in low-risk families (those without a family history of allergic disorders) and by 42 percent in infants with at least one close relative who has an allergy.[8]

Somehow breastmilk tightens the junctions of the gut barrier, so the allergens cannot penetrate as well. The immune factors and probiotics within breastmilk may be the primary participants in effecting this, with various prebiotics keeping those probiotics flourishing (see chapter 4 for a fuller discussion). Docosahexaenoic acid (DHA) also may help, with studies showing that the higher levels of DHA (intended to match those of breastmilk in US mothers) delay the onset of asthma, wheezing, and common respiratory illnesses.[9] Additionally, other factors that we are unaware of may have a role, and the avoidance of any exposure to the most common childhood allergens may help as well. Some physicians will also restrict soy and wheat, but that makes the mother's diet difficult and possibly may stop mothers from using their natural resources.

When breastfeeding can't be established, probiotics and either a partially hydrolyzed whey (Good Start) or a fully hydrolyzed formula (Nutramigen) have been shown to reduce the risk by 40 to 50 percent, at least for developing atopic dermatitis in the first six years of life.[10] Alimentum is probably similar in effect, though it was not used in the study. There is no evidence that soy formulas perform as well, and they cost approximately the same as Good Start (which is much less expensive than the fully hydrolyzed formulas). As a result, my recommendation is to use Good Start if you are not breastfeeding. The Protect variety has a probiotic and a prebiotic, and I would therefore recommend that particular product in this situation (figure 9.2).

The problem is that many of the symptoms you are trying to prevent might not show up until years after the formula has been used. Additionally, allergic symptoms often develop in infants and children who do not have a family history. The few tests on the general infant population do not show the striking differences seen in the infants at higher risk to suggest that using a partially or fully hydrolyzed formula would be helpful—which, of course, would take us away from formulas that are more closely matched to breastmilk.

There is still a debate about when to introduce infant purees (baby foods) to babies at risk for allergy in order to prevent allergy development. We'll discuss that in detail in chapter 13. Also, you can check our website, www.what 2feedyourbaby.com, where we will try to keep you abreast of the latest reliable information.

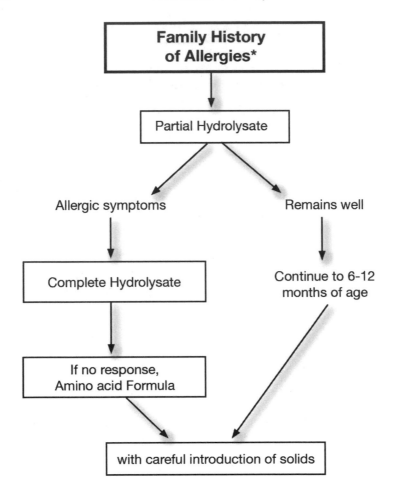

*In a first degree relative (parent or biological sibling)

Figure 9.2. For the infant with a family history of allergy.

SUMMARY

- Many reactions are mistakenly considered allergies when they come from another source.
- An allergy is a repeatable reaction to a specific substance or substances involving allergic antigens (allergens) and usually the antibodies to them.
- Allergies affect individuals differently.
- In infants, allergy testing is often expensive and does not appear to be consistently reliable for IgE allergies if the tests are negative. For non-IgE allergies, skin and blood tests would not be helpful.
- Allergies in the family increase the likelihood that other family members will also develop allergies. These odds increase if multiple family members are involved.
- But 55 percent of babies who have allergies do not have anyone in the family with documented allergies.
- Individuals who have food allergies may have them to more than one food.
- Symptoms improve when the cause is removed, whether it's a true allergy or another type of food reaction.
- Soy formula can be used initially in infants who demonstrate symptoms of cow's-milk allergy.
- Breastfeeding for at least four to six months best reduces the risk of future food allergies. Certain probiotics and the use of partially hydrolyzed whey or fully hydrolyzed formula appear to prevent later allergy symptoms. Good Start Protect is the least expensive of these and contains a probiotic as well. This formula should not be used if milk-allergy symptoms already exist or develop.
- When infant foods should be introduced to prevent allergies is currently unclear (see chapter 14)
- Many babies outgrow these problems by six months of age, when the intestinal cells knit closer together (known as gut closure), allowing less allergen penetration. When problems persist, another trial may be possible at a year. If that trial is not successful, or not performed because of the severity of symptoms, the problem and the need for food restrictions can persist for years.
- Slow, careful reintroduction of cow's milk should occur under medical supervision.

10

Underweight or Undergrown

Just looking at an infant will not automatically tell you if he is underweight. Even a normal, healthy baby can have prominent ribs, a protruding belly, and flat muscles. But looking at growth charts will show the differences immediately. The normal infant will be following the standard growth curves with little deviation. There are children, particularly those who were breastfed, who gradually shed their baby fat at two to three years of age and begin to slim down. But they continue to grow actively in height despite a temporary decline in the way they add weight. The continued growth in height despite temporary delay in weight gain classify these children as normal.

Infants who are underweight (and may have problems as a result) are very different. Their weight tapers off earlier. They don't stop growing entirely. But they gain less than expected in both length and weight. Their weight may start to slow down first, but length will follow if the situation is not corrected.

Lizzie Bishop was a perfect example. She was not the typical patient arriving in my office for evaluation of diarrhea. She was nine months old with little fat on her arms to hide her thin, atrophied muscle. She looked thinner. I was surprised that she was in the tenth percentile for weight, still in the normal range.

If I looked at those numbers alone, I would have missed the evidence of her failing growth. But fortunately I had copies of her pediatrician's records. Until four months of age she had been in the fiftieth percentile for height and weight. But she had steadily declined in gaining weight. At her six-month checkup, she weighed 15 pounds (in the twenty-fifth percentile), though not the 16 pounds that other infants in the fiftieth percentile for length weighed. But by her routine nine-month visit, she had only gained eight ounces over the intervening months. Her height had advanced, too, but at a slower rate, bringing her down to the twenty-fifth percentile.

Lizzie's falloff in growth was clearly abnormal. And that had triggered her parents' and physician's concern. Her parents wanted to understand if there was any danger for the baby. Was the brain being affected as well? What had caused the falloff? And how were we going to turn the situation around? These are all normal questions that deserve thoughtful answers.

WHAT PROBLEMS CAN UNDERWEIGHT INFANTS HAVE?

Fortunately, many children are simply slow gaining their weight—and that problem can be corrected with attention to the factors causing the problem(s) and focused effort on the details needed to resolve them. Infants and children who have more significant difficulties are generally those who are not just severely underweight but whose growth is affected as well. This combination of impaired weight gain and decreased growth was formerly known as *failure to thrive*, a term now considered negative and outdated. While the growth issues are significant enough themselves, they are often accompanied and caused by malnutrition. In fact, malnutrition is usually the real problem, and the issues of weight gain and growth are among the most visible consequences. (Fortunately, true malnutrition is relatively rare in industrialized countries, where a consistent food source is available.)

Infants who are behind in their growth will often remain undersized all their lives if the situation isn't corrected, challenging these children emotionally as they grow up. They often suffer far more than the overweight child, being treated as if they are fragile. They begin to think of themselves that way, too, and often are sidelined in athletic activities. They don't develop the self-confidence that actually does accompany body size. That poor self-image will frequently cause them to adopt a more passive role rather than an assertive, more confident one.[1]

The underweight, malnourished child is usually sickly. Malnutrition, or, more formally, protein-calorie malnutrition (where the child is not getting enough of the protein or energy sources needed), can impair the intestinal tract's ability to absorb nutrients, accelerating the level of malnutrition, and affect the intestine's function as a barrier, allowing increased intestinal infections that are harder for the malnourished child to fight because his immune capabilities also become progressively diminished. That malabsorption also leads to specific vitamin and mineral deficiencies (vitamin A, zinc, copper, selenium, and chromium among them), which further compounds the problems of intestinal integrity, infection, and growth. And, of course, the infections cause vomiting, diarrhea, and a decreased appetite, which cycle back into a devastating cyclone of more and more significant malnutrition, with greater and greater effect (figure 10.1).

The second question about whether undersized infants suffer any brain damage is really part of the same question about consequences. From the classic work of Dr. Myron Winick in New York, we know that infant rats that are starved or deprived of protein while inside the mother or even in the first several days of life

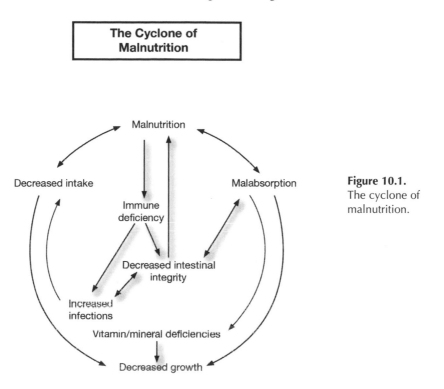

Figure 10.1.
The cyclone of malnutrition.

will have poor intellectual development and will not be able to advance as well as normally nourished infant rats.[2]

In these studies there is some meaning for the human infant as well. The loss of nutrients to the developing brain may be extremely detrimental, impairing intellectual function. In the rat this neurological development goes on for several days after birth, but in the human, brain growth and development that is so profound in the womb continues for several years, and some brain organization continues into adulthood. As pointed out in chapter 2, the brain's growth is rapid in the last trimester, with its weight increasing 260 percent; another 175 percent is added in the first year of life, and 18 percent in the second year, compared to only another 21 percent in the rest of childhood and adolescence. Thus there's that brief, important window during which we want to impact in a positive way. That's why vitamins, iron, and adequate nutrition are stressed for the expectant mother and why we want to nourish babies and toddlers particularly well.

We are uncertain as to how long the brain is susceptible to brain damage as a result of nutritional deprivation. But we do know that after an infant reaches six to seven months of age such susceptibility seems to be diminished. So you must be particularly careful about providing adequate nutrition for your baby during your pregnancy, as well as in the months that follow delivery.

HOW CAN I TELL IF MY BABY IS OR ISN'T
GAINING AS HE SHOULD?

You will probably need your physician's help in determining whether your infant has a disorder that may be interfering with his growth, but you can come to your physician with more insight and a better understanding of your baby's potential problem by starting at the same place as the physician. Look at the appropriate growth chart (see appendix).

The growth chart is a remarkable and invaluable tool, allowing you to evaluate the growth process that is going on with your baby compared to other infants. When the pediatrician weighs and measures your baby in the office, he learns what the baby weighs and measures at that particular time. Although helpful, that information is limited in scope. A far greater understanding is available if we plot those points on the appropriate growth chart, allowing the pediatrician to review your baby's growth pattern and compare it to normative data for infants the same age.

The World Health Organization's growth charts have become the standard for infants. They identify how children grow under optimal conditions, using lengths and weights measured at frequent intervals. They reflect growth patterns among children who were predominantly breastfed for at least four months and still breastfeeding at 12 months. These have replaced earlier Centers for Disease Control charts that were based on small sample sizes for the early months.[3]

Accumulating that growth information is one of the most important jobs for the pediatrician each time you visit for a wellness checkup. The growth chart compiles that information and shows your baby's continuous growth pattern. Height, weight, and head circumference can be compared with those of other infants the same age.

If, for example, Edna Millet is in the twenty-fifth percentile for weight, the seventy-fifth percentile for head circumference, and the fiftieth percentile for height, that simply means that if we placed 100 babies in order by their physical characteristics, Edna would be the seventy-fifth baby from the bottom (twenty-fifth from the top) as far as her head size, in the exact middle for her height, and the twenty-fifth child in line for weight. Her height would be the only physical characteristic that is exactly at the middle, or median, for her age. But all three characteristics are within the normal range for babies that age, because we consider the normal population to include everyone between the third and the ninety-seventh percentiles.

Of course, you want to make sure you are comparing to a similar group. If your baby was significantly premature, that infant didn't start in the same place as full-term babies born the same day. So instead we have a chart to evaluate babies' growth according to their prematurity (also in the appendix). Similarly, there are growth charts for babies who were born with certain genetic and developmental conditions (Down's syndrome and cerebral palsy, for example).[4] All of these charts recognize that there is no single healthy weight or length or head size; instead, there is a bell curve variation of normal weights, lengths, and head sizes.

For you to understand your own baby's growth, plot the points at which you have measurements and weights from his wellness checkups at different ages. Months are along the bottom; lengths and weights are along the sides of their respective charts. Once the graph is completed, look at the trajectory of his weight gain, and length.[5] If your baby was premature (which we will detail in the next chapter), use the premature growth chart and construct the same type of graphs, adjusting for how early he was.

Typically, a child will grow along the same percentile (also called isobars on the actual charts). If Edna is hovering about the median, or fiftieth percentile, on several measurements, she will probably continue to grow along that fiftieth percentile. For a child whose height is hovering at the tenth percentile, he will usually continue along the tenth percentile throughout his life.

Certain exceptions come into play later in childhood. Among those are children who sprout late in their adolescence with delayed maturation and children whose genetic makeup might limit their physical size. The major determinant of a child's eventual size is his parents' physical size. There is an inherited tendency to grow to a certain height. The same is true of head size and weight—in fact, it's true of all physical parameters and often the intellectual parameters as well. But these important factors do not play much of a role in an infant's early growth. The baby's growth inside the uterus does impact the baby's growth during infancy, as does breastfeeding. Smaller full-term *dysmature* babies tend to grow more slowly, while breastfed infants tend to increase their weight initially, then gradually readjust to their genetic potential over time.

With those exceptions considered, examine your baby's pattern. Concern should be raised when a child is not following a typical growth pattern. Carl Sand's weight may be normal at the twenty-fifth percentile and his height may be at the fiftieth percentile, but if he was previously growing in the range of the ninetieth percentile, and his weight and height have rapidly fallen to these lower percentiles, we must try to find out why. Remember, Carl did not lose weight; he is just not growing as rapidly. The twenty-fifth percentile and the fiftieth percentile are both entirely normal, but here the falloff suggests that the child's rate of growth has slowed dramatically. Usually, there is a reason behind it.

We can also get a little bit more specific, looking at the actual rate of growth, comparing it to other infants at the same age (which becomes valuable when we also look to see how effective our treatments are). The easiest way to evaluate the rate (or velocity) of growth is to construct a line between two points on the growth curve and compare it to the isobars of other infants at the same age. When the infant is paralleling infants in the third percentile, he is at least growing at a minimal rate; when it's less, he is still struggling and requires reevaluation; when he is gaining faster, he is actually catching up to some degree.

Additionally, you can compare his weight to what would be ideal for his height. To do so, plot his length so it falls on the fiftieth percentile (for example, if Rob Lowl is 25 inches and 13 pounds, 4 ounces, he is at the average length of an infant who is four months old, even though he is actually 5½ months of age and approximately at the tenth percentile for his own age). Now look at the fiftieth percentile of weight for the infant at the age plotted. For Rob at 25 inches, the average weight would be approximately 15 pounds, the weight defined as Rob's ideal weight for length. To take that one step further, we can look on a graph of weight-for-length percentiles (see the appendix) and find out he is at the tenth percentile, and that weight for length percentile can also be tracked over time to look for improvement or problems (the appendix also tracks that information for females). We can also define a percentage of actual weight to the ideal. In Rob's case, this is 90 percent—that is, 13 pounds, 8 ounces, or 13½ pounds (remembering there are 16 ounces in 1 pound) divided by 15 pounds. That number becomes useful when we are trying to determine whether Rob is malnourished and to what extent. Fortunately, he only shows evidence of being mildly malnourished, but if he weighed under 12 pounds (80 percent), he would be considered severely malnourished (table 10.1). For further assistance in plotting your child's growth curves and calculating various measures, please visit www.nutrition4kids.com.

Table 10.1. Stages of Wasting from Malnutrition

Malnutrition Level	Percentage Ideal Weight[a]
Mild	<90
Moderate	<80
Severe	<70

[a]Actual weight as a percentage of ideal weight for height.

Source: S. A. Cohen and A. Navathe, "Nutrition and Feeding for Children with Developmental Disabilities," in *Pediatric and Gastrointestinal and Liver Disease*, ed. R. Wyllie and J. S. Hyams, 4th ed. (Philadelphia: Saunders Elsevier, 2011).

WHAT CAUSES BEING UNDERWEIGHT AND/OR UNDERGROWN?

I usually group the causes into four categories that apply to infants and children alike:

- History
- Nutriture
- Absorption
- Metabolism

We've already recognized the genetic potential that the parents provide as primary, but also included within the historical basis is how well the fetus thrived inside the womb and whether there were any problems during pregnancy or with the baby's general health. Food availability is the most obvious component within the category of nutriture, but the caregiver's emotional and physical availability are also important to ensure they can understand and meet their child's basic nutritional needs. Beyond that, the infant's intestine and absorptive capacity takes over to digest and absorb the foods provided. And once that's accomplished, the baby or child must have a metabolism that can adapt, utilize, and store the various nutrients in an efficient, productive manner.

To be more specific, a group that does well includes infants who were slightly premature at the time of their birth and did not have any overwhelming problems with breathing or heart conditions in the nursery. After an accelerated rate of growth, they will reach a normal height and weight within the first years of life. They may gain most of their weight back by their first birthday, depending on how early they were born. But the general pattern is that usually for every month premature, it takes a year to catch up on weight gain, growth, and skills. If born one month prematurely, these infants catch up by one year of age; if three months early, by three years of age. Thereafter, they will generally continue to grow well as normal children, though sometimes they can actually become obese, gaining in weight appropriately but never quite growing fully.[6] Developmental skills in these same children often can be delayed as well. Their gains in development are usually similar to their nutritional progress, with these infants catching up at approximately one to three years of age. (Also review chapter 11 on premature infants.)

In contrast to the premature infant whose initial hours and days may have a stormy course, but whose growth is usually not impaired by problems, the dysmature infant represents many of the infants whose growth may be impaired later. Although small at birth, they usually do well in the nursery (except for occasional problems with low blood sugar in the first few hours of life). However, persistent short stature and learning disabilities are common. Their problems do not come from being delivered early but from an impairment within the womb. This may have resulted from a mother who had high blood pressure, malnutrition, or a chronic infection, or who smoked excessively.

From Dr. Winick's work we can determine that children suffer most if the mother's problem was severe, of long duration, or occurred early in the pregnancy. Thus, a child whose mother developed a relatively rare virus in the first trimester and passed it on to her unborn fetus or whose mother developed toxemia before the third trimester is at greater risk.

One of the best indicators of how these children will fare later on is not only the severity, duration, and timing of the problems in the uterus but the heredity the parents pass on as well. If both parents are quite tall, a child could have some growth retardation and still achieve a normal height. This child's genetic capacity might well have been to grow to 6'4", but the problems in the uterine environment stunted his growth; however, the child will still grow within the normal percentiles. However, the child whose parents are only 5'4" may have more significant growth problems since a deficit in his expected height will be more noticeable. Most of these infants will grow consistently, their weight gain and growth paralleling, but just under, the third percentile, with little response to increased calories or other measures to increase their weight and length other than growth hormones, which can be used when they are older.

Genetic and metabolic illnesses can result in a similar stunting of growth. These children may have normal weight and length at birth, but their diminished growth rate becomes evident in subsequent months. Often these children will not look like either parent but will have a look about them that is all their own. Unfortunately, these children often have other abnormalities that develop as well, which may take precedence over growth and nutritional concerns. And unfortunately, certain neurological and brain abnormalities can impose themselves on how babies accept the foods fed to them.

Cystic fibrosis is one genetic abnormality that is actually present from birth but may not show itself until months or years later, though now states screen for it in their metabolic panels in the baby's first days of life, so it is often diagnosed and treated quickly. With cystic fibrosis inherited from both parents, the child may develop respiratory difficulties or problems with absorption because of abnormalities in the intestinal tract, liver, or pancreas. Many of these children, as a result, fail to achieve an adequate height, particularly if the disease affects them when they are young. On the other hand, milder cases may not be recognized until adulthood. Previously, fat was often restricted in order to avoid problems with diarrhea. However, enzyme replacements are effective in digesting fat, making the calories from fat available for improved growth and better overall health. As a result, infants and children with cystic fibrosis are encouraged to eat as much as possible.

Celiac syndrome is another genetic disorder that is much more common than cystic fibrosis. As with Lizzie, the little girl described at the chapter's beginning, these children do entirely well in the first four to six months of life, at least until wheat is introduced into their diet. Shortly thereafter, diarrhea and irritability are often seen, and within several more months growth often falls off as well. Typically, these children come into the office looking stunted, with the muscles on their buttocks and limbs wasting away while their abdomens remain round and full. A mother may also note that her child has very little appetite. While this picture is true of infants who have celiac disease, many reach childhood with only a mild growth delay, or they present in adulthood with fractures, rashes, or infertility without diarrhea, diminished appetite, or growth impairment.

In this relatively rare illness, the diarrhea, irritability, and failure to grow are caused by wheat and certain other grains (rye and barley among them). A small fragment inside these grains, gluten, is responsible for literally wiping out a portion of the intestinal tract. The symptoms can be quickly and totally reversed with the simple avoidance of these grains and the products made from them. As if by magic, the child's irritability changes within a matter of weeks—if not days. The child becomes interested in eating once again, and slowly the child's muscle growth accelerates, often catching up to the potential the child originally had. The problem with grains is lifelong. If we place the intestine in a culture media with just the gluten, the intestine will once again deteriorate. And a patient with celiac disease will redevelop symptoms if he eats the gluten as a child or adult.

Too often parents who have heard of gluten intolerance eliminate these grains from their infant's diet if the child has prolonged diarrhea or undiagnosed abdominal pain or behavior issues. While this may be expedient at the time and may diminish the symptoms, the true diagnosis of this disease is often passed over and not firmly established. While this point may seem more of an academic interest than of clinical importance to parents who want to help their child feel better, making or excluding the diagnosis is crucial. Patients who do not have celiac disease might also improve for a number of reasons, but they are on a very rigorous and possibly unnecessary diet. More importantly, those who do have celiac disease are more difficult to diagnose and if they are not properly instructed and followed, they may be less compliant with their diet and reintroduce the different grains into their diet later, leaving them susceptible to adult manifestations, which can include intestinal cancer and unexplained abdominal complaints. Thus, it becomes extremely important to carefully establish the diagnosis of celiac syndrome to ensure that affected children will remain on the appropriate diet.

Numerous other gastrointestinal problems, both genetic and acquired, can compromise weight gain and growth, even in infancy, and some particularly so. As a pediatric gastroenterologist, I find it amazing not that so many medical conditions can affect infants (and children) but that so many children are healthy, escaping these conditions and their consequences. If I detailed them all here, this parent-friendly book would turn into a sleep-inducing textbook that might also contribute to excessive worry, so I won't put you through that. I will simply describe the general categories, working down through the infant's anatomy. (If you would like further information beyond what's provided here, please refer to the books and websites listed in the "Resources" section or visit our website, www.nutrition4kids.com.)

Oral and throat tumors can intrude into the mouth, making it difficult for infants to eat. Newer techniques are now demonstrating a variety of swallowing disorders that interfere with normal food movement. These and esophageal dysfunctions, even conditions as simple as gastroesophageal reflux, can lead to feeding aversions, where infants refuse what's offered and arch away to avoid it; and eosinophilic esophagitis, described earlier, is being recognized more frequently. Stomach problems are relatively rare for infants but can be related to the ability to propel food into the intestine. Pancreatic enzymes and bile (made in the liver and stored in the gallbladder) are released to break down (digest) the food into molecules that the intestine then absorbs. Certain, rarer intestinal illnesses can impair digestion or absorption such that malabsorption can occur. Even when elimination (defecation) is severely impeded (for example, with Hirschprung's disease), babies can lose their appetites. Unfortunately, other nongastrointestinal conditions (certain kidney problems or repeated infections) can also result in an impaired appetite or a change in metabolic functions that can start the cyclone of malnutrition (figure 10.1).

Of course, all of that presumes an available source of food (something we often take for granted, but those in other environments aren't always able to) and a physically and emotionally healthy caregiver. Knowledge about what to feed and how much can be learned (especially now), but the loving nurturing you provide is a true, innate blessing that will continue to benefit your baby.

HOW CAN THESE DIFFERENT PROBLEMS BE DIAGNOSED?

You have looked at your baby's growth chart and determined that his growth is not following a normal pattern. More than likely, that pattern falls into one of two general situations. Either his growth originally was normal and has now fallen off or his growth has never been normal, except perhaps in the first few weeks of life. In either case, these patterns should be reviewed with your physician. He will undoubtedly want your help, needing more information about the baby's activity, development, diet, and any previous problems. In addition, your physician will review your pregnancy with this infant (and any previous pregnancies). He will carefully examine the baby and may also need to obtain further laboratory tests. Several blood tests and urine studies may be ordered to look at the baby's kidney function, liver status, nutrition, and general chemical balance within the body. Stool samples may be obtained to look for malabsorption, infections, or blood within the intestinal tract, and a urinalysis may be requested to check the baby's ability to concentrate and acidify his urine and to check for infection.

Depending upon the results of these initial laboratory studies and dietary history, further evaluation may be necessary; the majority of these screening tests do not tell what the specific problem is, but rather where. Is this a kidney problem, or is the problem in the digestive system? Is it because of growth retardation when the baby was in the uterus, or is there a significant feeding problem that can easily be conquered? Once the general problem area is established, your primary physician or the specialist you're referred to will then go through an algorithm to pin down what specific cause is the actual culprit and determine the best way to correct it.

WHAT CAN BE DONE FOR MY BABY IF HE ISN'T GAINING?

Often, your primary care provider will be able to make changes in the baby's intake before the diagnosis is made and sometimes from the time of that first discussion. If you're fortunate, those changes will help the baby compensate for the problem he has and allow him to gain consistent weight. If so, that considerable diagnostic workup may be unnecessary.

The pediatrician will want to be sure that the baby does not have any other associated symptoms. Diarrhea, malabsorption, and vomiting require thoughtful evaluation and may require a temporary or enduring formula change. When these symptoms are not present and inadequate intake is the predominant symptom, changing the formula is generally not effective. Instead, the first step in the algorithm (figure 10.2) is to increase the calories the baby is receiving. Obviously, there's no way to feed the baby more formula since he's not taking enough as it is. So the way to accomplish that is to increase the calories in each sip. You can compare the concept to loading a baked potato. A naked baked potato contains relatively few calories (150), but load that potato with butter or sour cream, and suddenly you've tripled the calories, and each bite adds up to the calories of a deliciously dense chocolate cake.

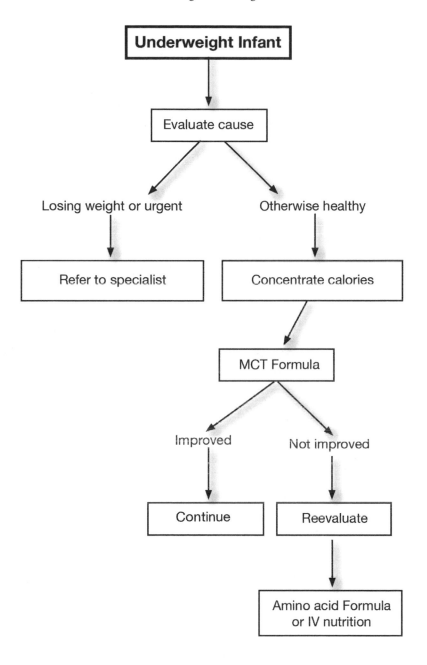

Figure 10.2. Helping the underweight infant.

The target is to increase the calories to approximately 110 to 130 calories per kilogram of ideal body weight for length (that's doctor speak for 50 to 60 calories per pound of the ideal body weight that we calculated). The easiest and most balanced way to add calories (and increase protein and all the nutrients at the same time) is simply to concentrate the formula. An additional scoop of routine formula powder in 8 ounces raises the caloric density by 25 percent, from 20 to approximately 24 or 25 kilocalories per ounce. That will also increase what the kidneys have to filter, but within a very safe range. The formula density can sometimes be increased further with careful physician guidance. If you are using a liquid concentrate, you can achieve the same results by lessening the amount of water you add to the 13-ounce can. Normally, you would add an equal amount of water, resulting in the standard 20 calories per ounce. If you add 11 ounces of water, the formula will be approximately 22 calories, while 9 ounces of water will bring this to approximately 24 calories in every ounce.

Alternatively, infant rice or oatmeal cereal can be added in small quantities to the formula (whether it is ready to feed or made from the powder or concentrate): 1 teaspoon yields 5 calories, accomplishing the same caloric increase. Remember that the cereal also thickens the formula, and a "Y" or cross-cut nipple may be needed to assist formula flow. A trick is to use a coffee grinder to make the cereal particles smaller, which will also ease the flow. But make sure you only mix as much as the baby is going to take at that feeding. When cereal stands in the formula, it tends to thicken further.

Both techniques add needed calories, though the additional cereal actually increases the carbohydrates relative to the other nutrients. When necessary, both techniques can be combined. Careful, ongoing monitoring is necessary to ensure that the increase does not precipitate any vomiting, diarrhea, constipation, or dehydration and that the increased calories result in the desired weight gain and not a further feeding issue.

To put the numbers into practical terms, you want your baby to consume 50 to 60 calories per pound of ideal weight.

at 20 calories per ounce = 2½ to 3 ounces per pound of ideal weight
at 25 calories per ounce = 2 to 2½ ounces per pound of ideal weight

Using Carl's example, ignore his actual weight of 13½ pounds and focus on the 15 pounds he should weigh at his ideal weight for length. At 15 pounds, he might need as much as 37½ to 45 ounces of regularly mixed formula to gain weight (and begin to catch up). Obviously that's a tremendous amount. By concentrating the formula to 25 calories per ounce, we can reduce that amount to 30 to 37½ ounces, and if we also add cereal to the formula at 1 teaspoon per ounce, we reduce that to 25 to 30 ounces per day (targeting the higher goal but being satisfied with the lower one as long as he gains weight).

WHAT IF INCREASING THE CALORIES DOESN'T WORK?

If increasing the caloric density does not result in weight gain, the baby needs to be evaluated for malabsorption and metabolic or other abnormalities. When actual weight loss or persistent lack of adequate weight gain is present, expeditious evaluation is important.

While awaiting the results and anticipating that malabsorption is likely, your physician may place the baby on a formula that is designed to be more readily absorbed. There are two: Pregestamil and Alimentum. Both have their protein (casein) fully hydrolyzed into peptides and their carbohydrates as sucrose or tapioca starch (which is quickly digested into simply absorbed sugars). Pregestamil has 55 percent of its fat as easily absorbed medium-chain triglycerides (MCTs), while Alimentum has MCTs as 33 percent of its fat. They are comparable in price, but Alimentum has a sweeter taste with its sucrose (table sugar) and modified tapioca starch, which is more appealing to infants. If this does not work, we often have to consider the formulas that have their proteins further digested into amino acids. All the other components are similar to the MCT formulas, but the reduction of the protein to amino acids makes them extremely expensive.

Some babies cannot take sufficient amounts of even that formula by mouth. They then require either intravenous nutrition or placement of a feeding tube, depending on the situation (see figure 10.1).

CAN I DO ANYTHING USING BABY FOODS?

Sometimes we can capitalize on your baby's diet and eating habits if your baby has already been introduced to infant purees. As with a child with cystic fibrosis, we may be able to achieve a somewhat improved weight gain by manipulating the child's intake of calories and protein.

To determine whether your baby might benefit from additional calories and nutrients, do what your pediatrician would do: review his intake pattern and your own role in his feeding. First, look at the entire aspect of eating. When does he eat best? Does he eat well in the evening, which is traditionally the adult American's time for the largest meal, or is your baby like many others who eat their best meal of the day at breakfast? If your child is a morning eater, it may help to make breakfast his major meal. He can get his protein-rich foods and high-density calories then and eat lighter meals during the day.

Or is your child one who is constantly grazing, constantly wanting something in his mouth? You may have tried to pacify him with some watered-down juice or a few crackers. If so, it may be wise to limit the child to only a small amount of any drinks for an hour or more before meals so that he is more interested in what you offer at mealtime.

As I indicated, we may want to concentrate the calories for the infant who is eating little rather than try to increase the total amount of food that is eaten. Several available products have been very beneficial in this regard. A teaspoon of canola oil can be added to 2 to 4 ounces of vegetable and meat purees, while an equal amount of cereal can be added to fruits. There are also commercial products available that can be added in small quantities to infant and table foods to increase their caloric density (table 10.2). They are effective but expensive. And you have to be careful with these calorie-dense foods and supplements, using a quarter teaspoon at first and then gradually increasing, because even a small bit extra can overfill your baby's stomach such that he'll develop vomiting or diarrhea or actually lessen his intake.

Remember, too, that we are dealing with children whose growth pattern is problematic. The baby is actually making a complicated but normal transition that we often ignore, going from drinking only liquids to swallowing solids. Some babies learn to chew and swallow as if it were the most natural event, while others struggle with the added complexity, having to figure out how to chew and use their tongues to move the food into position to go past their breathing mechanisms and into their gastrointestinal tracts. We will discuss this further in chapter 13, but please keep track of your efforts and your baby's response with the various foods, since that record may guide your physicians and any feeding therapists, should they become involved to help the process. A dietician can then review the calories consumed and determine whether the protein, vitamins, and other nutrients in the diet are adequate.

Table 10.2. Acceptable Additives

	Calories/ Tablespoon	Source
Infant formula powder	40	Variable
Nonfat dry milk for > 10 months old	22–30	Milk (protein 2.3g)
Infant cereal	15	Variable
Vegetable oil	124	Variable
MCT oil for malabsorption	115	Medium-chain triglycerides
Polycose	23	Glucose polymer
Benecalorie	110	Whey protein 2.3g, sunflower oil
Duocal	42	Hydrolyzed cornstarch, refined vegetable oils, fractionated coconut oil

Source: Adapted from S. A. Cohen and A. Navathe, "Nutrition and Feeding for Children with Developmental Disabilities," in *Pediatric and Gastrointestinal and Liver Disease,* ed. R. Wyllie and J. S. Hyams, 4th ed. (Philadelphia: Saunders Elsevier, 2011).

IS THERE ANYTHING ELSE I CAN DO
AS AN INTERESTED BUT WORRIED PARENT?

Perhaps you can consider your own very important relationship with the baby as he is being fed. Does your interest in your baby's eating come across in a positive or negative way? Do you smile and talk to the baby as you are feeding him, offering mild encouragement and showing pleasure when he is feeding well? Or do you perhaps unintentionally make the mealtime a challenge? One example of this is the anxious mother who coaxes each bite, saying, "Eat your beans, Jimmy," or who spoon-feeds the child who is looking around the room, quite content with what he's already eaten. In either situation, you have unintentionally set up a confrontation between yourself and your baby.

Believe me, your baby becomes very smart in the process. He recognizes that you will direct your attention solely to him if he refuses the feeding. He may make it into a kind of game, turning his head away while you are rushing your spoon to catch his mouth open. Such a feeding might well be fine for the 6-month-old who has just started purees, but for the 12-month-old, a more independent approach, allowing the child to feed himself almost completely, is usually far more appropriate and productive.

Or perhaps your attention is diverted elsewhere. Do you feed your baby while you are working or reading? Infants often do much better when they have a warmer, more direct relationship with the person who is feeding them. Rather than feeding the child while he is sitting in your lap but facing away from you, you might try turning him around and indicating your pleasure at his progress in eating and your joy in spending time with him.

These subtle changes create a more positive approach to eating—with gentle encouragement but no reprimands for not eating and no fighting to make the child eat—so mealtime can become less agonizing for both of you. Dr. Spock and others after him have pointed out that many of the children who want to eat between meals and have less interest at mealtimes see the meal just as their parents do—as a hated time when food becomes the focus. Meanwhile, during snack time there is little pressure, and food can actually be enjoyed. Changing the emphasis at meals, as well as the nuances of how the meal is provided, may encourage a happier and more successful mealtime.

SUMMARY

- Attention is required for children who are not gaining weight appropriately in order to understand and correct the problem.
- The pattern of an infant's growth must be examined to determine whether he is gaining sufficiently or at risk of becoming underweight.
- Underweight infants who are also falling off the normal growth pattern in height usually have a problem with malnutrition.

- Malnutrition can result in brain, intestinal, immunological, and growth impairment.
- Formulas can be concentrated to increase their caloric density proportionately.
- Foods and supplements are available to further augment your infant's calories.
- Formulas that are more easily absorbed may be needed.
- Additives are available to supplement the calories in infant purees.
- Your primary care provider should be involved in evaluating your infant and any decisions that need to be made, including the need to refer you to a specialist.

11

The Premature Infant

By definition, the premature infant is underweight and undergrown, but he also has other needs—for increased protein, calcium, and other micronutrients—that have to be met very cautiously. The growth-impacted preemie has only a relatively brief window of a year to catch up in head circumference and only three years for length, with a slim chance of catch-up growth later if it doesn't occur in those early years. But too-rapid weight gain for these fragile infants also has negative effects with an increased chance of high blood pressure, diabetes, heart disease, or osteoporosis later in life.[1]

Of course, you couldn't predict any of that looking at Sam, Nathan, and Ashton. The triplets, born at 31 weeks, could have easily been named Cute, Cuter, and Cutest in whichever order they were placed. A normal baby weighs an average of seven-ish pounds at birth, but the first two babies were each around half that, while Ashton was nearly another half pound lighter. They appeared tiny to their parents until they looked at the neighboring incubator, where another baby, Kobe, born even earlier at 26 weeks, was half their size, but fortunately was thriving as well as they were.

Their lungs were underdeveloped, as were their other organs, and all three required a brief stint of ventilatory support. But that was expected for babies born nine weeks early. Fortunately, they had been successfully weaned from the pressure that had been needed to expand their lungs—and now they were just on a small trickle of extra oxygen while they were gaining and growing, being carefully monitored. Of course, Ashton had stayed on the ventilator longer, but then he had also visited the operating room to have a small section of his intestine removed and an ostomy placed while he recovered from a condition called necrotizing enterocolitis (NEC), and he would return in several more weeks to have his ostomy closed.

NEC remains one of the most common conditions seen in premature (also called, neonatal) intensive care units, affecting 7 percent of the infants born at less than 1,500 grams (approximately 3 pounds), with too large a percentage of those dying or suffering significant consequences. NEC and optimal growth are two of the reasons neonatologists frequently research and debate how best to feed the infants under their care. For a while, neonatologists felt it was best to give all feedings intravenously, but studies showed that not only was it safe to place a tube through the nose and into the stomach to begin minimal feedings, it was actually better. These *trophic feedings*, which stimulate intestinal development in these particularly vulnerable, smaller infants, begin with tiny amounts (1 teaspoon dripped in over a few hours) and advance ever so carefully to larger, nutritious feedings.

It's a delicate balance for those first few months. Once a baby is delivered, it is hard to maintain the growth rate he had inside his mother initially (this is compounded further if the mother or the fetus had problems during the pregnancy, which is the reason mothers and babies are carefully measured prenatally). Studies have shown that babies whose growth is in the slowest group during their initial hospitalization will have increased rates of infection, NEC, and lung problems early on and greater risk for developmental delays later on.[2] So you would think that neonatologists would want to push nutrition maximally. But if they do, the rates of NEC go up as well. If they limit oral or tube feedings, instead delivering the nutrition intravenously, the risk rises for glucose instability and liver disease.

So neonatologists and nutritionists advance the diets of these tiny babies with caution and continuous calculations. The goal is to return each baby to the rate of growth in the womb (his intrauterine growth rate) and to match the rate at which he was accumulating various nutrients (the accretion rate), particularly for critical nutrients like protein, calcium, and phosphorus.[3] This can at first require intravenous nutrition, called total parenteral nutrition (TPN), meaning nutrition that comes into the body via a route other than the alimentary or gastrointestinal tract; this is also called hyperalimentation. But then trophic feedings are quickly added, and as those tube feedings are advanced, the TPN is slowly weaned, with the goal of maintaining stable fluids and nutrition for the baby.

The triplets' mother, Lauren, was able to provide enough breastmilk for the trophic feedings, but as they were advanced, her supply was insufficient. Two of her friends, Bernice and Mindy, were willing to contribute their excess breastmilk for the boys, but hospital safety policies required the milk to be pasteurized through a recognized donor bank, since these vulnerable premature infants need the level of protection that donor milk pasteurization provides in killing off potentially harmful bacteria that could contaminate the milk.

An infection that would not be harmful to older infants would be devastating to them, because their immune systems are far more fragile. It's the same reason that premature formulas are only available in sterile liquids, rather than in powders that can become contaminated with bacteria. So although pasteurization would simultaneously damage the breastmilk's cellular elements and the beneficial microbes present, the donor milk would still have immunological as well as nutritional benefits for the boys.

Lauren and her friends pumped their milk so that it could be mixed with a liquid milk fortifier, which added the additional protein, vitamins, and minerals needed for premature infants, and when that supply was exhausted, the babies were given premature infant formula, which is also designed to deliver the higher levels of protein, calcium, and other nutrients premature babies require.

WHY THE EMPHASIS ON PROTEIN, CALCIUM, AND PHOSPHORUS?

Protein is critically important to the small, premature infant after birth. Once he is brought into the world, he is suddenly without the source of his nutrition to build tissues and create the enzymes and structures that must begin functioning almost immediately. Studies have shown that increased protein concentrations improve the rate of growth,[4] and one study by B. E. Stephens and colleagues reported in 2009 that higher levels of protein in the first week actually increase mental development test scores at 18 months of age for extremely low-birth-weight babies.[5] As a result, most premature formulas now offer 20 percent more protein.

Infants accrue 80 percent of their calcium, phosphorus, and magnesium during the last trimester (roughly from the twenty-seventh week until they are routinely delivered at 38 to 40 weeks). If a baby is delivered early, he also misses a substantial amount of the elements that are important for growth and bone mineralization.

While breastmilk has low levels of these elements, the absorption is good. But even with this greater bioavailability, the amount the infant needs is greater than what can be provided by breastmilk alone. Therefore, supplementation is necessary with either a liquid or a powdered human-milk fortifier (table 11.1) that has additional protein, calcium, magnesium, and phosphorus to compensate. Formulas designed for premature babies similarly have increased amounts of the nutritional constituents that these babies need.

AREN'T FAT, CARBOHYDRATES, AND ALL THE OTHER MINERALS AND VITAMINS ALSO NEEDED?

Carbohydrates and fats are necessary for every infant to provide the substrate (building blocks) required for various cellular and chemical structures—and they each provide approximately half the calories the infant needs as his energy source. (If they are not receiving enough, some premature infants demonstrate that lack of energy supply by being unable to maintain their own body temperature.)

**Table 11.1. Estimated Nutrient Content of Preterm Human Milk (PHM)
and PHM Plus Enfamil Human Milk Fortifier (EHMF) Nutritional Supplement in
Powdered and Liquid Form**

Nutrient	PHM[a] per 100 ml ~20 cal./fl. oz.	Powdered EHMF 1 packet	Powdered EHMF + PHM 100 ml + 4 packets ~24 cal/ fl. oz.	Liquid EHMF 1 vial	Liquid EHMF + PHM 100 ml + 4 vials ~24 cal./fl. oz. Volume 120 ml
Calories, cal.	67	3.5	81	7.5	97
Protein, g	1.62	0.29	2.7	0.56	3.8
Fat, g	3.5	0.26	4.5	0.58	5.8
Carbohydrate, g	7.3	0.06	7.5	0.15	7.9
Vitamin A, IU	48	240	1,000	290	1,210
Vitamin D, IU	8	38	158	47	200
Vitamin E, IU	0.39	1.15	5	1.4	6
Vitamin K, µg	2	1.1	6.4	1.42	7.7
Vitamin B_1 (thiamine), µg	8.9	38	159	46	193
Vitamin B_2 (riboflavin), µg	27	55	250	66	290
Vitamin B_6 (pyridoxine), µg	6.2	29	121	35	146
Vitamin B_{12} (cobalamin), µg	0.02	0.05	0.2	0.16	0.66
Niacin, µg	210	750	3,200	920	3,900
Folic acid (folacin), µg	3.1	6.3	28	7.7	34
Pantothenic acid, µg	230	183	960	230	1,150
Biotin, µg	0.54	0.68	3.2	0.84	3.9
Vitamin C (ascorbic acid), mg	4.4	3	16.4	3.8	20
Calcium, mg	25	23	115	29	141
Phosphorus, mg	14.5	12.5	65	15.8	78
Magnesium, mg	3.3	0.25	4.3	0.46	5.1
Iron, mg	0.09	0.36	1.53	0.44	1.85
Zinc, mg	0.37	0.18	1.09	0.24	1.33
Manganese, µg	0.36	2.5	10.4	2.5	10.4
Copper, µg	38	11	82	15	98
Sodium, mg	28	4	44	6.8	55
Potassium, mg	50	7.3	79	11.3	95
Chloride, mg	58	3.3	71	6.9	86
Selenium, µg	2.4	None	2.4	None	2.4

[a]Values for preterm human milk compiled from nine sources; milk collected two to four weeks postpartum. Each vial of liquid HMF (human milk fortifier) increases volume by approximately 5 milliliters.

Source: Bailey Koch, RD, CSP, www.nutrition4kids.com.

The premature formulas contain fat blends that include medium-chain triglycerides to facilitate absorption (as 20 to 25 percent in the transitional formulas and higher in the premature formulas containing 24 calories per ounce). However, the amounts of docosahexaenoic acid (DHA) and arachidonic acid (ARA) in the different brands' premature formulas mimic the content of these two fats in the same brands' term formulas, with Enfamil EnfaCare and Good Start Premature having approximately twice as much as Similac NeoSure.

Various international societies[6, 7] would like to see even more added since most of an infant's DHA is transferred across the placenta in the last trimester of pregnancy. Therefore, prematurely born infants lack at least some portion of what they normally receive,[8] and infants are unable to make sufficient amounts of DHA to meet their own needs.[9]

Preterm infants also have low levels of the intestinal enzymes that break down lactose for absorption (34-week infants only have 30 percent of the function of term infants in that regard), but interestingly, they don't seem to have any clinical problem with the lactose in breastmilk or the lower concentrations in formulas designed for premature infants, where lactose makes up 40 to 50 percent of the carbohydrate, the rest being balanced by easily digested molecules of glucose strung together.

Iron is also a tricky issue for most premature infants, especially those who are very early, since frequent laboratory tests are needed to monitor their progress, but these blood tests lower their iron levels and their ability to transport oxygen. Transfusions or a red blood cell stimulator, erythropoietin, can help to maintain their supply of red blood cells, since the small volume of their TPN and iron-fortified formulas often cannot meet those needs alone. Fortunately, premature infants tolerate iron-fortified formulas well, without any problems or gastrointestinal upset.

Premature infants need the other minerals and all the vitamins at least as much as full-term infants do. The minerals are incorporated into different enzymes and cellular components that the baby must synthesize, and the vitamins serve as promoters or facilitators (cofactors) of many different enzyme processes or as chemical components themselves (please see chapter 15 for details). As a result, formulas designed for hospitalized premature infants (and transitional formulas for once they're discharged, as you'll see below) have higher content of many of the vitamins and minerals (table 11.2).

WHAT DETERMINES WHETHER A BABY CAN FEED FROM A NIPPLE?

The goal for most babies is to get them to feed by mouth. While that seems natural, it actually takes coordination in sucking, swallowing, and breathing in an ordered pattern so that infants will not aspirate formula into their lungs. Most infants can manage that patterning by 34 weeks of age, some slightly sooner. Those who are younger or still quite ill require a feeding tube of some sort.

Table 11.2. Comparison of Similac Preterm, Transitional, and Routine Infant Formulas per 100 Milliliters

	Term-Infant Routine Formula 20 cal./oz.	Preterm Transitional Formula 22 cal./oz.	Preterm In-Hospital Formula 24 cal./oz.
Energy, cal.	68	75	81
Water, g	90	90	88
Protein, g	1.4	2.09	2.42
Fat, g	3.65	4.1	4.38
Carbohydrates, g	7.57	7.54	8.31
Calcium, mg	53	78	145
Phosphorus, mg	28	46	81
Magnesium, mg	4.1	6.7	9.7
Iron, mg	1.22	1.34	1.45
Zinc, mg	0.51	0.9	1.21
Manganese, µg	3.4	7.5	9.7
Copper, µg	61	90	202
Sodium, mg	16	25	35
Potassium, mg	71	106	104
Selenium, mg	1	2	1
Vitamin A, IU	203	261	1,008
Vitamin D, IU	51	52	121
Vitamin E, IU	1	2.7	3.2
Vitamin K, µg	5.4	8.2	9.7
Vitamin B_1 (thiamine), µg	68	131	202
Vitamin B_2 (riboflavin), µg	101	112	500
Vitamin B_6 (pyridoxine), µg	41	75	202
Vitamin B_{12} (cobalamin), µg	0.17	0.3	0.44
Niacin, µg	709	1,455	4,032
Folic acid, µg	10.1	18.7	29.8
Biotin, µg	3	6.7	29.8
Pantothenic acid, µg	304	597	1,532
Vitamin C, mg	6.1	11.2	29.8
Choline, mg	10.8	11.9	8.1
Inositol, mg	3.2	26.1	32.3
Linoleic acid, mg	676	560	565

ml = milliliter; cal. = calorie; oz. = ounce; g = gram; mg = milligram (1/1,000g); µg = microgram (1/1,000,000g); IU = international unit

Source: Adapted from table provided by L. W. Williams, senior medical director, Abbott Nutrition, March 25, 2012.

Once they seem ready, the infants will be offered a small amount of water by mouth, often by a feeding specialist. They will be advanced to breastmilk or formula if they succeed, and the volume will be gradually increased. They will continue to receive the rest of what they need as *enteral feedings* through the feeding tube and perhaps with supplemental parenteral nutrition through an intravenous line as well.

Feeding tubes usually go through a baby's nose or mouth and into the baby's stomach in order to begin formula digestion there. The baby may be able to receive the feeding all at once, as if he had sucked it all into his mouth. But some babies can't handle that relatively quick *bolus feeding* and will instead require a slow, continuous delivery of the formula. For example, if Kobe needed 15 milliliters (3 teaspoons) of formula every 2 hours, instead of getting it over 5 to 15 minutes, he might receive 7½ milliliters each hour (approximately 1 tiny milliliter would be spread over 7 minutes).

If a baby has severe reflux or does not empty the stomach well (for any of a number of reasons), the tube might need to bypass the stomach and deliver the formula directly into the first portion of the intestinal tract (the duodenum). If the tube has to go farther because of a surgical or other condition, the baby may not be able to digest the formula nearly as well, in which case a more absorbable formula may be used. In either case, intestinal feedings must be done using that slow, continuous drip because boluses delivered into the small intestine can trigger diarrhea or nausea and vomiting.

CAN A PACIFIER OR THICKENER TRAIN THE BABY'S SUCKING AND SWALLOWING COORDINATION?

Often babies with feeding tubes will still be given pacifiers in order to learn how to suck and because the act of sucking by itself helps to propel formula through the gastrointestinal tract, though it can also increase air swallowing and generate some mild discomfort.

Thickeners were used until recently to prevent aspiration while sucking and swallowing. However, premature babies and their immature intestines are extremely vulnerable, and it appears that cornstarch-like thickeners can be associated with a greater risk of developing NEC. As might then be expected, the use of thickeners is better left until these babies are older and well past their originally expected delivery date.

CAN NECROTIZING ENTEROCOLITIS BE PREVENTED?

NEC seems to develop when feedings are introduced into a vulnerable intestine with an area of diminished blood supply. That vulnerability seems to be increased by the bacteria colonizing the intestine and any increased density of the feedings (like with cornstarch thickeners). As with so many other situations, breastmilk seems to provide the greatest protection when feedings are established. That may be due to its lower density, its immune factors, or its intrinsic microbial population. However, commercial probiotics have been repeatedly tested, and inconsistent results have emerged.[10]

Thus, trophic feedings and their cautious advancement are the current best recommendations available. New trials are under way using lactoferrin, one of the natural immune factors within breastmilk, but it is still too early to predict whether lactoferrin can modulate the antimicrobial and immune environment to make a clinical difference. Please follow the progress of this research on the website www.nutrition4kids.com or on one of the National Institutes of Health or other medical sites that track clinical trials.

WHAT IF MY BABY HAS REFLUX OR ANOTHER PROBLEM?

That of course depends on what the problem is. For the premature infant, one must consider when (at what age) the problem occurs and other factors contributing to the situation. Nathan, one of the triplets, was just such a patient. He wasn't gaining as well as he should have a month after birth, so his physicians and therapists cautiously increased the caloric density of his feedings. When that didn't work, the neonatologist tried to add a few more milliliters of formula to his feedings. That caused him to regurgitate. So the neonatologist evaluated the situation with stool studies (to look for blood or infection) and a number of blood tests, because any infant who has poor sucking after a period of feeding well might have a significant reason for the decreased intake. Fortunately, those tests were negative. A pH probe was ordered and found that Nathan was refluxing frequently. The treatment choices included changing to a rice-starch formula designed for infants with reflux, temporarily suspending or thickening the feeding by adding cereal to the premature formula, or using a medication for the reflux as well. Of course, using the rice-starch formula would eliminate the benefits of the premature formula, and thinning the formula would decrease the calories unacceptably. So a small amount of cereal was added to the formula he was already taking. The feeding volume was slowly advanced, and for good measure, a mild acid blocker was used as well. With that combination, Nathan gained weight and seemed to resolve his clinical reflux.

Nathan was an example of the unique feeding problems premature infants face. Had he been younger or smaller, or had there been any respiratory issues associated with the reflux, he might have required a duodenal (intestinal) tube delivering a slow, continuous feeding, or intravenous nutrition at the same time, with the parenteral and enteral feedings balanced daily to ensure adequate nutrition while trying to diminish the risks of both. If it was suspected that Nathan might have a milk allergy, he would have been placed on a protein hydrolysate, rather than a soy isolate, since soy infant formulas are not used in preterm infants weighing less than 1,800 grams (4 pounds) because of increased metabolic risk involving bone mineralization and lessened growth—issues that do not affect healthy, full-term infants.[11]

Just as Nathan's reflux required that his treatment options be reevaluated in light of the reflux as well as his prematurity, other gastrointestinal problems often cause a neonatologist to revert to the algorithmic progression for that problem and its possible solutions (figure 11.1), especially since many of the problems can be more frequent and significant in the preterm infant, sometimes necessitating prompt evaluation as well.

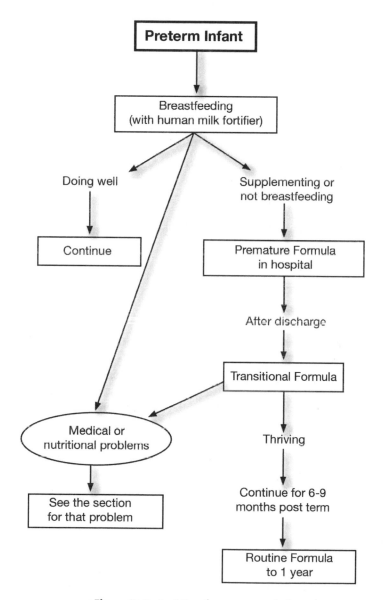

Figure 11.1. Assisting the premature baby.

HOW LONG DOES MY BABY NEED
TO STAY ON PREMATURE FORMULA?

Actually, two different formulas have been designed for premature infants. The ones used for early preterm infants (those younger than 36 weeks) are higher in protein and most vitamins and minerals, and they have 20 percent more calories (24 to an ounce) than routine formulas for term infants in order to assist growth and accretion rates. These are only made as sterile liquids and are only available in hospitals for premature infants in their nurseries and intensive care units.

Older prematures (those born around 36 to 38 weeks and often referred to as near-term) and most of the prematures who are finally growing well and getting ready for discharge from the hospital don't need nutrient levels quite that high. They still need more than full-term babies (again, full-term is considered 38 to 40 weeks, with complete gestation at 40 weeks).

So a second set of formulas, called *transitional formulas* by Abbott, Gerber, and Mead Johnson, the companies that make them in the United States, contain intermediate levels of protein (Gerber sticks with its 100 percent whey) but higher calcium and phosphorus, with most of the other vitamins and minerals placed at the levels for full-term infants. Because the babies are no longer as vulnerable (making bacterial contamination less of a problem), the formulas are available in stores in powdered as well as ready-to-feed versions. Both the ready-to-feed and powder versions, as they are routinely constituted, deliver 22 calories per ounce, 10 percent more than routine formulas.

The argument could be made that most of these infants could probably get by with routine formula that's concentrated an extra 10 percent or simply by taking 10 percent more formula (some infants automatically drink more when the formula has less density). Either strategy would increase the protein sufficiently, and the calories of the concentrate would be equivalent to the premature formula. Some of the vitamins and minerals would approximate the extra that near-term infants need, and any excess of the other vitamins and minerals would be trivial. But the concern is that some near-term babies are still at risk for NEC, so they have to be monitored more closely. Of course, we want to watch them carefully anyway, since some premature infants often take months to catch up to their peers in growth and development (usually up to a year for every month early, as stated earlier), and then they sometimes shoot to the other side of the spectrum with a tendency to obesity.

The real difference is that the calcium and phosphorus would remain low, just when babies need to mineralize their bone matrix as effectively as possible. And for that reason, I recommend the transitional formulas rather than concentrating routine formula or hoping that your baby is taking 10 percent more.

I continue the transitional formula until the babies are six months post term (six months past their original due date). Since term is considered 40 weeks, add the number of weeks the baby is early to the six months. Since the triplets at the beginning of the chapter were born at 31 weeks, they should remain on the transitional formula until eight-and-a-half months of age (six months, plus two-and-a-half extra to account for their prematurity). Their neighbor, Kobe, who was 26 weeks (14 weeks, or three-and-a-half months, premature), would thus remain on that formula six plus three-and-a-half months, for a total of nine and a half months. This six-month post-term concept is not set in stone, however, and I would monitor closely, prolonging the use of the transitional formula if I had any concerns about the triplets' or Kobe's intake, growth, or ability to swallow. And if one of the boys had a medical problem, I might use the algorithm for that problem to determine if the condition and solution might override my desire to keep him on the transitional formula.

IF MY BABY WAS JUST A LITTLE EARLY, DO I STILL NEED TO BE CONCERNED?

Of all the preterm babies, 70 percent are born between 34 and 36 weeks (a month to a month and half early). Yet they still have more severe illnesses and perform less well developmentally than similarly aged full-term infants. Some of them are smaller than they should be at birth, and even the ones who are normally sized are more likely to be underweight for that first year of life and maybe longer.[12] As a result, I would place these late preterm infants on a transitional formula of 22 calories per ounce until six to nine months adjusted age in order to continue to meet their increased nutrient needs and optimize their growth. Once the infant has reached six to nine months post term (adjusted age), the infant should be placed on a routine cow's-milk-based protein formula unless he has an additional problem requiring another type of formula.

SUMMARY

- Premature infants (born before 37 weeks) have unique feeding needs, and an algorithm can help you understand the requirements of this population.
- Small premature infants have an increased risk of remaining small if they do not catch up in their first three years of life (their heads should catch up in size within a year). If overfed, they are at risk for diabetes, high blood pressure, heart disease, or osteoporosis in later life.
- Babies born before 34 weeks may have difficulty swallowing successfully and may require tube or intravenous feedings.
- Small, trophic feeds through a gastric feeding tube can advance intestinal development and may be started shortly after birth.
- Fortification of breastmilk is indicated for the preterm infant to meet protein and mineral needs for optimal growth. Human-milk fortifier should be added until the infant has achieved a body weight of 1,800 grams (approximately 4 pounds) or nears the time of discharge from the hospital. Fortification may be needed for longer periods if the infant was very premature at birth.
- Vitamin D supplementation is required as well.

- Breastmilk may help to prevent necrotizing enterocolitis in early premature infants.
- If the mother makes the decision to supplement with formula or not breast-feed, a premature (transitional) formula should usually be prescribed once the infant has left the hospital and possibly before, depending on the age and size of the infant.
- The appropriate formula for the premature infant is determined by the infant's gestational age, post-term age, any additional problems, and whether the infant is in-patient or has been discharged (see figure 11.1).
- Preterm and immune-compromised infants are at risk for developing infection and should receive only commercially sterile liquid formula prior to hospital discharge.
- Milk allergy in preterm infants should be managed using protein hydrolysates. Soy formula should not be used for preterm infants because of metabolic risks affecting bone mineralization and growth.
- Upon discharge, most preterm infants will be placed on a transitional formula of 22 calories per ounce until six to nine months adjusted age in order to continue to meet the infant's increased nutrient needs.
- Once the infant has reached six to nine months post term (adjusted age), the infant should be placed on a routine cow's-milk-based formula unless he has an additional problem requiring another type of formula.

12

‿‿

Overweight or Just Plain Healthy?

Contending with obesity has become a national obsession among policy makers, and well it should. The facts about the obesity epidemic are not new, but they are frightening. Over the past several decades, the prevalence of obesity has doubled for children and adolescents in the United States. Of children between 6 and 12 years of age, 15 percent are overweight, and 18 percent of adolescents are obese. This percentage increases among some minority and economically disadvantaged groups, with more than one-fourth of African American and Hispanic children obese by eighth grade and with many of these children overweight by kindergarten.[1] The number of hospitalizations related to obesity for children 6 to 17 years of age more than doubled over the past decade, and the cost of caring for a child with obesity is 24 percent higher.[2] If you combine all the costs of this excess weight to our health-care system, they add up to over $114 billion a year, approximately the amount the government is trying to trim from the health-care budget.[3]

Cost is only a small part of obesity's impact. The first consequence these children often face is a crushing blow to their self-esteem and peer relationships. But they are also at risk for the medical side effects of obesity that occur later in adulthood, with hypertension and high lipid levels leading the list. Type 2 diabetes, which was previously seen in only middle-aged adults, is now being diagnosed decades earlier. Sadly, once obesity is present, losing the weight is difficult.

Understandably, much of the focus has been on preventing obesity in school-age children, but my observation, as the former cochair of the Taskforce on Obesity for the Georgia chapter of the American Academy of Pediatrics, is that this time frame may be too late for many children and that many parents don't understand the implications (which is the reason for this preamble).

Let me share the results of a research study I conducted for the Georgia WIC program to evaluate parents' concern about possible obesity in their children. I asked three groups of pediatricians to give parents of overweight children, two to five years of age, an algorithm that allowed parents to recognize the potential severity of obesity, listing potential outcomes (increased respiratory effort, diabetes, hypertension, heart disease, hyperlipidemia) to determine what would help them in addressing those concerns.[4]

I wonder if you can guess the results. Only a handful of parents filled out the evaluation. Many felt threatened by having their children classified as being at risk of obesity, and many of the pediatricians did not want to subject their patients to that concern. When the evaluation was filled out, only 29 percent were concerned about the weight or size of their child (and only 17 percent wanted nutritional guidance), though 58 percent did say they were concerned about their child's general health, and 58 percent were concerned about their own weight or size. However, 62 percent did say that they would "do something" if the problem worsened or it limited the child's activity. Unfortunately, I did not ask whether the parents were doing anything about their own problems.

I was appalled, and I am still distressed by the findings and what they tell us. But they certainly explain why obesity has become an epidemic. We are addressing the problem too late, and our efforts are often ineffective. However, I am writing this chapter because I do believe you can change the situation, at least for your own child.

WHEN DOES THE RISK BEGIN?

To many eyes, thin infants look underweight and unhealthy. We're used to seeing smiling, chubby babies on advertisements and in strollers on the street. But the reverse may be true: thin infants may be healthier, and there is a risk for that happy, well-fed infant to become overfed and overweight. The Institute of Medicine released a report in 2011 showing that 20 percent of two- to five-year-olds are overweight or obese (over the ninety-seventh percentile for age). That's 1 in every 5 children that age, an increase from 5 percent (1 in 20) in 1980. Among babies up to two years of age, over 10 percent are overweight and already beginning their trajectory toward obesity.[5]

Unbelievably, the problem may even begin before that, during pregnancy. Years ago, a comparison was made of children born before and after the mother developed type 2 diabetes. Those born afterward remained overweight throughout childhood and were approximately four times more likely to develop diabetes.[6] To lessen that risk, overweight women are cautioned to lose weight before they become pregnant so that they will have less chance of developing diabetes during pregnancy, and smokers are also encouraged to stop since their infants are usually small at birth but have a higher tendency to become overweight later. Interestingly, Dr. Dana Dabelea at the University of Colorado continued her research on the influence of diabetes and has now reported that breastfeeding for at least six months reverses that risk so that infants born of mothers with type 2 diabetes are no more likely to remain overweight as children.

CAN I ALTER FEEDINGS TO LESSEN THE RISK?

As stated previously, breastfeeding lessens the potential for later obesity, and the longer breastfeeding continues, the lower the risk.[7, 8] The secret of how it protects isn't clear yet, especially since breastfeeding also helps to increase weight for underweight children.[9] The composition of breastmilk or one of the bioactive substances may somehow program the metabolism that regulates growth and fat deposits.[10] Perhaps one of the hormones or a combination of the bioactive factors that cross from the mother to the baby has an effect. Insulin and a number of regulatory factors you may not have heard of, such as adiponectin, gherlin, and leptin, could be involved. Interestingly, an initial study showed that high levels of maternal-milk adiponectin were associated with thinner babies at six months of age.[11] This was logical since this factor is insulin sensitizing, and higher blood levels are seen in older individuals with less fat on their bodies. But another study failed to confirm these results,[12] and extending the study another year showed that the higher levels were associated with greater weight gain during the baby's second year.[13]

But breastmilk may not work just because of its content. It may help to lessen obesity by the way babies learn to feed—and those lessons can apply whether a baby is bottle- or breastfed. Breastfed babies feed vigorously when they are hungry and less actively when they're not. They don't watch the clock to see if it's time to latch on or look for ounce markings on the container. They turn the breast into a pacifier when finished, sucking with less intention, and fortunately mothers can't encourage the baby to finish the last ounce in the bottle.

Bottle-feeding mothers can adopt the same "on-demand" principles. When your baby wakes after a nap or it simply seems like a convenient time to feed him, try to resist that temptation and play with the baby instead, helping him develop his motor skills and letting him enjoy your voice and face. When he begins sucking, smacking his lips, bringing his hands to his mouth, or rooting with his mouth for a nipple, he's showing early signs of hunger. When he starts to fret, check to see if his diaper needs to be changed. Some authors note that a short, lower-toned cry that tends to rise and fall is characteristic of a hunger cry and much different from the higher-pitched, more exasperated cry of discomfort.[14]

And when he's pulling away or looking around the room, those are good indicators that he's full, that he has enough to satisfy him for the moment. There is no need for him to finish a certain amount. He may be hungry again in two, three, or four hours. He'll signal his interest and may take more or less at that next feeding or the one after that. The trick is to be sensitive to his needs, to recognize his hunger cues, and to distinguish those from signs of discomfort. If he's crying at the end of a feeding, you will want to check his diaper to see if it needs to be changed or offer a pacifier, and if those don't lessen his discomfort, consider giving a bit more formula. He may or may not want it. The important part is letting him take the lead—and not worrying about some preconceived notion of how much he should take or when he should feed. You'll know if he's getting enough if he's producing wet diapers throughout the day and if he has bowel movements once or twice a day (if he doesn't, it may still be a normal amount; see chapter 8 for clarification).

Additionally, the pediatrician will weigh the baby at his routine maintenance visits and let you know how he's gaining. The usual concern is with a baby not gaining enough, but he can also tell you if your baby's weight is accelerating too quickly. The usual, expected weight-gain pattern is as follows:

1½ to 2 pounds per month up to 4 months
1 to 1½ pounds per month from 4 to 6 months
½ to ¾ of a pound per month from 6 to 12 months

If the baby's weight gain is excessive, you may well be overfeeding him. It's often difficult to decrease the amount at a given feeding. You should not dilute the formula for a growing infant, because you'll also dilute important nutrients that your baby needs. Instead, offer a water bottle between feedings if your baby is consuming more than 32 ounces of formula per day at less than four months of age. Offer it if he begins to fuss before 2½ hours after the last feeding. If he won't take the water, you can add 1 teaspoon of juice to accommodate the baby's natural inclination for sweeter flavors. If you've added cereal to the bottle to help control your baby's reflux, you can try to reduce the cereal slowly. (You can also refer to chapter 6 for alternative solutions for the reflux.)

Also, check our website, www.what2feedyourbaby.com, to see if and when the lower-protein formulas are available. As discussed in chapter 4, standard infant formulas have higher protein levels in order to ensure the adequacy of essential amino acids, but metabolic changes result in increased insulin levels[15] and greater weight gain,[16] so some formulas with a different protein composition are being tested at the time of this writing.[17]

If your baby is over four months old, consider beginning infant foods (vegetables first, since they are filling and less dense calorically). And then follow the suggestions given in the next two chapters on how to moderate your baby's gain with the solids you introduce, remembering that babies' stomachs are usually about the size of their fists and that you don't want to restrict fat in order to lessen their weight gain (they need a careful balance of all components in order to achieve growth and long-term health).

Most importantly, recognize that you can work with your pediatrician or an expert in the area to help you determine the best strategy. There's reason for concern and much you can do but no reason to frustrate yourself worrying.

SUMMARY

- The tendency to be overweight may begin in infancy or even when the baby is in the uterus.
- Breastfeeding helps to lessen the risk of becoming overweight or obese. How breastfeeding exerts its effect is unclear. It may be due to the nutrients, some of the hormones, or bioactive substances in the breastmilk. It could be that the feeding patterns contribute as well.
- Bottle-feeding parents can adopt the same on-demand schedule, recognizing that well-fed babies don't necessarily finish the amount poured into the bottle and that the amount taken may be variable from feeding to feeding.
- Certain techniques with solid foods may also help to lessen the tendency to become overweight.

13

⌒

Infant Foods and
How to Introduce Them

You've become an expert on breast or formula feeding. You've provided all the nutrition your baby has needed since he left the womb simply through this magical liquid of breastmilk, or a formula that's been designed to function like it, or that's been adapted to compensate for your baby's specific requirements.

Now everyone, from your mother to your neighbor's best friend, has advice for you about when to introduce baby foods, because that's the way they did it. But the foods that are introduced and the timing aren't the same for every infant. Some should have their feedings at an older age (the potentially allergic infants, if they aren't breastfeeding) or earlier if they are breastfed or have reflux. Some need foods with lower calories (the overweight infants), others require higher calories (the underweight) or more fruits and vegetables if they have constipation, and the verdict is uncertain for the infant of a parent with celiac disease or gluten sensitivity. So the order and speed with which solids are introduced matters, as does the way they're prepared and stored at home. But does it make a difference if infant food is organic or does that simply reflect the parents' preference—and is it worth the additional expense?

WHAT ARE THOSE TIMING TRICKS?

The history of when baby foods were introduced is interesting. Before 1920, solids were often withheld until a year of age. In the 1930s, as now, feeding began at four to six months of age. It was only during the proliferation of and strong advertising for the frequent use of packaged infant foods (since the 1940s) that babies were exposed to foods earlier and earlier. The final absurdity was the introduction of cereals by three days of age, with vegetables, fruit, and meat soon to follow.

Fortunately, science has helped us establish the rationale for timing. Your own milk with added vitamins (and fortifier, if the baby was premature) or the similar commercial formula with added vitamins supplies all the nutrients your baby needs during those particularly crucial first months of life, supporting your baby even though he is growing rapidly. However, when your infant doubles his birth weight (at four to six months of age), or reaches approximately 13 pounds, his needs begin to outpace what you can supply with human or modified cow's milk alone. A good indicator is that he still seems hungry even though he breastfeeds 8 to 10 times or takes over 32 ounces per day (and isn't spitting up the excess).

There are developmental reasons as well. By five to six months of age, babies are able to sit well enough to support their heads, leaning forward when interested in eating and turning away when full or disinterested. They can use their lips to clear the food off spoons, and they can move the food with their tongues, so they have eliminated the risk of choking and aspirating solids that are fed. In addition, babies' developmental *extrusion reflex* to stick out their tongues and try to push out anything strange (including solid food) that is in the mouth goes away by four to five months of age. Thus, that seems to be the time when babies will accept solids most readily.

Internally, the intestinal tract is maturing as well. Dr. Allan Walker (whom I trained under at the Massachusetts General Hospital) established that early in infancy, large proteins can penetrate the intestinal surface. These proteins can sensitize the infant and allow food allergies to develop.[1] Of course, the story is far more complicated than that, since not all babies are susceptible, it seems, and the body somehow learns to tolerate most foods that are ingested. To me, it's a miracle that we can put foreign proteins in our bodies, and our bodies accept most of them. And babies do a good job of that after approximately six months of age, when, according to Dr. Walker, the intestinal cells knit together tightly and form a more effective barrier against these food proteins, lessening the potential to develop allergies. Before that time, the best we can do is limit exposure to food allergens and encourage breastfeeding because breastmilk has a protective effect.

Delaying the introduction of particularly allergenic foods, such as egg whites, cow's milk, citrus fruits and juices, and nuts, is controversial. Because of these foods' increased chance of causing allergies, the traditional approach has been that parents should wait a year before adding these to the diets of infants with a high risk of developing allergies (those who have parents or siblings with allergies or who have already demonstrated an allergy to another food).[2] However, an expert panel sponsored by the National Institute of Allergy and Infectious Diseases in 2010 provided guidelines for earlier introduction, indicating that even potentially allergenic foods may be introduced at four to six months of age.[3] A 2011 study takes this one step further, finding that infants whose parents had asthma or allergy actually had lower allergy antibodies to peanut and egg if they were introduced to these foods before four months of age.[4] Just as you may be able to prevent allergies by altering when solid foods are introduced into your infant's diet, you may also be able to reduce the risk of your child becoming overweight.

Why? Because an earlier introduction of solids does not substantially reduce the amount of formula or breastmilk that the baby takes. And the extra calories are simply added on, adding to the potential for a healthy infant to become an overweight child.

IS THERE ANY HARM IN INTRODUCING SOLIDS EARLIER?

I remember one mother whose parents were visiting from abroad and whose baby was two months old. Every day another argument ensued over whether the baby's fussiness was due to hunger and whether the mother should listen to her wise parents or some dumb pediatrician (namely, me). Due to all that pressure, several spoonfuls of cereal touched that virgin tongue. The baby tolerated it all quite well and maybe—maybe—was a little less fussy for a few minutes after the additional feeding. But the mother was afraid to tell me until the baby's four-month visit. Then she broke into tears.

I didn't reprimand her. I just listened and then explained that infants who are thought to be fussier often are started on solids before four months of age.[5] I was able to lessen her guilt. The baby didn't get sick or show any evidence of an allergy. We were able to modify the baby's diet by reducing his formula intake slightly. And while I support the American Academy of Pediatrics' guidelines advising that solids are most appropriately introduced at four to six months of age, your infant will survive even if you introduce solids earlier, as long as you do so sparingly.

There are two concerns. Babies have a higher incidence of developing or promoting allergies and eczema when foods are brought into the diet before four months of age. The problem is that this doesn't always become obvious right away but can affect them throughout their lives. The other concern is that babies who gain weight excessively have a higher risk (two to three times greater) of becoming obese when they are school age, and that risk increases their later risks as well. And there is that potential, since infants do not have enough neuromuscular control prior to six months of age to turn their head away and indicate lack of interest or satiation. Therefore, you should be particularly careful to avoid overfeeding and recognize that the baby's not going to grow any better with solids introduced before six months of age.[6]

WHAT FOODS FIRST?

Solid foods are added to the diet in order to provide what the infant cannot get from breastmilk or infant formula alone, and for that reason they are sometimes called complementary foods (some breastfeeding advocates even put infant formula in that category since it displaces breastmilk as a food). Solids also help your baby acquire oral motor skills, such as moving his tongue, swallowing thicker consistencies, and eventually chewing. And the solids expand his diet so that he can enjoy the other flavors that enrich life and bring pleasure.

Babies can experience a delay in their growth and development if baby foods are introduced much beyond six months of age.[7] By that age, they begin to outgrow what breastmilk or formula can provide alone. They need additional sources of protein, iron, zinc, and the B vitamins. As a result, the choice of foods to offer should include those nutrients (table 13.1). Babies could become deficient in vitamin D as well if they are breastfeeding and not receiving a supplement, but again, that potential deficiency exists throughout infancy and can be prevented with a daily supplement.

Iron-fortified cereal makes an excellent choice for most infants as a first food, with the fortification meaning that the precooked cereal doesn't provide iron from the cereal itself, so that element has been added. When iron was first added to cereals, a version was used that markedly limited its availability for absorption, but the iron phytate has been changed to electrolytic iron, which is more bioavailable. If your baby does show signs of anemia or low iron (this is generally checked by your pediatrician at six months of age), and your baby is taking more formula than he needs, my personal recommendation is for you to mix the cereal with diluted juice instead of breastmilk or formula or to combine the cereal with fruit since the vitamin C (ascorbic acid) helps iron absorption. Begin by adding three to four times as much fluid as cereal; then gradually lessen the amount of fluid (mixing twice as much fluid to cereal) to provide a thicker consistency.

There's an old wives' tale that cereal should be added sooner to help a baby sleep. In fact, I had one mother whose infant was sleeping through the night at one month of age, and the grandmother of that infant wanted her to have cereal because she was afraid the baby was sleeping too much; in her culture, cereal was added to keep the baby awake. For mothers who will try almost anything to get their baby to sleep through the night (after 4½ months, the time when babies usually start to do this on their own), I recommend a three-day trial of rice cereal (mixed as above with formula) at the evening meal. If the child sleeps through the

Table 13.1. Infant-Friendly Food Sources for Needed Nutrients

Nutrient	Food Source
Protein	Lean meats, beans, eggs
Iron	Iron-fortified cereal, meats, green vegetables
Zinc	Fortified cereal, meats
Vitamin A	Yellow vegetables
Vitamin C	Fruits, broccoli, leafy green vegetables, tomatoes
Vitamin D	Sun exposure, fortified cereal, egg yolk, cod liver oil
DHA	Eggs, fish (e.g., salmon)

Note: Iron, vitamins, and DHA are also available as infant drops.

Source: Bailey Koch, RD, CSP, www.nutrition4kids.com.

night, fine—we can attribute it to the cereal. But if he doesn't, then the parents are simply forced to wait for the baby to mature further before he, and they, have an uninterrupted night of sleep.

Irrespective of sleep, cereals often become an excellent introduction to solids, allowing infants to learn how to use their tongues to move the cereal from the front of their mouths to the back and, from there, past the epiglottis into the esophagus.

Rice has been the traditional choice initially because it's well tolerated by most infants, with relatively few who will develop allergies to it. The only problem is that it tends to cause constipation in some infants. For those babies, oat or barley can be used instead, at least in families who do not have celiac disease, since oats often have wheat flour as well, and we want to hold the exposure to wheat for those infants until after at least a few other foods are tried so that we don't confuse feeding issues with gluten intolerance or wheat allergy (see the section on celiac disease and food allergy in this chapter). In infants who have stooling problems and in whom we want to avoid other cereals, I will often introduce vegetables instead (which have protein) and start the cereals and other high-protein foods after vegetables and fruits are well tolerated. The infants tend to do better with more fruits and water easing their bowel evacuation.

IS THERE A BEST WAY TO INTRODUCE OTHER FIRST FOODS?

Nutritional science dissolves into art here, with a number of acceptable feeding schedules for introducing solids. All have two important concepts: (1) to introduce additional nutrients and calories to the infant who is rapidly growing and whose growth cannot be supported by breastmilk or formula alone, and (2) to adhere to the recommendations of when to introduce solid foods, as mentioned above, though these do change at times, often with some degree of controversy. This latter consideration is certainly more important for the child of allergic parents, but it is a general consideration for the population at large since we often do not know which other children are prone to allergies.

The one concession that we do make to the allergists and allergies in general is that foods should be introduced in a manner so that we can recognize the children whose reactions develop from foods and the foods that are causing those reactions.[8] For this reason, physicians generally recommend that your baby be introduced to only one new food every three to five days in the beginning (five to seven days for infants from families with allergies). This means that if the child is to be started on applesauce, he will start with a small amount the first time it's given, build up to full volume by the second or third day, and continue on the applesauce daily for another day or two. During that time, nothing else new should be introduced into the baby's diet. This allows you to recognize a rash or other reactions that may develop as a result of introducing the applesauce. If you see no reaction, you move to the next food at three days; if you question whether you are starting to see a reaction, five days should give you enough time to judge.

You can extend that to seven days for a child who has shown possible reactions to several foods. The intent of this careful introduction is not to confuse yourself when you introduce the next new food. Also, it gives the baby enough time to get used to a food, since it can take as many as 15 taste exposures before the baby readily accepts the food.

If a rash or other reaction does develop, the applesauce you just introduced may or may not be the cause. The only way to tell will be to stop using the applesauce for several weeks and then reintroduce it later at a time when nothing else is being added to the diet. Generally, if the same reaction occurs on three widely spaced trials, whether it's a rash on the face or vomiting, and it follows the introduction of the food within a period of 24 to 36 hours, you can assume that an allergy is present, and you should avoid that food for at least several months, if not several years. The severity of the reaction and whether the infant is showing a reaction to just that one food (a milder situation) will dictate how long to wait. Obviously, if the reaction is more severe (e.g., full-body eczema), or if the infant is globally allergic (i.e., has multiple food reactions), you will need to wait longer to have foods reintroduced. If a major reaction or even a minor one does develop, do discuss it with your physician to see if he or she thinks it was truly in response to the food and if and when the food should be tried again.

With these suggestions regarding the gradual presentation of new foods and the thoughtful monitoring that should accompany it, you should be able to work out a reasonable schedule for the introduction of foods. The schedule that I particularly like is one that provides variety for the child while introducing him to the various food groups in a rational approach.

Again, rice cereal is typically the first food I would start with. Introduce it once a day. Start with 1 teaspoon diluted with 3 to 4 teaspoons of formula or breastmilk, using less liquid (approximately 2 teaspoons) as the baby becomes proficient. After you give the baby one to two weeks to get used to the whole concept of a spoon and solids, I recommend introducing vegetables. A yellow (orange) first (carrots, squash, or sweet potatoes), because they all contain vitamin A, another of a baby's potential deficiencies beyond six months of age. They are well tolerated, create little gas, and rarely induce allergies. Once the baby has experienced the first, move onto another of the yellow vegetables and then onto two of the green vegetables in sequence.

Once four vegetables are tolerated without reaction, you can move onto fruits, again, one at a time for three to seven days. As the fruits are introduced, the cereal and any of the vegetables are still used. To make it easy, you can give cereal and a fruit in the morning and a vegetable with or without cereal in the afternoon, the cereal being used if you have a hungrier baby or one who prefers to have the taste of the two together rather than a vegetable alone.

You will want to introduce all of these foods as thin purees, often called stage 1 foods. A month or two later, when the baby seems to be handling the thin texture well, you'll progress to stage 2 foods, which are thicker, slightly lumpy purees.

The actual food within the group is left to your personal taste and the food's availability. If you are making the food at home, the season and whether you buy organic foods may make a difference in terms of availability.

Meats (and egg yolks) should be introduced in a similar fashion by themselves, rather than in the prepackaged mixtures with vegetables. Once the meats and vegetables are tolerated individually, without reactions, they can then be used in these convenient, but more expensive, combinations, if you'd like.

Always remember to be careful with storage. Unused portions can be refrigerated for up to 24 hours and then brought up to somewhere between room temperature and the baby's body temperature (a few seconds in the microwave should not hurt the foods, unless package instructions say otherwise, but hot spots can develop that can burn the baby's mouth, so it is often better to let the container sit in a small bowl of warm water for a few minutes).

WHAT ARE THE ALTERNATIVE PATTERNS?

Fruits can be introduced before vegetables, especially for babies on the slender side in order to increase calories, but my concern is that the sweeter taste of the fruits may lessen their acceptance of vegetables. So I prefer veggies first and will use cereal mixed in with the vegetables to modify the flavor of the vegetables if necessary or to bump up the calories until meats are introduced.

Other physicians and dieticians might begin an immediate rotation of all the food groups, introducing the cereal, then a vegetable, then a fruit (or vice versa), then a meat, and then repeating the cycle again and again until the baby has sampled a sufficient variety. This is perfectly reasonable, but I find babies are more reluctant to accept the vegetables and meats this way.

Babies can be somewhat reluctant to try the meats in the previous pattern as well. If they are, I wait until they are finger-feeding and then introduce shaved poultry or crumbled hamburger. There's no harm in waiting, since the iron and protein in cereal serves them well, with the meats merely serving as an alternative source for those nutrients in nonvegetarian families.

Other cultures have a history of making soups of their first foods and introducing vegetables and meats in that way. That's fine, too, as long as salt and seasonings aren't added, since babies don't need extra salt, and some babies' stomachs don't tolerate the seasonings. The only problem is that it is harder to recognize allergies to a particular food.

DO YOU HAVE A BRAND PREFERENCE?

In terms of cost, yes, I do. Homemade baby food is much less expensive. However, it is time-consuming for mothers who may already be exhausted from taking care of their infants and trying to contend with other children or other work as well.

Nutritionally, either home-prepared or commercial (Gerber, Beechnut, organic, etc.) foods are fine. I have less concern today about utilizing the packages of baby foods that are available on the grocer's shelves than I did several years ago. The high salt content, the use of extensive additives, and the addition of excessive sugars have been corrected in response to public opinion, as well as pressure from the physicians and nutritionists who lobbied for these changes. As a result, the commercial infant foods are safe and acceptable.

If you should choose to prepare your own fruits and vegetables for your infant, there are several books available that will provide recipes and further instructions for you (see the "Resources" section). But there are certain basics you should know:

- Use only fresh fruits and vegetables. Those that are canned often have a high salt or sugar (or syrup) content and are not designed for infants. Fresh frozen foods will be fine, but those that have been precooked or blanched may lose many of their vitamins.
- Prevent vitamin and nutrient depletion by not overcooking and by blending lightly or simply mashing the foods (such as ripe bananas) with a fork.
- Do not add sugar or salt to your baby foods. These are potentially the most detrimental of all additives and do little to improve your baby's interest in eating the foods.
- Spill out excess juice from the puree so you offer the nutrient-dense food itself. (Homemade foods usually have fewer calories and nutrients than the more concentrated infant foods[9] and this technique helps to ameliorate that concern.)
- Avoid allergy-inducing foods in the beginning (wheat, citrus fruits, eggs, and peanut products) and vegetables such as spinach, beets, turnips, and collard greens that are high in nitrates.
- Egg yolks are often best given from one of the commercial brands, since it can be difficult to successfully remove all of the allergy-provoking egg whites. Additionally, some brands use yolks higher in docosahexaenoic acid (DHA).
- Peel fruits before cooking or pureeing them to lessen the potential for the baby choking.
- Organic foods are often more costly. You might want to spend the extra amount for foods you cook entirely, like green beans, or foods with thin skins, like peaches or plums, to avoid the pesticides that may have been sprayed on them while they were growing.
- Please be especially careful to ensure the cleanliness and safety of both your home-prepared foods and those you purchase in the store. Avoid spoilage and bacterial contamination by meticulous food processing and storage.
- Some prepared foods can be frozen in ice cube trays, allowing you to use a few cubes at a time. You should bring them up to somewhere between room temperature and the baby's body temperature when you are ready to serve them. Again, letting the container sit in warm water is preferable to using a microwave.

WHEN SHOULD I FEED MY BABY?

From six to about eight months of age, infants generally require only two meals a day. If solids are begun before that, one meal a day should suffice. In the first meal, you can provide the cereal and add the vegetable when your baby is ready. When you add the fruit, make that a separate meal. And it doesn't matter at what time those occur (what matters far more is that you get great pictures or videos). But most parents will end up giving one morning and one early-evening meal. Truly, babies are unconcerned with whether they have vegetables for breakfast or dinner.

It is important, however, that you not offer the breast or a bottle until after the feeding, since the fluids will fill the baby up before he gets to the solids; and if you breast- or bottle-feed too soon after the solids, the baby again will be overfull and have a tendency to regurgitate. So it's usually best to wait perhaps an hour and let the baby play and enjoy in an upright, inclined, or seated position in that interval and for at least a half hour after both are consumed.

At eight to nine months of age, meat can be added to both the evening and an additional midday meal. Most infants begin to want the midday meal at about the same age that meats are introduced. The calories (and other nutrients) these solid foods provide your infant are listed in table 13.2, which should help you

Table 13.2. Calories in Infant Foods

	Amount	Calories	Amount	Calories	Also Provides
Breastmilk/ Formula	4 oz.	80			Complete nutrition
Dry cereal	1 tbsp.	15			Protein, iron, zinc
	Stage 1		Stage 2		
Vegetables (most) Carrots, Squash Sweet Potato Green Beans Peas	2.5 oz.	15–20 40 80 40 60	4 oz.	25–40	Protein, vitamins, minerals, fiber
Fruits (most)	2.5 oz.	30–40	4 oz.	40–70	Vitamins, minerals, fiber
Meats Beef, Liver Lamb Ham, Pork Turkey Chicken	2.5 oz.	65–80	2.5 oz.	65–80	Protein, minerals
Fruit juice (100%)*			4 oz.	60	Vitamin C, some minerals

*Juice is not recommended.

Source: Bailey Koch, RD, CSP, www.nutrition4kids.com.

understand the nutritional balance you want to acheive and may help you avoid overfeeding your baby.

I should stress that with the increase in solid foods, formula should be limited to no more than a quart per day or reduced further if the child is taking excessive quantities of the other foods or spitting up but still gaining weight well.

Should the child still be hungry, water may be given between meals. Babies actually require very little additional fluid, except in hot weather, since breastmilk, formula, and the water in baby foods is generally adequate. Juices themselves have very little additional value. The vitamin C they provide can be obtained from breastmilk, the formula, fruits, and vegetables (please see table 14.1 for additional insight). However, since many babies seem uninterested in plain water, diluted fruit juices can be offered. This can present problems for a baby's weight and teeth, since a child who constantly drinks juice bathes his teeth in sugar and risks cavities and the destruction of his developing teeth. So dilute the juice well, using between 1 teaspoon and a ½ ounce per 4 ounces of water if he won't accept water by itself.

WILL ANYTHING IMPROVE MY BABY'S ACCEPTANCE OF THESE NEW FOODS?

Offer the new food when your baby is hungry. If he's just had a bottle, he's going to be reasonably satisfied and less interested; if he's just had his favorite fruit, he'll want more of that instead of a flavor that's foreign to him.

Also, your attitude can affect your baby's acceptance of the foods you offer. If you know the baby should try peas, but you hate them and show that with your face crinkled in disgust while you are offering them, you can imagine that your baby may pick up on those cues and be less accepting. Your smiling face and your eyes focused on his will tell him much more about your pleasure at seeing him eat well.

Equally important is to be responsive to your baby's hunger and satiety (fullness) cues. Hunger cues to watch for include lip smacking or interest when you or other family members are eating. Crying is often a late indicator, with the baby already filling himself with swallowed air and becoming more fretful while you're preparing his meal. When he's full, he'll start having less interest in eating and begin playing with the food or looking around to see what now captures his attention. And instead of leaning forward for another bite, he'll turn away, bring out his lower lip, or pout in his usual expressive way to communicate that he's ready to be changed or to play.

Sometimes feeding your baby can take a great deal of patience, as well as encouragement (as just one aspect of thoughtful, compassionate parenting). It does help if you can minimize other distractions and talk to your baby during the feeding. If he routinely pushes out everything, you can gently place your finger under his chin once you put the food in his mouth, since that will help him move the food backward, but be careful not to force too much with either the spoon or your finger, since that might instead cause him to be more resistant and feeding averse.

WHEN SHOULD THE PATTERN CHANGE?

I find it interesting and somewhat problematic that many infants \
off their normal growth curves when solids are introduced. Some v   ...
underlying condition that introducing solids exposes. A quarter of infants with
undiagnosed cerebral palsy will show up with feeding problems (though they
will often have increased muscle tone that is present earlier). Infants with celiac
disease may show problems once they are started on cereals that contain wheat or
barley. Infants with oral sensory issues or oral motor delays will have difficulties
bringing their food to the back of the mouth and swallowing. So it's a good idea
to have your physician evaluate the baby and refer you to a specialist if necessary.
Most of the time, fortunately, he or she will inform you that there is no underlying condition that you need to worry about, and you can simply follow his, her,
or my recommendations for getting the baby used to this new experience.

On the other hand, babies with reflux often improve because the thicker solids
hold the formula down better, and they often do well by moving the solids and
then the formula closer together so that the solids will help to hold the formula
down—as long as they are not overfed with the combination. Babies with constipation or infrequent bowel movements can improve as well—but they can also
worsen, depending on what they are fed. Cereal, particularly rice, is more constipating, while vegetables and the "p" fruits (peaches, plums, pears, prunes, and
papaya) usually provide more bulk and ease bowel movements.

And as discussed below, there are specific pattern changes that can help the
underweight infant, the infant who's at risk for becoming overweight, and the
child from families with allergies or celiac disease.

WHAT CAN HELP MY BABY GAIN MORE WEIGHT?

The task, remember, is first to prevent malnutrition and then, as my mother
would say, "to put meat on his bones" and help him grow, not to make your baby
fat, with a goal at 6 to 12 months of approximately three-quarters of a pound per
month (compared to a more rapid weight gain of 1 to 2 pounds per month in the
first six months).

The logic is to emphasize foods that have higher caloric density while maintaining a well-balanced diet. Fortunately, breastmilk or formula helps to maintain
that balance of the various nutrients (the macronutrients, protein, carbohydrates,
and fat, as well as the micronutrients, including all the vitamins and minerals, that
we will discuss in chapter 15).

To put that into action:

- Begin on the earlier side, adding solids to the diet around four months of
  age, if he is already having difficulty gaining or when that difficulty begins
  to manifest.
- Include at least one vegetable (preferably two) each day once the baby has a
  full diet.

- Add meat or cereal to the vegetables because of their much higher calories (seen in table 13.2) if your baby will accept them that way (after they have been individually introduced).
- Add egg yolks twice a week or more often if you do not have a high incidence of cholesterol problems or heart disease in your family.
- Hold his bottle or breastfeeding until after mealtime so that he will be hungrier for his solids. You can give the fluid immediately afterward if he is a champion spitter. Otherwise, wait an hour or so.
- Follow the instructions in chapter 10 on how to increase formula density.

If changing the pattern does not make a real difference or your baby doesn't eat much of the solids, please make sure that your physician reevaluates him. You can also bring along the list of acceptable calorie enhancers (table 10.2) in case he or she wants you to start with one of those, using the recommended quantities (if you add too much, they unbalance the diet and may not be tolerated well).

WHAT IF MY BABY SEEMS TO BE GAINING TOO MUCH?

As we've discussed, in infancy it's very tricky differentiating the healthy, normally fat-cheeked baby from the baby who has too much fat and will have a tendency to put more weight on. And it's somewhat of a trick to slow rapid weight gain down, when we want to be sure babies get enough to sustain optimal growth of their bodies and brains. That's aided by the baby's intake of breastmilk or formula, which will help to keep daily fat content at approximately 25 percent of daily calories.

The major ways of helping here are as follows:

- Delay solid-food introduction until six months of age.
- Begin with only a small quantity of cereal (just 1 to 2 teaspoons with twice to three times as much formula, breastmilk, or water) or begin with vegetables first.
- Maximize vegetables.
- Lessen cereal and fruits to a single serving daily (unless the baby's constipated—then give the "p" fruits twice a day).
- Avoid juice and give the baby water (or, later, vegetable puffs) if he's hungry between meals.
- If your baby is eating well but often wanting extra servings, try giving him his formula or extra water 15 to 20 minutes before his meal so he won't be ravenous.

WHAT IF WE HAVE CELIAC DISEASE OR FOOD ALLERGIES IN OUR FAMILY?

The only family members who count in this instance are those in your immediate family. If your aunt and three cousins have celiac disease or your spouse's entire family has various severe allergies, but you and your spouse and your children don't, then you needn't worry. You can feel comfortable introducing solids in the normal pattern. On the other hand, if you, your spouse, or even one of your other children has allergies or celiac disease, this section is intended to help your baby (because he has a first-degree relative with one of those conditions).

As stated in chapter 9, the single best prevention for allergies or celiac disease is to continue breastfeeding while new foods are introduced. The immune properties in breastmilk seem to modify potential allergic factors and produce food tolerance instead of allergy. And since you never know if there is going to be some illness or situation that reduces your ability to breastfeed or your desire to, I also suggest introducing first foods a little early (around five months) rather than later, though this is contradictory to most recommendations, which suggest exclusive breastfeeding until six months of age.

There is no study to support my approach in which breastfed babies given new foods before six months had fewer atopic (allergic) reactions than those who had foods added later, but a study showed that infants who had their solids introduced while they were breastfed (even before six months) had lasting protective effects against type 1 diabetes and celiac disease.[10, 11]

For babies who are not breastfed, I take the opposite approach and wait until six months, when the intestinal cells create tighter junctions and permit less penetration of potential allergens between the cells. Active research hopefully will show whether pro- and prebiotics also limit allergen penetration to prevent food allergies.

The newest recommendations from an expert panel of allergists indicate that delaying the introduction of foods beyond six months does not prevent food allergies[12] and merely delays the inevitable. The European Society for Paediatric Gastroenterology, Hepatology and Nutrition's Committee on Nutrition concurs, stating that while we know that eggs, nuts, and seafood (more than other foods) are associated with food allergies in Western societies, there is "no convincing scientific evidence" that delaying their introduction reduces allergies for the general population or for those at risk.[13] But what often happens is that early skin rashes or allergic symptoms often delay the introduction of dairy until later, and that delay is associated with more rashes developing.[14]

As I indicated earlier, this area remains controversial, with active research and new pronouncements being brought forward on a regular basis because many of the early studies were flawed due to the study design or nonadherence to the diet. At www.what2feedyourbaby.com, we will try to keep you informed of new studies or analyses that can help sort through the issue. Meanwhile, a slight delay in introducing common food allergens seems warranted—at least until you see how your baby responds to other foods. This is not a hardship for most infants, since plenty of other good sources of protein, calories, and most nutrients are available—with one exception, DHA. The natural source of DHA is fish (that eat the algae that make the DHA), and so most physicians would encourage the introduction of fish at one year or sooner if babies are not getting DHA in some other way. Interestingly, however, using fish oil in high-risk infants did not prevent childhood allergies either.[15]

What I find fascinating in this controversy is that various countries have different food allergies that are most common. In the United States, we often focus on milk, soy, eggs, wheat, fish, peanuts (which grow on bushes and are more related to legumes like peas than other nuts), and tree nuts (like walnuts, pecans, and almonds). However, in France, the predominant allergy is to fruit, while it is sesame in Israel, where many baby foods include sesame seeds, and rice is a common allergen in Asia.[16]

Peanut allergy has attracted particular attention, since even breathing peanut proteins in closed spaces (an airplane, for example) can potentially cause problems for some individuals. What's interesting here is that peanut oil in some skin preparations has been associated with developing the allergy, and some consider soy milk or soy formula as a possible contributor, though to a lesser extent.[17] Interestingly, however, peanut allergy is less common in China than in the United States, though peanuts are used about equally, possibly because the methods of preparation differ; the allergy is only one-tenth as common in Israel as in the United Kingdom. The difference may be that Israeli infants and toddlers from eight months on are frequently eating peanut protein (and apparently, so are their mothers when they are pregnant).[18] Israel's low rate of peanut allergy has prompted studies that are under way to see if gradual, small exposure will help to lessen later food allergies.

Again, stay tuned to www.what2feedyourbaby.com for updated information. And please review the additional discussions in the next chapter about diagnostic food challenges and reintroducing foods.

In the meantime, and irrespective of when solids are introduced and whether the baby is breast- or bottle-fed, I have parents slowly introduce the new food, perhaps 1 or 2 teaspoons the first day or so, then gradually increase, until the baby is eating full amounts by the third or fourth day. This is the same pattern for babies from nonallergic families. The difference is that I extend the introduction for allergic babies, and we continue the same food for perhaps seven days before going to the next one.

For babies from a family in which a first-degree relative has celiac disease, the normal pattern for most foods differs for wheat and barley, which both contain gluten. While oats do not have gluten, many of the foods that have oats also contain wheat or are tainted by it (families with gluten intolerance already know this, so they do not use many oat products or, for that matter, any products that are not labeled gluten-free).

So the issue becomes focused on introducing wheat and barley. Dr. Ed Hoffenberg at Denver Children's Hospital, who recognized the increased prevalence of gluten intolerance—we used to think it occurred in 1 out of 3,000 to 5,000 people until his group's research showed it is an amazing 1 in every 133 people—published a study in 2005 showing that babies who were exposed to wheat, rye, or barley in the first three months had five times the risk of demonstrating positive blood tests for celiac disease compared to infants who were introduced to those grains between four and six months, while babies who did not have those foods until they were over seven months of age had four times the risk.[19] So he introduces grains in small amounts sometime between six and seven months and gradually increases the amounts, irrespective of whether the infant is breastfeeding or not.[20] Another expert, Dr. Alessio Fasano at the Mass General Hospital for Children (who is working to find an alternative to the very strict diet), similarly introduces gluten into the diet after six months of age, adhering to the American Academy of Pediatrics guidelines.[21] But I must tell you that the advice of these two experts differs slightly from what they do in Sweden, which has a high rate of breastfeeding (97 percent of mothers breastfed there in 2007, with 56 percent continuing exclusively until four months of age).[22] Dr. A. Ivarsson and colleagues noted that from the time when exclusive breastfeeding was encouraged to extend to six months, the rate of celiac disease was increasing. So they've begun introducing small amounts of wheat into infant diets between four and six months of age and asking mothers to continue breastfeeding for at least a month afterward.[23, 24] While this may not totally prevent celiac disease from developing, it may delay its presentation. As a result, the European Society for Paediatric Gastroenterology, Hepatology and Nutrition in 2008 recommended introducing wheat products between four and seven months of age, while continuing breastfeeding for at least that long, in order to lessen the risk of celiac disease and wheat allergy.[25]

SUMMARY

- Once your baby has doubled his birth weight and weighs at least 13 pounds, he begins to need more protein, iron, zinc, and vitamins than breastmilk or formula can provide alone.
- Your baby can display his hunger and fullness (satiety) cues best once he can support his head while sitting and when his tongue no longer automatically pushes food away (because of his tongue extrusion reflex).
- Internally, the intestinal cells knit together tightly by six months of age and lessen the potential for food allergies.
- Breastfeeding while new foods are introduced seems to be the single best means of preventing food allergies because of the immune and protective factors in the milk.
- The first foods should be thin purees, with gradual thickening and lumps, so your baby first learns to move food back into his mouth and then to chew.
- Homemade baby foods are less expensive, but they can be lower in calories and nutrients.
- Organic foods (especially thin-skinned fruits and vegetables and meats) may be worth the additional expense, particularly if you are preparing your own foods. Parents who eat organic foods themselves similarly may wish to purchase commercial organic foods for their infants as well.

- Unused portions of infant foods can be refrigerated until you are ready to use them and then warmed to somewhere between room temperature and the baby's body temperature, depending on preference.
- Fortified cereals provide most of the additional nutrients that your baby needs, although cereals can be constipating.
- Breastfeeding and introducing vegetables before fruits may help your baby accept flavors better, and together they provide additional calories and nutrients for your baby.
- Up to 15 tastes are needed for some babies to accept a new food.
- You should only introduce new foods gradually over three to seven days so that you can determine if your baby does not tolerate a new food.
- Underweight infants benefit from calorically rich foods and holding their fluids until after mealtime.
- For infants who are gaining too rapidly and tending toward becoming overweight, you can sometimes reduce their intake by having them drink before eating and by an emphasis on lower-calorie vegetables.
- Babies with firmer bowel movements will do better with more fruits, vegetables, and water in their diet.
- Your smile, encouragement, and eye contact will help your baby accept the new foods you try to introduce.

14

~~

Transitioning to the Real Stuff

Your baby is truly amazing, isn't he? Look at how much he's grown and what he can do now. He's sitting and smiling and has even learned to chew the soft lumps in baby food.[1] He may be picking up objects and bringing them to his mouth to explore, since his mouth and tongue have become this fascinating way to experience new things. The downside to that, of course, is that if he's crawling, he may be picking up the nasty things he finds on the floor and bringing those to his mouth as well.

Is he ready for table foods, even if he doesn't have any fancy new teeth yet? You bet. He'll use his gums to mush most soft foods to death and then swallow them without choking if you follow the guidelines here.

WHAT ARE THE GUIDELINES?

Babies like the crunchy kinds of foods that they can pick up using the *pincer grasp*—that is, with their thumb and first finger. When they can manage that skill, usually around seven to eight months, I recommend starting with puffed cereals, like Cheerios or puffed rice that saliva will dissolve in their mouths if they don't manage to mash them completely. You can also use the more expensive versions that come in convenient containers (but you can always make the cereal varieties convenient by using plastic bags or containers).

Once your baby has mastered the pincer grasp, you can begin offering soft, skinless, Cheerios-sized pieces of foods the baby has already accepted as a lumpy puree, such as cooked, diced carrots, mashed banana, peeled bites of soft fruits, or crumbles of hamburger, if your baby likes, or you are now willing to try, beef. Then you can expand the diet to other foods, like pasta, small pieces of avocado, small bites of bread, or shaved chicken.

Give him only a few bites at a time so he doesn't stuff his mouth or begin to play with the pieces and scatter them all over your floor. Again, give him each food multiple times (up to 15) so that he has an adequate chance to accept it.

Watch as he moves the food around in his mouth to be sure that he does so safely. You don't want to be feeding him as he is running or playing, stopping for a brief snack before returning to his laps around the house. Not only will that increase the risk of choking, but it will also discourage good mealtime behavior.

Most babies adapt well to the thicker foods, so I usually recommend going directly to them rather than through stage 3 baby foods, which are a combination of purees with larger pieces in them. I think these are actually harder for new eaters to handle since they must contend with two different textures simultaneously.

Your infant may soon want to control his eating, preferring to take the spoon himself or assist you with it, since he's picking up the finger foods himself. Encourage his help with the other table foods you're feeding him, making sure that he gets enough by providing nutritious foods at mealtimes and snacks. Remember that his stomach is only the size of one or two of his fists, so don't expect him to eat a large amount at a single meal. And also remember to have your camera and cleaning supplies handy.

ARE THERE ANY FOODS TO AVOID?

Some babies do have a harder time learning to chew, and some have texture issues. If yours falls into this category, revert to the intermediate step of stage 3 foods. And let your child progress more slowly to finger and table foods. There's no rush and no deadline for when your child has to accomplish this task.

Be sure, though, to mention the situation to your doctor, particularly if your baby gets full after just a few bites, vomits more, or repeatedly coughs and chokes when trying various foods. The fullness or vomiting could suggest a problem with allergies or with the foods exiting the esophagus or stomach, warranting a gastrointestinal X-ray series or a referral, while the coughing and choking suggest problems with oral motor skills, which might trigger a different set of X-rays (swallow studies) and a different evaluation.

Of course, almost all babies will have difficulties with foods that are hard to chew (even with a few teeth) or that can be difficult to swallow. Reserve these until at least three years of age, and give them under your direct supervision:

- Popcorn or pieces of nuts
- Unpeeled fruits or vegetables, including grapes or raisins and peas
- Hard, raw vegetables
- Hard or gummy candies

Also avoid honey during the first year, not because it is hard to swallow but because honey and corn syrup can contain botulinum spores. This powerful toxin can create a dangerous illness that surfaces 6 to 36 hours after the toxin has been consumed. While it can also occur in children and adults with immune problems, infants are particularly susceptible and present at first with constipation, a weak cry despite irritability, and excessive drooling; they can progress to muscle weakness, with floppy movements and trouble controlling the head, tiredness, and drooping eyelids, then difficulty sucking or feeding and possibly even paralysis. Fortunately, most cases of infant botulism are diagnosed and treated quickly, lessening the progression of the disease. Because parents are more aware of this situation, fewer than 5 percent of the cases in the United States are now due to honey.

WHAT CAN I DO TO PREVENT ALLERGIES WITH SO MANY INGREDIENTS IN SO MANY FOODS?

The issue of preventing food allergies again comes up, particularly as wide choices abound in the grocery store and as you begin to let grandparents and other caretakers offer some of the meals.

The following six groups of foods are considered to be most often associated with food allergy in North America (this differs in other Western societies, as noted in chapter 13).

- Milk
- Soy
- Eggs
- Wheat
- Peanuts and other nuts
- Shellfish and fish

If you are still breastfeeding, bravo—you can lessen allergy risk if you slowly introduce these foods while you are breastfeeding, and you then continue to breastfeed for at least a month afterward. If you are using infant formula, guilt is not necessary. Instead, delay these foods until you have assessed whether your baby has had allergic symptoms with other foods. If your baby has tolerated routine formula and has no evidence of other allergies, he is unlikely to have allergies with these foods, and they can be introduced in the same gradual process that you followed for earlier introductions. If he had problems, delay the introduction of these foods until after he's a year old—and then introduce them gradually.

Some allergists would prefer that you wait even longer for allergic infants (two years with shellfish and peanut butter), though data from Israel suggest that peanut-based puffs introduced early into infant diets seem to lessen and not increase allergy to peanuts (as described in chapter 13). So this is causing us to rethink the timing for introducing various potential allergens. If you want to be kept up to date, visit our website, www.what2feedyourbaby.com, or other websites, like that of the Food Allergy and Anaphylaxis Network (www.foodallergy.org).

WHAT ARE MY BABY'S CHOICES OF DRINK?

You may be well aware that John D. Rockefeller continued to drink human milk throughout his lifetime,[2] but wet nurses are hard to find. So I generally suggest that breastfeeding stop sometime before children go to kindergarten. Quite seriously, there is no specific age at which one would want to stop breastfeeding. I have seen mothers continue until either they have another child or the infant wants to stop at about 18 months of age. In selected situations, this has resulted in a decrease in the child's intake of solids, which precipitated decreased weight gain; for most infants, however, mothers can breastfeed as long as they wish to.

There is no advantage, however, to continuing infant formula beyond a year. The question then becomes what to transition to. In decades past, there wasn't much choice. Cow's or other animals' milks were the only offerings. But now, shelves of other drinks are available—they call themselves milks because they are whitish drinks with various nutrients, but they are not truly *milk* (which is the substance produced by the female mammary glands of different species), and as detailed in the appendix (table A.2), they do not contain much of what your growing child needs. Then again, nutrient deficiencies and protein content generally make the milk of many other species less wholesome than vitamin D–enriched cow's milk (as discussed in chapter 4).

So cow's milk is generally the best choice, at least for the healthy toddler with a broad diet. Because toddlers need additional energy sources to continue their still rapid growth, whole milk is recommended until at least 18 months of age, at which point they can be transitioned to 2 percent milk, which has the same amount of protein, vitamin D, and lactose but half the fat content of whole milk. Skim milk should not be used even for overweight children, because after the fat is removed, the relative protein content is high, and also because these children still need essential fats and fat calories in their diets. So 2 percent should be used. If the child is an abundant drinker (over 32 ounces a day), you can dilute the milk, using 1 extra ounce of water for every 7 to 8 ounces of the 2 percent milk.

For children with restricted diets because of allergies, one of the milks in table A.2 can be used, recognizing that these children will need to acquire many of their nutrients and calories from other foods in their diet (please see chapter 15 on vitamins and minerals for good choices).

For picky eaters with poor diets, a number of commercially available milk-based beverages are now supplemented with vitamins and minerals. The one most parents are familiar with is Pediasure, but it has a high sugar content that brings it up to 30 calories per ounce (240 calories for the usual 8-ounce bottle). The same manufacturer, Abbott, has a better product, Similac Grow and Go, available as a powder, that tastes more like milk and is only 20 calories per ounce (160 calories for 8 ounces). It has docosahexaenoic acid (DHA), much more iron, zinc, vitamin C, and vitamin E than cow's milk, and approximately the same amount of calcium and vitamin D. Of course, Mead Johnson has a competing product with similar vitamins and minerals but higher DHA. I recommend either of these products instead of Pediasure and further suggest that parents continue to offer a variety of nutritious foods to broaden their child's tastes and nutritional sufficiency so that they won't have to rely on these expensive alternatives (more about this topic shortly).

Unfortunately, the child with milk, soy, and nut allergies doesn't have these choices and is often restricted to one of the other drinks. Both Neocate and EleCare come as formulas for children over a year old. Those make very acceptable but very expensive substitutes. They provide adequate vitamins and minerals because some children rely solely on these drinks for their total nutrition. If your child does have an adequate diet otherwise, then perhaps you can try one of the less expensive products, like hemp milk, recognizing its deficiencies and having a dietician help you compensate for them through a selection of other foods and supplements.

WHEN CAN I START MILK PRODUCTS OR SUBSTITUTES?

A suitable time to change to whole cow's milk or an alternative beverage would be at approximately 10 to 12 months of age. By this time, most infants are able to tolerate the increased protein load from whole cow's milk, and the problems with allergies or milk-induced iron deficiency are lessened by the intestine's maturity and the use of supplemental foods. A good guide is when your baby is consuming three good meals of table foods a day (again, that's at about 10 to 12 months of age).

For the infant who had problems and was switched from routine formula to a specialty solution, the transition is best made at the end of this time frame, at 12 months of age. But you should speak to your doctor about when to make the change and what beverage to transition to. Most infants will tolerate whole milk, but as stated in the previous section, some babies need one of the other alternatives.

Drinkable and spoonable yogurts have become popular and can be included in the diet by 8 to 10 months of age for the milk-tolerant infant who is still hungry after two containers of infant food (at least 8 ounces) at a meal. Small bites of cheese can be offered at about the same time (try them in series, not simultaneously). I've been surprised by how well some infants on soy or partial hydrolysate formulas have done with yogurt and cheese. The infants who tolerate yogurt and cheese usually make the transition to whole milk quite easily and without evidence of allergy developing.

You can usually substitute a serving of whole milk for a serving of formula when you are ready, and you can make the switch by continuing to substitute an additional serving each day. But parents often find that once the baby makes that initial change, he no longer wants his formula and wants to go straight over to the whole milk. If you are concerned that your baby might have a problem, only introduce a small amount the first few times, offering a few sips or milk-wetting a cracker or some of the baby's bread to see how he will do with it. Then gradually offer more until you reach a full serving. If you are successful with that amount, you can then proceed with substituting serving for serving over the next few days. Babies who have had allergic reactions to milk should proceed even slower and should receive their initial introduction under medical supervision (as suggested by the European Society of Paediatric Gastroenterology, Hepatology, and Nutrition and summarized in chapter 9).[3]

Do recognize that dairy products, particularly milk and cheese, are constipating, or "binding," in my mother's words. Your baby only needs 270 milligrams of calcium from 7 to 12 months and 500 milligrams from one to three years of age, and 275 milligrams of phosphorus in the last six months of his first year and 460 milligrams per day from one to three years of age. That amount is met with one to two servings of dairy products per day in total, so you can give the baby only a single glass of milk if you are giving yogurt or cheese and meet his major needs (assuming he is meeting his goals for protein and vitamins through other foods) in order to avoid the tendency to constipation.

WHAT ABOUT JUICE?

Parents love to give their infants juice. They're always asking when they can start or how much their baby needs. The truth is a baby doesn't need any juice and often would be better off without it.

As detailed in table 14.1, juice provides vitamin C but does so with lots of sugar. Apple juice has 10 teaspoons in 12 ounces, the same amount as in a can of Coke, and it has more calories (160 to 180) in 12 ounces compared to 140 calories in that Coke. Grape juice has 50 percent more sugar and calories. That's natural, 100 percent juice, not the sweetened kind or the 10 percent juice to which extra high-fructose corn syrup has been added. Fruits also have high sugar content, but the advantage is that they are filling and contain other vitamins and minerals. So it becomes more logical to offer fruits instead of their juices.

Table 14.1. Fluid Calories and Nutrients (Per 8 Ounces)

	Calories	Sugar (g)	Protein (g)	Other Nutrients
Water	0	0	0	Water itself
Milk	160	12	8	Vitamins A and D, calcium, phosphorus
Apple juice	105	26	0	Vitamin C
Grape juice	160	58.5	0	Vitamin C
Carrot juice	43	10	1	Vitamins A and C, minerals
Celery juice	40	5	1	Vitamin C, minerals
Sports drinks	50	10–14	0	Sodium and potassium
Coca-Cola	94	26	0	Water

g = grams

Source: Bailey Koch, RD, CSP, www.nutrition4kids.com.

Vegetable juice does have fewer calories, and it has the vitamins and minerals of the actual vegetable. But the juice lacks the vegetable fiber that is so filling and particularly beneficial when you are trying to lessen your child's desire to eat more.

During hot summers, when infants and children have higher fluid needs, 4 ounces of juice per day is certainly permissible, either as a treat or to flavor the water they are drinking. For infants, it's best to water the juice down by at least half or just to use as little as 1 teaspoon with 4 ounces of water.

Now that you know about the high sugar content of juices (which at least serve as a good source of vitamin C), you probably don't really want to think about sweet tea, lemonade, and fruit-flavored drinks—and their totally empty 140 to 200 calories per 12 ounces. The frequently advertised sports drinks that athletes consume are beneficial for athletes who deplete their electrolytes after an hour of sweating profusely, but for infants and toddlers they simply add more unneeded sugar and half the calories of a Coke.

Yet juices and fruit drinks (not counting the other non-nutritious drinks) replace milk in an estimated 55 to 67 percent of 9- to 11-month-olds' diets and in 62 to 100 percent of the diets of toddlers between 19 and 24 months of age.[4]

WHEN SHOULD I START MY BABY ON A CUP?

It is better to start weaning your child away from the bottle and introducing him to a cup early on for several reasons. First, most infants who begin to take the cup reduce their milk and formula intake at about the same time. This helps to prevent overfeeding. Moreover, the dependence infants develop on their bottle is more difficult to break the longer they remain attached to it.

In many instances, babies are handed the bottle as they are dropped into their crib for a nap or their night's sleep. The bottle acts as pacifier. Infants can develop a pattern of seeing food and the bottle as a means of pacification, a worrisome pattern when we consider the emotional precursors to obesity later in childhood. In addition, the bottle, whether it contains fruit juice or milk, exposes the teeth to sugar for a prolonged period when babies suck on it in bed. Bacteria in the mouth feed on the sugar and produce acid that destroys the teeth, causing cavities and tooth decay, or what the dentists who have to treat it call *nursing bottle caries*.

The problem of nighttime weaning is definitely worse for the bottle-fed infant since the breastfed infant can't usually take the breast to bed with him. So if you can, switch your child from bottle to cup at 10 to 12 months of age, when you are also switching to milk. That way you can offer milk in the cup instead of in the bottle. If your baby doesn't accept it at first, you can give him diluted formula in the bottle. Progressively dilute the formula or milk until only water is there. If your baby still wants his nighttime bottle, begin to reduce the amount of water in the bottle.

For some babies, taking the bottle away may be worse than allowing them to keep it temporarily. The child who is moving or has a new sibling may need the security of a bottle. For that child, water is still the preferred contents. And if he needs the bottle to go to sleep, let him take it on your lap rather than in the crib. You, and not the bottle, will help his sense of security this way. And while you are holding him, particularly at that age, have him sit in a more upright position rather than lying down. The suction from the bottle alone is enough to pull fluid toward the *eustachian tubes* and predispose the child to ear infections as well as reflux.

Occasionally, I will continue the bottle for underweight toddlers who only take small amounts from a cup because I am interested in assuring that the child consumes adequate nutrients and the extra calories.

SHOULD I OFFER SNACKS?

Most babies are hungry a few hours after their main meal. This could be because of their small stomach size (one to two of their fists is all their capacity), because of a drop in blood sugar and hormonal changes, or because of earlier patterning with frequent bottles or breastfeedings. Either way, babies will often display hunger cues several hours after a meal, so a snack is important to sustain their energy levels and meet their needs. For many infants, this means they are then eating five to six small meals a day.

The real question is what to feed him, but you probably know the answer: wholesome nutritious food that isn't given just to fill him up and prevent his crying but nourishment that contributes value to his diet. If he's not getting enough fruits or vegetables during his meals, snack time is an appropriate time to offer them (table 14.2).

Sadly, that's not the way some parents think. An unbelievable 17 to 33 percent of infants and toddlers between 7 and 24 months of age consume no vegetables whatsoever, and of those who do, french fries are the most common vegetable by 15 to 18 months of age (though many three-year-olds in my office tell me their favorite food, not just favorite vegetable, is carrots). Even more unbelievable is the fact that in the same age range, 23 to 33 percent of infants and toddlers do not eat

Table 14.2. Healthy Snacks (in Order of Preference)

Fruits and vegetables
• Small bites of fruit
• Cooked, diced pieces of vegetables (once child is older, you can coat pieces in hummus, cream cheese, or dips)
• Avocado
More fruits and vegetables
More fruits and vegetables
(Do I make my point?)
Yogurt (after eight to ten months)
Cheese (after eight to ten months) and crackers (preferably whole grain)
Fruit smoothies with yogurt or juice

any fruit, whereas almost half of seven- to eight-month-olds consume some type of dessert, sweet, or sweetened beverage; by 19 to 24 months, 62 percent consume dessert, and 20 percent consume candy.[5]

But you are reading this book as an interested, nutrition-conscious parent or child advocate. So you know that while fruits and vegetables are expensive, they are worth it, and that you can usually find locally grown seasonal fruits for less cost. (I hope you also remember, when you or others travel in foreign countries, to carefully select the fresh fruits and vegetables you eat and wash them carefully before consuming them—because you'll then remember that many of the out-of-season fruits and vegetables are imported from other parts of the world, so you'll take extra caution before consuming the out-of-season fruits and vegetables that are imported from other parts of the world in order for the grocers to have them for you.)

Since fruits and vegetables and healthy sources of protein are worth the cost, you'll understand the mantra I often repeat to parents and picky eaters: if there's no room for fruits and vegetables, there's certainly no room for dessert. Thus, I allow desserts in the diet, but not as at the expense of healthy foods. And I take care to make sure that the desserts are not seen as a reward for eating the other foods. I don't want to make them seem exalted or better than other foods, because I'd rather encourage healthy foods, not cookies and cakes, as "treats." Remember the three-year-olds coming to my office who tell me their favorite food is carrots.

WHAT ELSE CAN I DO FOR MY PICKY EATER?

First, understand that picky eaters are often made, not born. You may think otherwise when your baby refuses his first vegetable. But how many times did you offer it? He may need as many as 15 tastes to accept it. And did you smile or wrinkle your face into a frown or a give quizzical look when you fed it to him? And was chaos breaking loose, with other children wanting your attention to change the television channel, distracting the baby?

In other words, a number of factors can predispose the baby to the tastes he acquires, particularly if the caretaker doing the feeding was also a picky eater. He may have specific preferences for sweet or salty foods, as many infants do, or a specific dislike for a particular vegetable, but as long as that does not become a total distaste for vegetables, other choices can provide similar nutritional value.[6, 7]

So what can you do? Several things. As I've said elsewhere, make sure your baby is hungry when you feed him. Try to offer the food when you first see the hunger cues so that he's not cranky and crying when you feed him. Do not fill him up with fluids before you offer the food you want him to try. Offer the food several times at a sitting and then again a few days later. Don't force the issue and get into a food fight or control battle. Do know that if he doesn't eat, he'll make up for it later (sometimes at the next meal, sometimes a day or so afterward). And also know that most infants do become more erratic in their eating when they are two- to three-year-old toddlers exerting more independence.

Hopefully, you will be able to maintain the calm composure that you normally have. Studies show that an authoritative approach ("Let's try these tasty peas") eventually accomplishes the task most of the time, while a permissive approach ("Since you don't like the peas, here are some french fries instead") doesn't, and an authoritarian approach ("You can't play until you eat the peas") has a greater association with obesity when children reach first grade.[8]

IS THERE ANYTHING FURTHER TO DO FOR OVERWEIGHT OR UNDERWEIGHT INFANTS?

The main points have already been reviewed in the specific chapters on these two conditions and in the previous chapter on early solid-food introduction. There's little else you need to do at this age other than follow the same principles, especially for the well-filled-out infant whom you're afraid could one day be considered overweight. Continue to emphasize vegetables and whole-grain foods, avoid fruit juice and replace it with water, and let him have ready access to water before and during his meals. And just as you would with any infant, encourage his activity and mobility.

For the truly underweight infant, you may want to add extra calories in the various ways proposed and follow the guidelines in the section on the picky eater to make sure his appetite isn't accidentally being hindered. Additionally, review your baby's progress with your physician on a regular basis to ensure that your baby's weight gain and development are steadily improving.

SUMMARY

- Soft "table" or "people" (adult) food can be gradually introduced to infants when they master eating and swallowing soft, lumpy purees at approximately 8 to 10 months of age.
- Babies do not need teeth to begin learning how to mash solids with their gums.
- Bite-sized finger foods can be offered, small amounts at a time, once infants learn to pick up small objects using a pincer grasp.
- Puffed cereals are excellent choices to start with because they will dissolve in saliva if they are incompletely chewed.
- Foods that the baby has eaten before as a puree can be diced into bite-sized pieces that can be cooked and given as the next step in exposing him to a wider diet.
- Infants will often have more interest if they have first seen a food on their parent's plate.
- Healthy snacks can add nutritional value to the diet.
- Yogurt and cheese can be added into the diets of non-milk-allergic children at approximately 8 to 10 months of age, while milk itself should be delayed

until your baby has been eating three good-sized meals per day (generally at 10 to 12 months of age).

- Honey and corn syrup should be avoided until after a year of age.
- Foods that can cause choking should be avoided until three years of age. These include popcorn, nuts, hard foods and candies, and foods with pits or peels.
- In infants with allergies, introduction of other potentially allergic foods may need to be delayed until after a year of age.
- Effective strategies can be followed to minimize the chance that infants will become overly selective, picky eaters.
- Specific foods and the amounts offered can be modified to help infants who are gaining slowly or too much.
- An infant who is not eating, chewing, or swallowing well should be examined by his physician to determine whether testing, further assistance, or both are needed to help the infant progress developmentally.

15

⌒⌒

Essential Nutrients

Throughout *What to Feed Your Baby*, the need for various nutrients has been mentioned. When these were relatively obscure, like docosahexaenoic acid (DHA) or prebiotics, they were discussed in some detail. But often the need for nutrients like protein and iron was merely mentioned, since you're probably somewhat familiar with those requirements already.

Each of these important molecules generates books of information. This chapter summarizes the nutrient's major functions, the food sources for the nutrient, and requirements for infants and breastfeeding mothers (who must consume enough to provide for their infant while meeting their own needs). Many other resources are available if you wish to read in more depth, since new information is becoming available (and accessible) at a rapid rate. And it's actually quite fascinating, if you're like me, and find an apple unceasingly intriguing and milk awe inspiring.

The term infant's and breastfeeding mother's requirements, or Dietary Reference Intakes (DRI), are stated as the Estimated Average Requirement (EAR) and Recommended Daily Allowance (RDA), as determined by the Food and Nutrition Board of the Institute of Medicine of the National Academies and Health Canada. (Please see table 3.2 for the breastfeeding mother and table 3.3 for term infants.) The EAR represents the amount needed by at least half of children, and the RDA provides the amount that approximately 97 percent of children that age need. When neither is available, an adequate intake (AI) is the estimate of a sufficient intake. Too often, for infant nutrition, only the AI is available—and it's entirely based on the amount provided by breastmilk.[1]

Several years ago, it seemed rational to base these recommendations on the amount in breastmilk. But it was recently recognized that breastmilk needs to be supplemented in order to provide enough vitamin D, and so the recommendations for vitamin D were increased for infants.[2] Of course, the solid research on vitamin D (like most research) brings up more questions than it answers. Does that mean that scientists and physicians now need to investigate the sufficiency of the other vitamins and minerals needed for infants? Or are the other recommendations on target because they represent the amount in breastmilk—and breastmilk is considered the gold standard?

Except maybe it isn't always. We've already explored how variable DHA can be based on the mother's diet, with those eating more fish having higher levels; as a result, DHA supplements are recommended for pregnant and breastfeeding mothers whose intake of DHA may be lacking. And the recommendations for vitamin D are continuing to evolve, with supplemental vitamin D being recommended (so we will discuss it in more detail, along with vitamin C, because it too has been controversial).

This chapter will provide you with an understanding of the need for the various nutrients and their sources.[3] The Institute of Medicine's recommendations are current at the time of this writing. Recommendations for preterm infants are based on a composite committee of neonatologists' determinations. These amounts for preterm infants are usually stated as grams or other units per kilogram of body weight needed daily.[4] For the purposes of this book, the amounts have been recalculated per pound, so there may then be a slight discrepancy between the two numbers.

But stay informed. Research and future thoughtful, evidence-based recommendations will continue to advance science, answering and posing important questions. Hopefully, www.what2feedyourbaby.com and other reputable resources will keep you updated.

THE MACRONUTRIENTS
(WHAT YOUR BABY NEEDS IN LARGE AMOUNTS)

Protein

Amino acids contain nitrogen, hydrogen, oxygen, and carbon in related structures that link together into peptides, which then link together into proteins. The proteins then form the basic structure of all enzymes and hormones and every cell in the body, either by themselves or in combination with sugars (glycoproteins) or fats (lipoproteins). Dietary proteins are broken down (digested) into their component amino acids and then reused by the body, being synthesized into the various proteins the body needs. The excess cannot be stored as protein itself and is instead converted to fat and sugar (glucose) or metabolized and lost through the urine and sweat.

Nine of the amino acids are indispensible (the others can be made from these) or conditionally indispensible in situations like infancy and particularly prematurity, when they cannot be made in enough quantity to meet the infant's needs at that time[5] (see table 15.1).

Breastmilk proteins are efficiently digested and absorbed, and breastmilk contains 20 percent or more of its nitrogen as amino acids and amino acid breakdown products. Because even the whey in cow's milk is digested less well, more cow's-milk protein (predominantly whey) has to be added to infant formula to compensate, provide sufficient protein, and approximate the ratio of whey to casein in human milk. Soy proteins have lower digestibility still (table 15.2); thus soy formulas must have an even higher protein content to ensure protein sufficiency for infants. Methionine is added to the soy formula to prevent a protein deficiency, since an imbalance of amino acids can interfere with the ability to use the proteins (correcting an amino acid imbalance is required for any situation, not just soy, and not just during infancy).

To understand and use these recommendations, let us take the example of a 20-pound eight-month-old, who needs 0.5 to 0.6 grams of protein per pound, or 20 × 0.5 to 20 × 0.6, which equals 10 to 12 grams of protein per day. Preterm

Table 15.1. Daily Protein Requirements (Grams per Pound of Body Weight per Day)

	EAR	RDA	AI
Premature infants[a]			1.5–2
0–6 months			0.75
6–12 months	0.5	0.6	
12–36 months	0.45	0.5	
Breastfeeding mother	0.5	0.6 (or a total of 71g/day)	

Note: Sources include breastmilk, infant formula, dairy, meats, vegetables, beans, and peanuts.

EAR = Estimated Average Requirement; RDA = Recommended Dietary Allowance; AI = adequate intake

[a]This is a consensus recommendation rather than AI. *Source:* Reginald C. Tsang, *Nutrition of the Preterm Infant: Scientific Basis and Practical Guidelines* (Cincinnati, OH: Digital Educational Publishing, 2005), 417–18. The remaining recommendations are established by the Institute of Medicine.

Source: Adapted from J. J. Otten, J. P. Hellwig, and L. D. Meyers, eds., *Dietary Reference Intakes: The Essential Guide to Nutrient Requirements* (Washington, DC: National Academies Press, 2006).

Table 15.2. Sources and Quality of Proteins for Infants

	Digestability (%)
Cow's milk	95
Beef, cooked	94
Egg	97
Soy	95
Wheat, refined	96
Wheat, whole	86
Rice, cooked white	88
Beans, cooked navy	78

Source: Adapted from R. E. Kleinman, ed., *Pediatric Nutrition Handbook*, 6th ed. (Elk Grove Village, IL: American Academy of Pediatrics, 2009), 333.

infants have greater needs, relative to their body weight, with those needs becoming higher the younger they are. As children (and adults) age, that need decreases, stabilizing after puberty, then increasing for women who are pregnant or breastfeeding. There are advocates for even higher protein intake to increase growth and muscle mass, with little risk unless that intake is truly excessive, while there is also some evidence (pointed out in chapters 4 and 12) that higher protein intakes during infancy can contribute to later obesity.

For infants, good sources of protein are breastmilk or formula, meats, and vegetables. If an infant is on a vegetarian diet, indispensible amino acids can come from alternate nonmeat sources, such as lysine from cereals or methionine and cysteine from peas.

Carbohydrates (and Fiber)

Carbohydrates provide energy to all of the cells in the body. They are not hydrates of carbon but carbon, hydrogen, and oxygen combined into saccharides, a term for simple sugars, and the more complex polysaccharides, which are commonly referred to as starch and dietary fiber. Their simplest forms are simple sugars, like glucose and fructose. The rest are combinations of these that must be digested into these simple sugars in order to be absorbed and used. Fiber, however, resists that digestive process and, as a result, will be discussed separately. Any excess carbohydrates and those that the body can't digest or absorb (like the starches and sugars in beans and mushrooms) will continue downstream to the large intestine, where they will either be converted into absorbable fatty acids or become food for the microflora, which will metabolize them into waste water and gas.

Lactose and sucrose have individual enzymes, lactase and sucrase, to cleave them into their component parts. These enzymes reside on the tips of the *villi* in the upper intestine, and when the villi have been damaged, these enzymes can be lost temporarily. Genetically rare infants are born with a lack of sucrase. Lactase levels are low in 25 percent of one-week-old term infants; interestingly, feeding lactose usually induces the enzyme (causes it to develop more) and rarely causes problems. The gradual loss of lactase, which occurs as an inherited condition, usually does not show up until six or so years of age.

If the digested and absorbed sugars cannot be used immediately, they are formed into glycogen, effectively chains of glucose molecules, that can be stored in the liver and muscles for later use, or they will be metabolized and combined with protein or fats (glycolipids) to form nucleic acids (such as DNA), structural elements, and numerous hormones or enzymes.

While requirements have been written in terms of the grams needed each day, in infancy they are not based on what infants actually need but rather on what they usually consume from breastmilk in the first six months and then when other foods are added. It's more useful to recognize that approximately 40 percent of the calories in formula and breastmilk are from their sugar component, while carbohydrates represent 50 to 60 percent of diets for the average American (with the leading source of added sugars coming from nondiet soft drinks).

Fiber, often referred to as roughage or bulk in the past, is the part of plants that we, as humans, don't have the enzymes to digest (see table 15.3). (Pandas thrive on bamboo; we can't metabolize it.) Current dietary recommendations for infants balance the need for fiber with the potential that the phytates in fiber can bind to various minerals the baby needs, lessening their absorption. As a result, fiber should be gradually introduced between 6 and 12 months of age in the form of whole grains, vegetables, and legumes to a total of 5 grams per day by one year of age (see table 15.4). Thereafter, the amount of fiber can be steadily increased (www.nutrition4kids.com discusses this topic). The passage of soft bulky bowel movements is normal and can be accompanied by considerable amounts of gas, whereas overconsumption often results in feelings of bloating and discomfort.

Table 15.3. Sources of Fiber

	Type	Benefit
Soluble	Oat, psyllium, fruit, legumes (beans)	Lower cholesterol
Insoluble	Whole grain, vegetables	
Both		Lessen risk of obesity Lessen constipation

Source: Adapted from www.nutrition4kids.com.

Table 15.4. High-Fiber Foods

Fruits
Each serving has approximately 2 grams of fiber. Older infants should have one or two each day. Avoid giving fruit with pits to infants. Remember to remove skins and seeds.

Apple, 1 small	Cantaloupe, 1 cup[a]	Pear, ½ small
Apricot, 2 medium	Cherries, 10 large, pitted	Plum, 2 small
Banana, 1 small	Dried figs, ⅓ cup	Strawberries, ½ cup
Blackberries, ½ cup	Peach, 1 medium	Watermelon, 1–3 cups[a]

Cooked Vegetables
Each serving has about 2 grams of fiber. Children should have two servings or more each day. Children 6 to 12 months should have one to two fistfuls per day; children 1 to 3 years, half a cup of vegetable per day.

Avocado, fresh, ½ medium	Carrots, ⅓ cup	Potato, 2-inch diameter
Broccoli top, ⅓ cup	Green beans, ½ cup	french fries, 20
Beans, 2 tbsp.	Peas, ¼ cup	Sweet potato, ½ medium

Bread and Cereal
Infants need iron from infant cereal or meat, approximately 2 ounces per day. Each serving has about 2 grams of fiber (but these foods are not needed for infants).

Cheerios, ⅔ cup	Animal crackers, 3 boxes (2 oz. each)	
White bread, 3 slices	Whole-wheat bread, 1 slice	Graham crackers, 10 squares
Infant rice cereal and puffs have minimal fiber		Infant oatmeal, 12 tbsp.

[a]Estimates vary widely.

Source: Adapted from S. A. Cohen, *Healthy Babies, Happy Kids* (New York: Delilah Books, 1982), 168.

Fat

Fats have gotten a lot of bad press. Saturated fats have been associated with high cholesterol levels, and both saturated fat and cholesterol have been thought to increase the risk of heart disease later in life. But frankly, we are uncertain when this starts and whether restricting these fats in childhood will make any difference. In fact, breastmilk is higher in cholesterol than cow's milk. This may mean that a high level is intended to teach the body from the beginning how to break down cholesterol later on.

In fact, fat is absolutely necessary for your baby and represents approximately 50 percent of the calories in breastmilk and formula. It has high energy value and spares protein from being used as an energy source. It carries the fat-soluble vitamins and becomes a part of cell membranes and brain cells. Fat also improves the taste of food and slows the stomach emptying—making us all feel full in much the same way as high-fiber foods do.

Fats, also known as *lipids*, are absorbed from vegetable oils and animal fats after they have been digested by a combination of bile from the liver and enzymes from the pancreas. Following absorption, the smaller fatty acids are transformed into triglycerides and other lipids that are then used by muscle for fuel, with the excess building the fatty tissues of the body.

Infants do not contain sufficient amounts of the enzyme that creates DHA. They receive it intact from breastmilk and across the placenta during pregnancy. In order to match the optimal brain and eye development seen in breastfed infants, DHA and its omega-6 balancing partner, arachidonic acid (ARA), are now added to infant formula, since infants lack the ability to synthesize sufficient amounts for their needs (thus, I would describe them as conditionally essential, though they have not yet been defined as such). Alpha-linolenic acid (an omega-3 oil), from which DHA is made in adults, and linoleic acid (an omega-6 oil), from which ARA is made, are the essential fatty acids (originally dubbed vitamin F) since humans cannot manufacture them and must obtain them in their diets. When they are absent, essential fatty acid deficiency develops, resulting in diminished growth and scaly skin.

These essential fatty acids are present in breastmilk and formula. The infants' dietary recommendations for DHA are based on actual consumption rather than actual need for the fats in general. The estimated need for DHA is shown in table 4.1, with breastfeeding mothers estimated to need 300 milligrams of DHA daily (which can be best obtained from fish or a supplement of DHA or omega-3 oil).

Parents who are afraid of their children becoming obese often restrict fats, polyunsaturated as well as the saturated. But this can be detrimental to a developing infant or toddler. Please remember that fat in the body does not just come from the fat that your child eats. It comes from excess calories, whether those calories are from fat, protein, sugars, or starches. All excess calories contribute to being overweight. Infants need fats for growth and for their brains to develop appropriately. And many weight-reducing plans for teens and adults depend on higher levels of fat and protein to reduce the desire to eat and to help trim extra pounds while not trimming too much muscle protein.

Water and Fluids

Most people don't think of water as a nutrient, but remember that water contributes 60 percent of the body's weight, maintains the blood volume, transports other nutrients, removes waste, and acts as the body's cooling system when sweat is produced. In order to keep the body's total water stable, losses must be matched by sufficient intake. Those who are physically active or live in a warm environment require more fluid at those times, since the body balances fluids continuously (as opposed to vitamins, like B_{12}, which are balanced over long periods, so that vitamin deficits can take months to present clinical symptoms).

As previously stated, infants require water, which they consume in the form of breastmilk or formula. Water by itself usually isn't necessary but forms the fluid component of both. This is best demonstrated by the fact that you add formula powder to water in order to constitute the formula so your infant can drink it. And offering water can interfere with establishing breastfeeding. The water can slake an infant's thirst and thus lessen his interest in latching on or feeding.

If a full-term baby is getting his formula as recommended on the can (one scoop per 2 ounces, yielding 20 calories per ounce), he is receiving 150 milliliters of water for every 100 calories he's consuming. This is based on the normal ratio of calories to water in breastmilk. For babies on preterm formula, that ratio is changed in order to deliver more calories (24 calories per ounce). Similarly, infants who have more powder in their formula, in order to increase calories, receive less water. And babies who have cereal added for reflux also have a different ratio of calories to water. All of these infants should be monitored routinely for their hydration status.

The best way to tell that an infant is receiving adequate fluid is to examine his mouth, ensuring it is moist, and to examine his diaper for the color and amount of urine. If the urine is dark or the amount seems less than usual, you can alter the feeding pattern. If you are breastfeeding exclusively, offer the breast more frequently (and make sure you remain well hydrated). If you are formula-feeding or have already introduced infant foods, you can offer water between feedings or meals (particularly if it's a hot day or your infant has a fever). The maximum should not exceed 3 to 4 ounces per pound of body weight.

THE MICRONUTRIENTS: VITAMINS AND MINERALS, NEEDED IN SMALLER QUANTITIES

Vitamins and certain minerals are chemicals that the body requires in small amounts in order to have a normal metabolism (hence the term *micronutrients*). You hear and read about the need for iron. But do you know how much iron is in your body as an adult? A pound, perhaps? Actually, not even an ounce. Four grams—that's considerably less than would fill a thimble. And a quarter of that is stored. That means that three grams is all that your body has available to carry oxygen in the bloodstream and to serve as a part of enzymes and proteins that transport energy and oxygen to each of your cells.

Your children have even less iron. An infant is born with less than 10 percent of that iron and must continue to acquire it throughout his life. Though so small as to seem almost inconsequential, the amount does not count alone; the role it plays in the body is most important.

The best way to see its importance is to look at the consequences of your child's not having enough iron. The obvious result is iron-poor blood, or anemia. But his lack of iron will cause him to act anemic, too. With less oxygen being delivered by the blood, and with enzyme systems working at diminished capacity, muscles tire more rapidly, school performance declines, the ears have a ringing sensation, and the heart is required to work harder and beat faster to deliver what oxygen is available. The child's appetite may falter. He may be irritable and have a shortened attention span—making him seem like a hyperactive child. And he may even develop a strange habit of craving ice, dirt, or laundry starch. (No one knows whether kids and pregnant women who do this are trying to get more iron that way or whether the low iron and oxygen levels derange their taste buds or a part of their brain, causing this strange behavior.) Some children with severe iron deficiency may not grow at a normal rate unless supplemented with additional iron.

That explanation is to help you understand the necessity for these micronutrients. It is also necessary to understand that the body is usually unable to make these substances. They have to be consumed in the diet or as a supplement.

The difference between a vitamin and a mineral is simply in the chemical structure. Remember your high school chemistry: vitamins are organic substances (made from carbon, hydrogen, oxygen, and nitrogen). Minerals are best remembered from your early science classes as part of the inorganic classification "animal, vegetable, or mineral."

By definition, the body needs these substances only in small quantities in order to carry out normal metabolism. The requirement for a vitamin is calculated by how much a person actually needs of that vitamin in order to provide for adequate metabolism. It takes into account not only how much is used internally but how much is necessary in order for a person to actually absorb that much. In other words, if I need 2 milligrams of a substance in my body every day, but I only absorb 10 percent of that amount from what I actually eat, I need to consume 20 milligrams of the vitamin each day.

That requirement varies from individual to individual. In order to account for that difference, EARs and RDAs have been established as well. Here these are listed again by age and for the breastfeeding mother. They differ from what you find on the required nutrition labels for processed foods, where the amount in the food is noted as a percentage of the daily value, which is based on a reference 2,000-calorie diet.

The RDAs purposefully overestimate our daily needs to account for variations within the population—making sure that the requirements will be met for 97 percent of the population. Because these figures are intentionally high, nutrient deficiencies should not be seen. In fact, many people who consume less than the recommended amounts will do quite well.

Vitamins

Basically, vitamins can be separated into two groups, depending on whether or not they dissolve in water. Vitamin C and the B vitamins dissolve in water and hence are considered "water soluble." Because of this, they penetrate cells well, and any extra that the body doesn't need is removed by the kidneys.

Vitamin C is important in the formation of certain types of protein, including collagen, the body's most abundant protein. Many of the B vitamins (including B_6, B_{12}, and folic acid) are important for the formation of proteins, too. They act somewhat like laces on a shoe, making sure it fits and is used properly. (As trivial as that sounds, try to wear a pair of tie-up boots without those laces!) The other B vitamins, thiamine (B_1) and riboflavin (B_2), are important for the breakdown of sugars and other nutrients for energy. The body cells that require increased energy need these vitamins the most and suffer more if the vitamins are not available.

Vitamins A, D, E, and K are not soluble in water but instead penetrate cells that have a high fat content and are stored there. Because excessive amounts of these vitamins cannot be eliminated from the body easily, they continue to be stored. Vitamin D has a well-known role in regulating calcium and phosphorus in order to keep our bones in good shape. Vitamin K aids in forming the protein needed to help our blood clot. Vitamin A is important for our eyesight, and with vitamin E, it also stands guard to protect cells from antioxidant effects and being broken down. However, vitamins A and D are known to cause severe illnesses if they overaccumulate. And prolonged supplementation with high-dose vitamin E is associated with an increased risk of heart failure in adults.

The formula-fed infant has little need for any vitamin or mineral supplementation because these are sufficiently provided in commercial preparations. As previously discussed, breastfed infants require additional vitamin D to meet their needs. The preterm infant will require multivitamin supplements because stores of the various vitamins have not built up in his own system.

In the preterm infant, as well as in the older child and even the adult, other nutrients influence vitamin needs as well. This can be best understood by considering a malnourished African child. Those frail infants actually have very little need for vitamins. The reason is simply that they are not growing, and they are not eating very much. As they eat more and begin to grow, their needs for vitamins increase. In such a situation, the vitamins must be balanced because of vitamin and mineral interrelationships. For example, vitamin E protects vitamin A from oxidation, meaning that a deficiency of vitamin E may also result in a deficiency of vitamin A. Moreover, little vitamin A, or pyridoxine, is needed when that malnourished child has little protein in his diet. But as he eats more protein-rich foods, he will need more of these vitamins. And he will need more thiamine as he receives more carbohydrates.

Table 15.5 summarizes some of the important facts about the various vitamins, but a brief section reviews each of the vitamins and minerals for those readers who desire a fuller understanding of these essential chemicals.

Table 15.5. Vitamins in Brief

Water Soluble/Required	Importance	Sources
Thiamine (B_1)	Carbohydrate and amino acid metabolism, nerve and muscle membranes	Grains, nuts, potatoes
Riboflavin (B_2)	Energy use, cell respiration and repair	Dairy, meats, green vegetables, eggs, yeast
Pyridoxine (B_6)	Enzyme activation and cofactor	Meats, vegetables, fruits, nuts, grains, legumes
Cyanocobalamin (B_{12})	Formation of genetic code, amino and fatty acid metabolism, blood cell and nerve development	Meats, eggs, milk products
Folate	Formation of genetic code, utilization of protein	Green vegetables, nuts, liver
Ascorbic acid (vitamin C)	Collagen formation/wound healing, immunity	Fruits, vegetables
Water Soluble/Conditional		
Niacin (B_3)	Protein and energy utilization	Grains, poultry, fish
Choline	Cell transport signaling and integrating	Milk, eggs, liver, peanuts
Biotin	Energy metabolism activation of folate	Intestinal bacteria, organ meats, yeast, soy, nuts, cereals
Pantothenic acid	Fat metabolism	Meats, whole grains, legumes, vegetables
Fat-Soluble Vitamins		
Vitamin A	Vision, skin integrity, gene expression	Fruits, vegetables, fortified milk, fish oils
Vitamin D	Calcium and phosphorus absorption, possible immune regulation	Sun, fish, eggs, fortified milk products
Vitamin E	Cell membrane stability, antioxidant	Fruits, vegetables, meats, oils
Vitamin K	Clotting	Intestinal bacteria, meats, green vegetables

Source: Adapted from S. A. Cohen, *Healthy Babies, Happy Kids* (New York: Delilah Books, 1982), 139.

Vitamin C

Man is one of the few animals that does not make its own vitamin C. We need it in our diet. Very little is required to prevent scurvy (only 10 milligrams per day). An intake of 30 milligrams a day appears to provide adults with adequate storage of the vitamin, and 45 milligrams per day (the equivalent of eating an orange a day) has been shown to give the body as much as it can hold. This is easily achieved for children and adults who eat adequate fruit daily or drink juice. Pregnant women do require slightly more (as do smokers). Moreover, certain people are at risk of having a minimum intake of, or increased need for, vitamin C: adolescents and picky eaters who totally avoid fruits and other vitamin C–rich foods, children with malnutrition, and infants who are fed cow's milk as the main source of nutrition in the first 6 to 12 months of life.

Infant recommendations are based primarily on what they should receive in breastmilk. That amount of the vitamin is added to infant formula. As a result, infantile scurvy is rarely seen in the absence of malnutrition.

Vitamin C did receive considerable attention in the 1970s and 1980s, when large doses were seen as a cure for colds, the flu, and even cancer. And while not applicable to infants, the continued controversy begs further explanation. Because of the popularity of the concept, manufacturers began producing megavitamins that contain large quantities of ascorbic acid and other vitamins. Prior to that, science was focused on this vitamin for its ability to prevent scurvy (remember your health class lectures about the depressed and weak sailors who bled easily and had loose teeth until the British began eating limes and other citrus fruits on board to prevent the scourge of scurvy, hence the nickname "limey"—at least, that's how I remembered it).

Vitamin C also helps in the production of collagen (which has been referred to as the cement between cells and also provides the structure for our connective tissues—the ligaments, tendons, and cushiony parts of our joints). Vitamin C also has a role in iron metabolism and in synthesizing the neurotransmitters that signal between nerve cells. Its capacity to help relieve the body's oxidative stress also suggested that, in higher doses, it could possibly protect against viruses, and there was hope that it could help prevent cancer.

Unfortunately, we are still contending with viruses and cancer with little help from high-dose vitamin C, though those larger doses still sell well. Two studies are particularly interesting. J. L. Coulehan and his coworkers reported their work in the *New England Journal of Medicine* in 1974 and in 1976. In those studies, more than 600 Navaho children between the ages of 6 and 15 in Arizona boarding schools were examined during the winters. The kids were given either 1 or 2 grams daily of vitamin C or a placebo and were watched for a period of 14 to 18 weeks. The number of colds did not differ between the two groups, and there was no difference in the complications that arose from the colds, such as bronchitis or ear infection. Symptoms were somewhat alleviated by the vitamin C in a small percentage (9 to 26 percent) of the children. Thus, while the vitamin C did not appear to prevent colds, it may have helped a few individuals feel slightly better.[6] Further analyses of all the studies that have been done show no difference in cancers or colds in adults.

Vitamin B Complex

In comparison to the controversy surrounding vitamin C, the questions that vitamin B has generated seem dull and academic. The B vitamins have been important in preventing diseases such as beriberi and pellagra for centuries. These diseases seem so distant, occurring in undeveloped countries in days of yore. But these same diseases still exist in rare instances today when diets have been inappropriate or adequate nutrition is simply not available. These B vitamins help to form many enzymes that are important in protein manufacture and metabolism.

Thiamine (known as B_1 because it was the first B vitamin to be described), riboflavin (B_2), and pyridoxine (B_6) are all considered vitamins that must be supplied to man because we cannot make these vitamins within our own bodies. The other B vitamins are required in some circumstances but not in others (and they are therefore classified as conditional vitamins). But B_1, B_2, B_6, B_{12}, and folate are always required.

Thiamine is involved in the metabolism of carbohydrates and certain amino acids. Very little is required in our diet since only 30 milligrams (one-thousandth of an ounce) are stored in an adult's entire body. Thiamine is easily absorbed; any extra is excreted in the urine. Recommended amounts are adequately supplied in a single serving of grains, such as peas or beans, or organ meat from either pork or beef. Yet those who subsist on polished rice alone or ingest large quantities of fish (such as raw carp, herring, or shellfish) or tea (as in an Asian diet), which contain large antithiamine factors, are at risk for a thiamine deficiency.

Riboflavin helps to form numerous enzymes that are important in allowing the cells to breathe and repair themselves. A deficiency can be detected by an inflamed area at the corners of the mouth and some thickening and purplish discoloration of the tongue. This syndrome is rare because of the wide availability of the vitamin in diary foods, meats, eggs, yeast, and green vegetables.

Pyridoxine, like the other required B vitamins, is used as an enzyme activator in protein and glycogen metabolism and as a cofactor needed for other enzymes to work. Various forms of pyridoxine are widely present in meats, vegetables, fruits, whole grains, and legumes. However, cooking does destroy much of the vitamin's activity. The requirement for pyridoxine seems to be proportionate to the amount of protein you eat, as with riboflavin. Therefore, in periods of increased growth, when one is consuming more protein, increased amounts of pyridoxine and riboflavin are needed but are usually eaten along with the protein.

Vitamin B_{12} is critical to the metabolism of certain fatty acids and amino acids. This is most evident in the development of red blood cells and the nervous system. As a result, a deficiency in B_{12} (and/or folate) shows up with a particular kind of anemia, where the red blood cells are larger but there are fewer of them, and with tingling in the legs, difficulty walking, and changes within the brain that result in sleep disturbances, difficulty concentrating and remembering, and possible mood changes. Bowel and bladder control can also be affected. Vitamin B_{12} deficiency can also develop for others who have absorption problems because of previous surgery, an intestinal illness, or long-standing diarrhea. Additionally, since the main source of B_{12} is animal proteins (meats, milk products, eggs), a deficiency can be seen in breastfeeding infants of vegan mothers who do not eat enriched grain products or take sufficient supplements. These infants' stores of the vitamin may be low at birth, and they may receive only small amounts from their mothers' milk. It is also important to note that the B_{12} in milk is greatly diminished with cooking.

Folate is important in creating the genetic code (nucleic acid) contained in every cell nucleus. Growth diminishes in each cell when suboptimal amounts are in the diet. The cells that are growing most rapidly are first affected by their absence. Thus, red blood cells, which are continuously repopulating themselves, will increase in size but decrease in number.

However, it is most interesting that problems do not develop for many months from the time when diminished intake starts. In a classical experiment, Dr. Victor Herbert deprived himself of folate-containing foods and folic acid (the more easily absorbed form used in dietary supplements and fortified foods). Low blood levels of the folate were seen at approximately three weeks, but anemia did not develop until 4½ months into the dietary restriction. The reason for the slow occurrence of the symptoms is that folate is stored in the body in more-than-adequate amounts. The adult needs such a small amount that less than a millionth of a gram of folate is required each day (30 grams make 1 ounce), making a natural folate deficiency hard to come by

When deficiency does occur in pregnant mothers, however, their infants can be severely affected, with severe spinal defects (spina bifida) and even worse brain abnormalities. Supplementation of women able to become pregnant has reduced the frequency of those birth defects, and it has been associated with a decline in cleft lips, heart defects, and limb abnormalities as well. As a result, women of childbearing age are encouraged to take 400 micrograms of folic acid daily, in addition to their normal dietary intake, to bring their total intake to 600 micrograms daily. A woman who is pregnant should continue this supplementation to avoid depleting her own stores of folic acid in order to supply this much-needed vitamin for her child's growth. Her needs for folate increase to two times what she would normally use and remain at 25 percent more than the normal requirement while she is breastfeeding. Mothers carrying or breastfeeding more than one baby may have needs even greater than the RDA.

Many people derive folate from bacteria in their systems in adequate quantities to meet their minimum daily requirements. Fortunately, folate (chemically known as pteroylglutamic acid, which is why it is commonly known as folacin or folate) is widely available in leafy green vegetables, liver, asparagus, lima beans, nuts, and lentils. However, diets that are poor in vitamin C are also generally poor in folic acid as well. Not uncommonly, drugs interfere with the absorption or utilization of folic acid. This is true with several antibiotics, anticancer agents, and antiseizure drugs.

The remainder of the B vitamins are considered conditional vitamins: though they are essential in certain circumstances, often they are manufactured within the human body. For example, niacin can be made from the amino acid tryptophan (assuming adequate tryptophan is in the diet). Moreover, biotin and pantothenic acid are made in our intestines by the bacteria that are normally present there. Only when those bacteria do not exist or when there is an increased binding of the vitamins within the intestinal tract (blocking absorption) is there any necessity for additional quantities in the diet.

Niacin is the most widely known conditional vitamin. It was long thought to be absolutely necessary in the diet. However, it can be manufactured in small quantities from the essential amino acid tryptophan. It is also widely available in grains, meat, poultry, and fish, with little change from cooking or exposure to light, making a deficiency of niacin uncommon. The use of corn as the only grain in the diet does present a problem, however. Though niacin is present in corn, the vitamin there is basically unavailable to the body. Interestingly, in Central America, where tortillas are made with limewater added to the corn, the lime seems to liberate adequate amounts of niacin, preventing deficiency.

A niacin deficiency can occur in infants with malabsorption or chronic diarrhea, where niacin passes rapidly without adequate absorption; children whose dietary sources of niacin and protein are generally limited; and patients with prolonged high fevers, increasing the need for niacin. Others at risk include patients with pyridoxine (B_6) deficiency because the B_6 is needed for the conversion of tryptophan to niacin.

Bacteria that reside in our intestines can manufacture *biotin*, which is used in the activation of folate, as well as in certain specific reactions in the metabolism of protein, fat, and carbohydrate. Children at risk of developing problems include those who are on very restricted diets, such as tube feedings with inadequate vitamins, or who consume large amounts of raw egg whites. The reason in the first case is that the intestinal bacteria may change, and in the second, the egg whites have a factor that binds to the biotin, making it unabsorbable by our intestines. More biotin may be needed in pregnant women, the elderly, athletes, and children who suffer burns. The bumpy red rash of seborrhea that is common in infancy may be related to biotin, since the administration of biotin shots has been helpful in controlling this mild problem, as well as a severe, scaly rash around the eyes, nose, and mouth that occurs far more rarely in infants. Eye inflammation, alopecia, lethargy, and abnormal sensations in the arms and legs can also be present in biotin deficiency.

Although *choline* was discovered in 1864, it was not classified as an essential nutrient until 1998. Since it is water soluble, choline is usually grouped with the B vitamins. It is indeed essential, being involved in the structural integrity of all cells and in chemical signaling and transport between cells. Choline may be a conditionally essential nutrient, since the body may be able to manufacture it. But it is also readily available from milk, eggs, liver, and peanuts. Without it, liver damage occurs, but too much choline is associated with sweating, increased saliva, low blood pressure, a fishy body odor (from bacteria metabolizing the choline), and liver damage.

Pantothenic acid is another B vitamin that is synthesized by the intestinal bacteria. It too is an important part of enzyme systems that are involved in fat metabolism. Experimental diets that have eliminated pantothenic acid have produced headaches, fatigue, lack of coordination, tingling sensations in the hands and feet, and some vomiting and diarrhea. Prisoners of war in Asia labeled this the "burning-feet syndrome." Fortunately, it was corrected by pantothenic acid. However, with a normal diet consisting of meats, potatoes, tomatoes, broccoli, whole grains, or legumes, including peas and other vegetables, pantothenic acid deficiency is distinctly unusual.

Fat-Soluble Vitamins

Fat-soluble vitamins are so called simply because they dissolve in oils. Because of this property, they are generally deposited and stored in the tissues, particularly the liver, rather than left floating about in the serum like the water-soluble vitamins that are filtered out by the kidneys. This storage leads to concern about the fat-soluble vitamins' potential to cause significant damage when taken in high dosages, while at the same time, we're learning more about their therapeutic potential (particularly vitamin D, as you'll soon see).

Vitamin A is well known for its importance in keeping vision optimal. In its absence, night blindness occurs. Recently, however, vitamin A has been found to be vital to growth, reproduction, immune function, gene expression, and maintenance of healthy skin and the membranes that line the mouth, respiratory, gastrointestinal, and urinary tracts, thus protecting against infections.

Among infants, a yellow tint to the skin, particularly of the nose or the palms, implies adequate vitamin A levels and healthy intestinal absorption. More extensive yellowing of the skin might warrant a vitamin A blood-level test. But toxicity is rarely an issue in infants, since it arises from large doses in supplements, not from cantaloupe, yellow (and green) vegetables, and fish oils, which are natural sources of the carotenes that are converted to the vitamin in the body (and that also serve as antioxidants themselves), or from milk products fortified with the vitamin. Birth defects can occur when pregnant women take high doses, and breastmilk transfer might be of concern (at least theoretically) for women who are breastfeeding. For this reason, stick to levels near the RDA if supplementation is needed at all. And remember, supplementation is usually not needed since milk is fortified with vitamin A, and yellow or leafy green vegetables, animal meats, and freshwater fish usually meet everyone's needs.

Eight different forms of *vitamin E* (*tocopherol*) occur naturally (with some then included in vitamin supplements). The problem is that they aren't equal in their bioavailability. That makes the recommendations for vitamin E especially tricky, since it is an important antioxidant, and you want to be sure you and your baby have enough (but not too much, as you'll see). Because only one form, alpha-tocopherol, is functional, the recommendations are stated in terms of that form (dietitians can calculate an equivalence factor for the other forms). More problematic, at least for me, is that the criteria for determining the infant's requirements are again based on the amount present in breastmilk. Since that method was proven wrong in the case of vitamin D, I'm hoping that eventually the science will focus on the need to readdress how to better establish true requirements for infants.

Most interestingly, the need for vitamin E in the premature infant was recognized because many of these infants became anemic shortly after birth. When iron was given, instead of improving as expected, they became more anemic. It was then recognized that iron, acting as an oxidizing agent, was destroying the polyunsaturated fats in the red blood cell membranes. Adequate doses of vitamin E prevented this from occurring.

With the recognition that it worked there, vitamin E was utilized in other aspects of the care of newborn premature infants as well. With anemia, the iron could be removed and vitamin E given to improve the blood count. There is hope that adequate doses of vitamin E may prevent oxygen damage to these infants' eyes and lungs. But there is also concern that premature infants are particularly vulnerable to the vitamin's toxic effects at higher doses.

The fact that vitamin E is an effective antioxidant, protects lipids (particularly the polyunsaturated fatty acids), affects gene expression, and has a role in platelet and neurological function has led to its being tried in treating a number of different adult conditions, often yielding disappointing results or requiring too high a dose, which then revealed toxicities that could develop.

These problems don't exist when normal amounts of the vitamin are consumed in the various oils, fruits, vegetables, and meats or in normal multivitamin supplements. So the standard recommendation is not to take a routine supplement of vitamin E unless you are being treated for a particular condition and being carefully managed by your physician. In older infants and children, the main need for vitamin E supplementation is only in those with liver disease or cystic fibrosis, who are unable to absorb their fat-soluble vitamins well, and premature infants, as discussed.

One question that has arisen is whether the use of vitamin E in these special cases makes this compound a true vitamin. Is it truly a nutrient acting in this regard, or is it just another drug that is treating illnesses? As Victor Herbert has often pointed out, just because your child develops an ear infection and requires penicillin to treat it, that doesn't mean that your child is penicillin deficient. It only means that penicillin is a good drug to correct the problem. That may be equally true with vitamin E as well.

Although the other vitamins were named by the order in which they were discovered, *vitamin K* took its name from the German word *Koagulation*, meaning clotting. Indeed, its function is exactly that. Vitamin K is necessary for the liver to make the proteins used to form a blood clot or even a scab on an open wound. Without the vitamin, uncontrollable hemorrhaging can occur.

The vitamin is widely available in green plants, as well as in animal meats. However, our own intestinal bacteria are responsible for making most of our vitamin K. In much the same way as with the other fat-soluble vitamins, problems with vitamin K can occur if fat is not well absorbed within the intestinal tract because of diseases of the pancreas or the intestine itself or if there is a problem with inappropriate formation of the vitamin by intestinal bacteria.

Such a situation exists in the newborn infant when the vitamin K from the mother is not passed through the placenta to the infant and intestinal bacteria are not yet developed. As a result, babies in American and European nurseries receive an injection of vitamin K shortly after birth to prevent any possible bleeding in those early days of life.

Vitamin D (the Special Case?)

Our initial understanding of vitamin D grew out of the recognition that cod liver oil and sunlight could cure rickets, a disease causing bent and weakened bones. Vitamin D would help in the absorption of calcium and magnesium and in utilizing these minerals to form teeth and remodel bones. But recent data are beginning to suggest that vitamin D has a far broader role in preventing high blood pressure, some autoimmune diseases, and even cancer.

Many people can also obtain this vitamin freely from the sun. It takes only 20 minutes a day of intense sunlight on the face to provide adequate levels of vitamin D, without any dietary therapy, to prevent rickets (for fair-skinned individuals who live in warm climates and are foolish enough not to wear sunscreen). The radiation from the sun acts as an enzyme, converting one of the products of cholesterol metabolism into vitamin D. Further metabolism in the liver and kidneys converts the vitamin (whether from diet or the sun) into its most active form.

The problem with depending upon the sun's irradiation with ultraviolet light is that unless one is light skinned and constantly exposed to the sun in an intense manner, the rays lose their effect. Sunscreens with a sun protection factor (SPF) of 30 block 98 percent of the solar radiation needed to covert the cholesterol, the dark pigmentation among African Americans reduces this capacity naturally by 90 percent, and the angle of the sun's rays during winter in areas north of Atlanta markedly reduce the vitamin D that can come from the sun.[7] So, if you are black or living in Minneapolis in the middle of winter with only your face exposed to the less-than-clear sky, further vitamin D is going to be necessary. But the amount is crucial.

We don't judge vitamin D sufficiency based on intake anymore, in part because the sources of the vitamin are both sun exposure and diet, but also because we can objectively look at blood levels that tell us how much is in the bloodstream, and those levels correlate with levels of parathyroid hormone, which regulates calcium and bone health. And, of course, the concern isn't just rickets in the young but also preventing osteopenia (decreased bone mineralization) and osteoporosis (a weakening of the bones) with advancing age. So the Endocrine Society established that a vitamin D deficiency exists with low blood levels (less than 20 nanograms per milliliter of the commonly measured 25-OH form of vitamin D), sufficiency exists when those levels are greater than 30 (with an ideal level between 40 and 60), and insufficiency exists in individuals with levels between 20 and 30, putting them at risk.[8]

Using those definitions, the Centers for Disease Control released a report in 2011 that showed deficiency among up to 11 percent of one- to eight-year-olds, 22 percent of older children and adolescents, and up to 28 percent of adults.[9] Those statistics are even worse among teens in the southeastern United States (using a slightly different measurement). According to one study, 56 percent had insufficiency and 29 percent were deficient—and those statistics worsened again for black youths and those who were overweight.[10] Going north, the numbers worsen again, with 42 percent of black and Hispanic Boston teens and 48 percent of white girls in Maine deficient.[11, 12]

With all of this, the Institute of Medicine in 2010 revised its recommendations to increase consumption of vitamin D (as seen in table 15.6), still recognizing that toxicity can result at too high a dose. There are two concerns: these levels are hard to achieve with just diet alone (it would take two to six dairy servings a day to reach the 600 IU recommended at the current levels of supplementation), and these levels may still be too low.

Why? In Japan, 1,200 IU of vitamin D per day during the winter reduced the risk of having the flu by 42 percent; babies receiving 2,000 IU per day during their first year were 88 percent less likely to develop diabetes over the next 30 years, and black teens on that same dose reduced their potential for high blood pressure and atherosclerosis, whereas 400 IU did not produce the same effect.[13, 14, 15] And in a US study, pregnant women who took 4,000 IU in their second and third trimesters had a reduced rate of pregnancy-related diabetes, infections, high blood pressure, and premature births, with no ill effects, compared to women who took the usually recommended 400 IU of vitamin D every day. And the babies had higher vitamin D levels as well.[16]

As chairman of the Committee on Nutrition for the Georgia chapter of the American Academy of Pediatrics (AAP), I recommended that we follow the new guidelines established by our national organization, giving 400 IU to all infants (including infants who are breastfed) and 600 IU to everyone older, including pregnant and lactating women.[17] I am no longer convinced that's enough (see table 15.6). It appears that 2,000 IU daily is safe for at least a year and that toxicity can occur with 4,000 IU. As a result, I am now more in line with the Endocrine Society's Clinical Practice Guidelines, which recommend at least 400 to 1,000 IU for infants; in fact, 1,200 seems reasonable based on the Japanese data. I also support the Endocrine Society's recommendations of 1,500 to 2,000 IU for pregnant or lactating women, preferring the higher range of values, with the note that maternal supplementation of 2,000 IU while lactating achieves vitamin D levels for infants comparable to infants receiving 400 IU daily.[18]

I would use the lower amounts cited in the range if anyone in the family has had kidney stones or kidney disease (or at least discuss the options with your doctor), since excess calcium can promote stones and damage. And particularly in infants and pregnant and lactating mothers, I would follow blood levels to ensure calcium and vitamin D levels are within the optimal range, since these higher doses do involve some risk.

I do understand that in Britain, levels of 4,000 IU of vitamin D per quart of milk were used in the 1950s. Rickets was prevented, but toxic reactions to vitamin D resulted. Initially, large segments of British children lost their appetites and began having vomiting and constipation with weakness and weight loss. Approximately half of those affected had increased urination and an increased thirst as well. Calcium was deposited throughout the tissues. High blood pressure, kidney stones, kidney failure, and even death also developed. The pregnant women who drank the highly fortified milk in accordance with their general prenatal care seemed to produce infants who had high calcium levels and heart murmurs, though these

Table 15.6. Recommendations for Vitamin D Daily Intake (International Units per Day)

	Institute of Medicine				Endocrine Society	
	EAR	RDA	AI	UL	DA	UL
Premature infants[a]			20–75 IU/lb.			
0–6 months[b]			400	1,000	400–1,000	2,000
6–12 months			400	1,500	400–1,000	2,000
1–3 years	400	600		2,500	600–1,000	4,000
Breastfeeding mother	400	600		4,000	1,500–2,000[b,c]	10,000

Note: Sources include sun exposure, fish, eggs, and supplemented dairy products.

EAR = Estimated Average Requirement; RDA = Recommended Dietary Allowance; AI = adequate intake; UL = tolerable upper limits; DA = daily allowance for patients at risk for vitamin D deficiency

[a]This is a consensus recommendation rather than AI. *Source:* Reginald C. Tsang, *Nutrition of the Preterm Infant: Scientific Basis and Practical Guidelines* (Cincinnati, OH: Digital Educational Publishing, 2005), 417–18. The remaining recommendations are established by the Institute of Medicine.

[b]See the text for personal recommendations.

[c]The Endocrine Society recommends 600 to 1,000 IU for lactating mothers who are under eighteen years of age.

Source: Adapted from M. F. Holick, "The D-Lightful Vitamin D for Child Health," *Journal of Parenteral and Enteral Nutrition* 36, no. 1 (2012): 9S–19S (based on Dietary Reference Intakes for calcium and vitamin D, Institute of Medicine, released November 30, 2010), and M. F. Holick et al., "Evaluation, Treatment and Prevention of Vitamin D Deficiency: An Endocrine Society Clinical Practice Guideline," *Journal of Clinical Endocrinology and Metabolism* 96 (2011): 1911–30.

findings now appear to be caused by a genetic abnormality that can be worsened with increased calcium or vitamin D. As a result, I do not recommend the 4,000 IU dose; rather, I recommend the 2,000 IU levels that seemed to nearly match the 4,000 IU dose in effectiveness.

Please understand that you should not depend on skin exposure alone and that whatever is not consumed in the usual diet should be provided by using a supplement. If you have any question regarding your child's or your vitamin D status, a simple blood test can monitor the effectiveness of your efforts. Additionally, a scan can translate that into a measure of your bone density, particularly if you have insufficient blood levels or a condition that might impair calcium or vitamin D absorption or metabolism.

Those recommendations for pregnant women are particularly important since vitamin D deficiency has been shown to be associated with increased preeclampsia and an increased risk of needing a Caesarian section. Moreover, daughters of women who had vitamin D deficiency while pregnant have flattened pelvic structures, putting them at greater risk of needing a Caesarian section when they deliver. And do remember that too much vitamin D can cause nausea and vomiting, loss of appetite, excessive thirst, frequent urination, constipation, abdominal pain, muscle weakness, muscle and joint aches, confusion, and fatigue, as well as more serious consequences, like kidney damage. And know that the AAP still recommends a supplement of 400 IU of vitamin D a day for a child who is not receiving that in the diet,[19] and the Institute of Medicine recommends 600 IU for everyone from 1 to 70 years of age, including pregnant and lactating women.[20] Do remember that the total amount needed includes the dietary supply and thus any amount to be supplemented has to consider your baby's intake. If your child is on infant formula or if you have questions about how much to give, check with your pediatrician before giving your child vitamin D (or other) supplements.

Minerals in Brief

Iron (which is a wonderful example) and most other metals come from the soil. Plants that grow in the soil and animals that eat those plants contain sufficient iron for everyone. Sure, an average portion of spinach has 2 milligrams of iron, which should be enough for one to two days' worth—if all were absorbed. But phytates in plant fibers bind that iron so tightly that we can only extract a small fraction (about 2 percent) of it.

Thus, we have to think not only of a food's mineral content but also of that content's availability (*bioavailability*). For example, a normal portion of corn and veal both contain the same amount of iron; however, 20 percent of the iron in the veal is absorbed, while only 4 percent of the corn's iron is absorbed.

Again, as an example, iron from animal sources is better absorbed than iron of vegetable origin. Part of this is due to the phytates and fiber that bind the iron. Part is due to other metals (such as zinc and cobalt) from the soil that compete

Table 15.7. Minerals in Brief

	Importance	Source
Calcium	Bone formation, nerve signaling, hormone secretion	Dairy, broccoli, kale
Copper	Creation of bone structure, energy metabolism	Seafood
Chromium	Sugar metabolism	Meats, fish, grains, Brewer's yeast
Fluoride	Strengthening of teeth, bone formation	Fluoridated water, toothpaste, mouth rinses
Iron	Transportation of oxygen and energy	Meats, green vegetables, iron-fortified cereals
Magnesium	Bone metabolism, metabolic processes	Grains, nuts, leafy vegetables
Manganese	Protein and fat metabolism, bone formation	Vegetables, grains, organ meats
Potassium	Regulation of fluids in cells, nerve signaling, heart contractions	Fruits (bananas, oranges), vegetables
Selenium	Antioxidant (similar to vitamin E), part of enzyme system	Vegetables, meats, fruits, milk products
Sodium	Regulation of hydration and fluid in blood vessels	Salt in food preparation, processed foods
Zinc	Protein and fat formation, processing of genetic codes	Fish, meats

Source: Adapted from S. A. Cohen, *Healthy Babies, Happy Kids* (New York: Delilah Books, 1982), 163.

with the iron to enter our bodies. And part is simply due to a more efficient absorption process of iron from animals.

Foods eaten at the same time as iron-containing foods may also influence the absorption of iron. Vitamin C (ascorbic acid) and the stomach's own hydrochloric acid allow iron to enter the intestinal cells more easily, probably by releasing iron bound by fiber and by preventing the iron from binding to other iron particles. Eggs (and coffee and tea), on the other hand, bind the iron and therefore interfere with its absorption.

The absorption of iron is also determined by the proteins in the cells lining the intestine. In fact, they serve as the regulators of the body's iron content. When there is sufficient iron in the body, the proteins hold the iron in the intestinal cells until it is needed, at which point it is released into the bloodstream. The more a person needs iron, the more efficient the protein is in releasing it. Those proteins also protect us from iron poisoning by keeping that excess in the intestinal cells, eventually eliminating it from the body when the cell dies and is replaced by new intestinal cells.

Over 99 percent of the body's *calcium* is located in the bones and teeth, though it is also important in achieving muscular and blood vessel contractions, neurological messaging, and hormonal secretion. The bones, too, participate in maintaining blood calcium levels, releasing the mineral when circulating calcium levels are low. That release can result in a loss (osteoporosis), making the bone fragile unless dietary calcium and vitamin D–assisted absorption are increased. Again, that requires adequate levels of vitamin D, but even then calcium absorption declines with aging and cannot keep lactating women from losing bone while breastfeeding. Fortunately, breastfeeding mothers appear to compensate and return to normal bone health after weaning. This can become more of an issue for mothers breastfeeding multiple infants, so additional calcium and magnesium are worthwhile (since calcium and magnesium need to be balanced, given that lower levels of one of these minerals will often cause lower levels of the other).

Dairy products are ready sources of calcium, but that becomes a problem for those who are lactose intolerant or on vegan diets. Certain vegetables, such as kale and broccoli, are good sources of calcium, but vegetables such as spinach and sweet potatoes release only approximately 10 percent of their calcium because of the oxalic acid they contain, and the phytic acid in soy, grains, nuts, and beans limits calcium absorption as well (approximately half of the calcium in dried beans is released). Additionally, caffeine and high sodium intake may increase calcium losses, and the phosphorus in soft drinks can lower calcium absorption.

At the same time, it is important to remember that as with vitamin D, which increases calcium absorption, an excess of calcium can cause kidney stones and kidney damage, and high levels can interfere with absorption of other minerals. Since the needs for calcium are often stated along with those for vitamin D, and so you can compare the levels to what you might find in the foods you offer your infant, table 15.8 shows the levels needed.

Table 15.8. Daily Calcium Requirements (Milligrams per Day)

	EAR	RDA	AI	UL
Premature infants[a]			45–90 mg/lb.	
0–6 months			210	
6–12 months			270	
12–36 months			500	2,500
Breastfeeding mother		1,000[b]		2,500

Note: Sources include dairy, broccoli, and kale.

EAR = Estimated Average Requirement; RDA = Recommended Dietary Allowance; AI = adequate intake; UL = tolerable upper limit

[a]This is a consensus recommendation rather than AI. *Source:* Reginald C. Tsang, *Nutrition of the Preterm Infant: Scientific Basis and Practical Guidelines* (Cincinnati, OH: Digital Educational Publishing, 2005), 417–18. The remaining recommendations are established by the Institute of Medicine.

[b]This number is higher (1,300) for teenage mothers.

Source: Adapted from J. J. Otten, J. P. Hellwig, and L. D. Meyers, eds., *Dietary Reference Intakes: The Essential Guide to Nutrient Requirements* (Washington, DC: National Academies Press, 2006).

Magnesium, to my mind, is calcium's younger brother. It, too, plays a role in bone metabolism, and its absorption is regulated in part by vitamin D. It also has a role in hundreds of other metabolic processes and an interactive relationship with vitamin D, calcium, and phosphorus so that their blood, and possibly their tissue, levels affect each other. Thus low magnesium levels can cause low calcium levels and their deficiency states can look similar, causing muscle cramps, tremulousness, and seizures. High levels, on the other hand (usually from the many over-the-counter and prescription medications that contain magnesium), can interfere with vitamin D metabolism and also cause low potassium levels and an inactive intestine.

Fortunately, magnesium is readily available in grains, nuts, and leafy green vegetables. Mothers who are breastfeeding multiple infants may need additional magnesium during the months they are breastfeeding and to replenish their stores afterward.

To now be more specific about *iron*, the requirement depends on the individual's needs. A certain amount of iron that the body has available each day is recycled from old red blood cells that are trapped and broken down in the spleen and bone marrow. The iron is then freed from these cells to be reutilized. However, we must also bring enough iron into the body to replace what is lost and needed for growth each day. Much depends on gender (women need more because of regular blood loss with menstrual periods) and growth.

Pregnancy increases iron requirements even further. A large portion of iron from a pregnant woman's body is transferred across the placenta to satisfy the constantly increasing needs of her unborn infant, whose blood cells and enzyme systems are being built. Less obvious are her own ongoing daily iron losses and her increasing blood volume, which is rapidly expanding to circulate nourishment through the placenta to the baby.

By the time her unborn infant reaches full term, his iron content is roughly 250 milligrams, compliments of his mother. If the mother's nutrition is not adequate to meet these demands, the iron stored in the mother's system is transferred preferentially to the infant, depleting her stores while protecting the baby's.

When born, a baby has the iron that his mother has provided during pregnancy, with an extra load given at the time of birth—some of the blood from the placenta is delivered through the pulsing umbilical cord to the infant. Thereafter, his needs must be met by what is fed to him. His requirements roughly parallel his growth rate. As his size increases, so does the amount of blood circulating through his body. The active and storage forms of iron grow, too.

Iron needs during breastfeeding are essentially those of nonpregnant women, but continued supplements for the mother for two to three months after delivery are advisable in order to replenish the stores depleted by pregnancy.

To ensure that these needs are met for whatever age or situation, the principles of mineral sufficiency must be remembered. The balance between losses and absorption are in part dictated by the mineral's bioavailability as well.

Several errors in iron nutrition have occurred when these factors were not thoroughly considered. Women breastfeeding their infants were told to supplement their infant's intake with iron, because the small quantity of iron in human milk was thought to be inadequate to meet the infant's needs. Based on the usual 10 percent absorption of the iron in milk, this advice was correct. But nature outsmarted the scientists, making 50 percent of the iron in human milk available, giving breastmilk the highest bioavailability of any food and therefore providing enough iron to meet an infant's daily requirements.

Thus, a breastfed infant needs no supplementation until his growth exceeds his mother's ability to supply his needs at approximately six months. The infant receiving commercially manufactured formulas is no different. The formulas now have adequate iron included and meet iron needs for the same period. When an infant doubles his birth weight at approximately four to six months of age, however, his size and blood volume require larger amounts of iron. This will mean using greater quantities of formula (or human milk—more than most women can provide) or turning to other sources for the iron.

It would be a mistake, however, to continue to use more and more formula to meet these needs because this establishes a pattern of excessive milk drinking later in life, when a diet relying largely on cow's milk (with its lower iron content) will not be adequate. Iron-rich foods are a simple solution. Meats, vegetables, and iron-fortified cereals, together with a quart of human milk or formula, do meet these requirements nicely.

Just a few decades ago, that might not have been true. The infant cereal and flour industries erred in calculating bioavailability from the iron phosphates and pyrophosphate added to infant cereals. This supplement had no taste, odor, or ill effects and provided high iron content in the food, satisfying everyone—until nutritionists found that the iron in this form was almost totally bound, making it unavailable to the infant. That problem has now been corrected, and a more absorbable iron has replaced the previous forms in infant cereals.

A premature infant is somewhat different, however. As discussed, the transfer of iron across the placenta to the infant generally follows an infant's rate of growth. A fetus's growth in the uterus is slow at first, occurring much more rapidly later in the pregnancy. If pregnancy is interrupted by a premature birth, an infant does not receive his full maternal supply of many nutrients, including iron. An infant born two months early, for example, will have only two-thirds of his iron requirement. Instead of the 250 milligrams of iron that a normal infant would have at birth, this infant could be expected to have only two-thirds of that, or 175 milligrams. This deficit needs to be replaced (but it will take longer to add the iron outside the womb) and has to be balanced by vitamin E.

In the premature infant who is breastfeeding, however, other factors must be considered before beginning treatment, particularly with regard to increased susceptibility to infections. Breastfeeding gives an infant additional protection by providing lactoferrin, a transport protein that binds iron and also participates in immune protection. This protein partially prevents certain bacteria from growing in the large intestine. Once saturated with iron, however, lactoferrin can no longer compete and prevent that bacterial growth, especially for the vulnerable premature. As a result, most neonatologists now use only small quantities of iron drops for the young premature and then transfuse the infant with fresh red blood cells if he should become alarmingly anemic. This controls the anemia and possibly allows lactoferrin to continue its protection.

Since most other infants receive adequate amounts of breastmilk or iron-fortified formulas, the next period of concern is after a child has just been weaned onto regular cow's milk. The content and availability of iron in cow's milk are very low. As a result, the child who is gaining and growing from all of the protein and calories in cow's milk may still be lacking in his iron supply. By making sure that he is also eating meats, vegetables, and iron-fortified cereals, this problem may be avoided.

As with so many other nutrients, you must also recognize that an overabundance of iron can become a problem, with high-dose supplements causing gastrointestinal distress, such as nausea, vomiting, and changes in bowel habits (a change in bowel color to black is not a problem and is an expected result of taking iron supplements). Iron overload can result in increased stores in the liver and even the heart, so now men and older women are told to avoid iron supplements.

Zinc, like iron, is important as a part of many enzymes that help to make proteins, carbohydrates, and fats; it also helps process the genetic codes. Therefore, it is not surprising that a zinc deficiency can cause a lag in growth and sexual development and, in the very young, a lag in brain growth as well. Diarrhea, poor appetite, and decreased resistance to infection may result. Because of the importance of zinc in forming skin and hair, its lack may cause skin rashes, hair loss, and poor wound healing.

Even the most common causes of a zinc deficiency appear to be rare, however. Fish and meats are good sources of zinc, since the availability of zinc is high in these foods. As with iron, zinc availability is poor in vegetables that are high in fiber and phytates, and the zinc in grain is often removed during milling. So a child's supply of zinc will depend on his diet, with vegetarian children often requiring 50 percent more because of lessened bioavailabilty.

Breastfed infants have a good zinc source but begin to outgrow what breastmilk alone can provide by seven months of age. If an infant or child has severe diarrhea, poor absorption, excess sweating, or kidney disease, his requirement for zinc will increase.

Detecting zinc deficiency is still a formidable task if the blood levels are normal. Hair samples have been collected for zinc levels in adults and can show a mild, ongoing deficiency, but our knowledge of the amount of zinc in children's hair is still limited. However, physicians can examine one of the enzymes (alkaline phosphatase) that zinc influences to see if that enzyme level is low and whether the addition of zinc increases the enzyme's activity.

Excessive supplementation, however, also poses problems, with adverse gastro-intestinal effects (decreased appetite, nausea, vomiting, pain, and diarrhea) among the first to develop. Ongoing zinc excess can lessen immune responsiveness.

Copper is another mineral that is involved in the structure and function of different enzyme systems, though two-thirds of the body's copper is found in the musculoskeletal system. Unlike with iron and zinc, vegetable fiber does not interfere with the absorption of copper. In fact, vegetables are excellent sources of this nutrient. Seafood, nuts, seeds, and whole grains also contain bioavailable copper. Dairy products are only a fair source of copper (and many of the children with copper deficiency in Peru began their symptoms when milk was used to combat their malnutrition). As long as your baby has a mixed diet or is on formula containing copper, a deficiency should not develop. Even though copper levels are low in breastmilk, a normal infant's body supply of copper should last until he has begun solid foods at six months of age.

As a result, copper deficiency is truly rare in infants and children unless they have an underlying problem, such as prolonged, severe malabsorption, malnutrition, or prolonged intravenous feedings of copper-poor solutions. The exception is the premature infant who has small storage pools of copper and may not be provided any additional copper unless his pediatrician makes certain that he receives it in his feedings or in his intravenous fluids.

Chromium appears to be important in lowering blood sugar by helping insulin allow sugar to enter the body's cells. Except in infants with severe malnutrition, few problems with chromium deficiency have been observed in children. Whole grains and meats are good sources of chromium, while fruits, vegetables, and eggs contain little. Vitamin C appears to enhance chromium absorption, while phytate and antacids may decrease absorption.

We do not know how much *manganese* is required for children or adults, since no problems of manganese deficiency have ever been observed in humans. Vegetables, grains, and organ meats all contain adequate manganese content.

That is not to say that manganese is not important. It is used in several enzyme systems, in forming bone, and in nutrient metabolism, and lack of manganese in animals has caused problems with regard to the bones, ear, and brain, as well as with growth, stillbirths, and sterility. When manganese was eliminated from the diet experimentally, a scaly skin condition developed, and cholesterol levels fell.

Selenium is another nutrient that is only present in trace amounts in the body but appears to have an important role as part of several enzyme systems. Its presence in food is highly dependent on the soil content where the foods are grown and where the animals graze. Although selenium deficiency has mainly been seen in children with severe malnutrition or infection, toxicity can be seen at relatively low levels, with gastrointestinal complaints or hair and nail changes.

Researchers speculate about possible uses for this metal. The reason is that selenium is very similar to vitamin E in its action. In fact, those with adequate selenium seem to require less vitamin E. Both of these nutrients protect the body and its cells from oxidation and peroxidation (the reaction that occurs when hydrogen peroxide is added to anything). Additionally, selenium has an active role in regulating the actions of vitamin C and thyroid hormone. And some studies have begun to explore the possibility that selenium, as a potent antioxidant, might have an effect in preventing cancer or lessening its impact.

Sodium and *chloride* are usually coupled in their consumption as well as in the body. Together they provide the solute (substance) that keeps fluid in the blood vessels and allows it to be filtered by the kidneys. As a result, they regulate hydration and blood pressure so that, in a healthy state, what is consumed closely matches what is lost in sweat and urine. When strenuous physical activity occurs, particularly in a hot climate, excess losses can occur, and the individual has to compensate quickly to avoid dehydration. This is quite different from most other nutritional states, where losses can be replenished at a slower pace.

Since sodium intake is largely related to how food is prepared, the amount of salt in the diet, which often comes from the way the food is prepared or processed, varies widely among various cultures and can cause a problem with fluid retention or high blood pressure, particularly if there is an underlying problem or tendency toward kidney or heart disease. Those problems may begin in childhood, though they may not show up until much later.

For infants and children, the more common situation is dehydration when a baby develops vomiting, diarrhea, or both. Rehydration is required, which is more easily accomplished if vomiting is not part of the picture. As long as the salt and sugar rehydration solutions, such as Pedialyte, are provided in adequate quantities, intravenous therapy is rarely needed, and the infants and children recover quickly without any sodium imbalance.

So while there are sodium RDAs for normal healthy individuals, it is most important to avoid excesses (in order to lower the potential for high blood pressure) and to make sure sodium is adequately provided along with water to prevent and treat dehydration.

While sodium maintains the fluid in the vascular space, *potassium* maintains the fluid volume inside cells; in doing so, potassium allows functions as diverse as signaling between nerves and muscle (including heart) contractions. As a result, one of the most significant signs of a high or low potassium level is its impact on the heart and other muscles, though milder insufficiencies can affect the blood pressure and bone metabolism.

Fortunately, potassium is widely available from fruits (bananas and oranges are rich sources) and root or leafy vegetables. As is the case with almost all other nutrients, the adequate intake for infants is based on the amount in breastmilk, and that becomes the basis for the nutrient concentration in the various infant formulas, modified by the bioavailability of the nutrient in that formula.

Fluoride is incorporated into the enamel of teeth before and after the teeth erupt, strengthening the teeth and preventing cavities across the life span. It similarly promotes bone formation and can bind with calcium there. As a result, it has been added to drinking water (though not to all sterile or bottled waters) and toothpaste. So infants on powdered or concentrated formulas usually receive sufficient amounts. Breastfed infants similarly have little need for fluoride beyond the amount that is transferred from the mother. However, for both bottle- and breastfed infants, a 0.25 milligram supplement is recommended daily after six months of age where the water supply contains less than 0.3 parts per million of fluoride.[21] And that should probably continue until the child has the opportunity to see a dentist (and receive fluoride treatments) at two to three years of age. Excesses should be avoided to prevent pitted and darkened teeth, which can occur with high levels.

SUMMARY

There is no question that these macro- and micronutrients are necessary and their best sources (and functions) are compiled in this chapter's tables. Vitamins and minerals, although only present in small quantities, are obviously important to your baby's nutrition and overall health. The question becomes how much is enough and whether supplementation is necessary. Over the decades, research on iron bioavailability changed the perspective on the requirements for iron, and, more recently, a different understanding of how to assess vitamin D has led to suggestions that more of the vitamin is needed, while the recommendations regarding vitamin C vary widely, depending on which opinions are considered more valid. But for most other vitamins and minerals, little has changed, and the amount your baby needs is sufficient in breastmilk, infant formula, and the solids he will take in during the first year.

As your baby becomes a toddler and his preferences change, a healthy, balanced diet should maintain micronutrient sufficiency. A deficiency of any of these elements is not difficult to manage but important to recognize. Consider whether you or your child fit into any of the high-risk categories. Then examine your diet for its adequacy and consult your doctor or a dietician for help in evaluation. And we will do what we can to keep you updated at www.what2feedyourbaby .com. Reliable resources are available, but do exercise your best judgment, since what your neighbor's aunt read on the Internet may not be the best information. As always, discuss any doubts, comments, or questions with your child's doctor.

16

⤳

Transitioning to Toddlerhood

You watched with wonder and excitement, no doubt, as your baby watched you and responded, while you, in turn, did the same. The small infant who has so enriched your life, while you've enriched his, has grown and gained skills, and now it's hard to believe he's almost not a baby anymore.

If he's a year old, he's probably tripled his birth weight and increased his length by ten inches or so. If he was a preemie, he may have exceeded those parameters and your expectations. While I congratulated you in the first chapters on the new baby in your home, I now applaud you for all you've contributed to your baby and what you may have given up in order to do so. Too often those efforts and sacrifices are assumed as an appropriate trade-off and go unrecognized. To my mind as a pediatrician, they are part of the martyrdom of motherhood and fatherhood, and your efforts and love deserve recognition and gratitude. Gratitude because all that you've done to enrich your child physically and emotionally will benefit him and, through him, the world he'll enter and further enrich.

You've truly nourished and nurtured your baby. Since you're reading this book, you've accepted that responsibility and are making sure that your nutritional decisions are sound. You want to benefit your child and lessen the impact on your budget.

It was relatively simple in those first few months: either you chose to breastfeed and watched your (or his mother's) diet, avoiding foods and substances that might affect your baby, or you were able to select an appropriate formula that had undergone rigorous testing and oversight in order to be available on the store's shelf. Complexity was added when you began to select or make infant foods to expand your baby's diet. The small section of baby foods in the grocery store provided a few choices, and the baby tasted new flavors and supplemented his intake with nutrients his body needs. He began to feed himself with foods he could pick up himself, and within the next few months, he'll test his skills and your patience with a spoon and then a fork.

Wonderful, but guess what: the task has now gotten harder for you. The rest of the grocery store just opened up to you, and so you have to sort through all the products on the various aisles to entice you with their packaging and marketing. Your job is to select nutritionally beneficial foods that, hopefully, will appeal to your baby. Strike that—to your emerging toddler.

Some parents choose the foods they think their children will like and hope they meet their child's nutrient needs, or they supplement with a daily vitamin in case they don't get it quite right; other parents (and since you're reading this book, I think you're one of these) will plan their children's meals based on the child's needs and do what they can to ensure that what they serve appeals. They may still add a vitamin, but if so, it's intentional insurance to supplement the picky toddlers who may be more stringent in their choices than the parents are.

The latter approach makes sense. I have never met a toddler who drives himself to the grocery store or offers his own credit card at the cash register. Nor have I met a toddler or child who drives himself to McDonald's. They may watch television (only occasionally, I hope, with those instances as infrequent as the occasions we celebrate, like birthdays, New Year's, and the Fourth of July), and they may "demand" what they see on the commercials, but remember, parents can exercise a choice in how they respond.

I promise you: you are in charge, at least in the beginning, in toddlerhood. And how you respond will either allow you to continue in that role or cause you to give way to your child's dictates. Not that I am advocating an authoritarian approach. As already stated in chapter 12, that adamancy leads to a greater risk of obesity by first grade.[1] Instead, a high level of sensitivity to your child's emotional and nutritional needs will allow you to guide your child through decisions (yours and his) that should be more effective and satisfying in the long term.

WHAT IF MY CHILD HAD PROBLEMS IN HIS FIRST YEAR?

I hate to say this, but most of those problems will persist, and some may get worse. Reflux usually gets better sometime between 8 and 18 months of age. The babies who are able to keep down solids usually outgrow the condition sooner, but in some babies it will continue on into childhood and adulthood. Underweight children will often return to a normal growth curve with appropriate attention, though the timing is variable, and that often assumes a thorough understanding of the cause of the slower gain. The timing for premature infants to match their peers nutritionally is much better understood. For every month (or four weeks) a baby is premature, it takes a year to catch up and reach a normal growth pattern.

But unfortunately, the same cannot be said for infants with allergies, who may or may not improve and often march forward to other allergies later in life. Nor can it be said for the overweight infant, whose risk of obesity may increase—unless continued attention is focused on the situation, since some of the patterns that contributed to his increased weight may not disappear just because he is now walking and more active (though the increased activity will help to control it). And the constipated infant may actually worsen, depending on his diet.

Fortunately, all of these ongoing problems can be tended to and potentially improved by following many of the same principles that have already been reviewed. And other problems that may arise later—like lactose or gluten intolerance, inadequate school meals, and all the advertising and television time that can lead to unhealthy habits—can also be improved with well-timed, appropriate attention.

However, this book focuses on infants and is not the guide you need. For that reason, a list of resources (books and websites) is provided. Other resources are also available, but please be careful as you peruse the Internet. Just because three children got better after someone metaphorically swung a chicken over their heads doesn't mean that will work for your son or daughter. So use trusted references, like the ones here, or come to our website, www.what2feedyourbaby.com, where we intend to continue to update useful nutrition information for children and their families. I can't promise the humor will be any better, but I can promise you will find worthwhile information to help nourish and nurture your family. I also promise to thank you for raising healthy children and for giving them tools that will help them navigate through the problems that will continue to arise.

Appendix

WORLD HEALTH ORGANIZATION GROWTH CHARTS FOR INFANTS

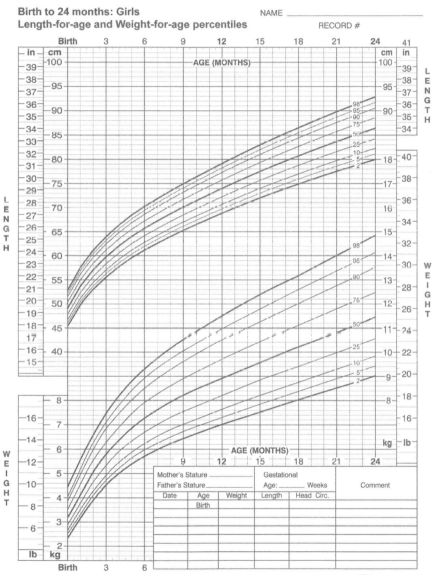

WHO infant female growth chart.

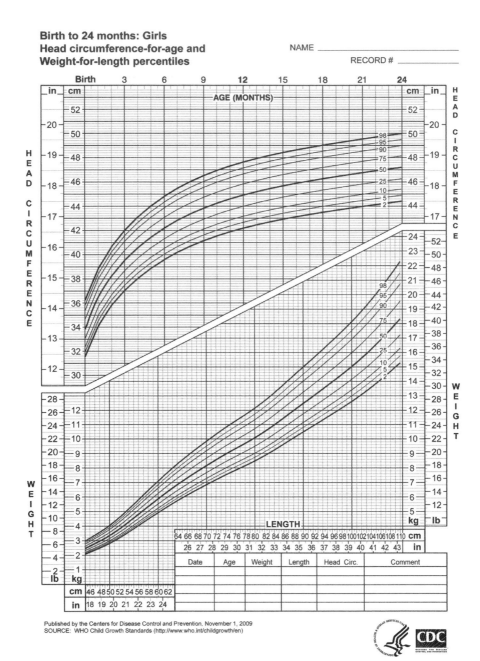

Birth to 24 months: Girls
Head circumference-for-age and
Weight-for-length percentiles

NAME _____

RECORD # _____

Published by the Centers for Disease Control and Prevention, November 1, 2009
SOURCE: WHO Child Growth Standards (http://www.who.int/childgrowth/en)

WHO girls weight-for-length percentiles and head circumference-for-age.

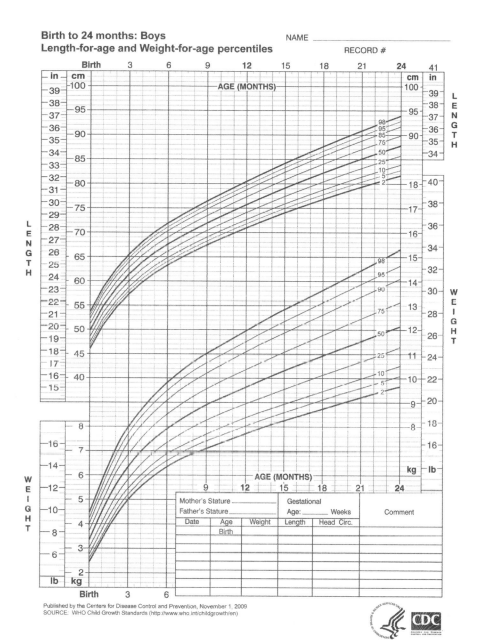

Published by the Centers for Disease Control and Prevention, November 1, 2009
SOURCE: WHO Child Growth Standards (http://www.who.int/childgrowth/en)

WHO infant male growth chart.

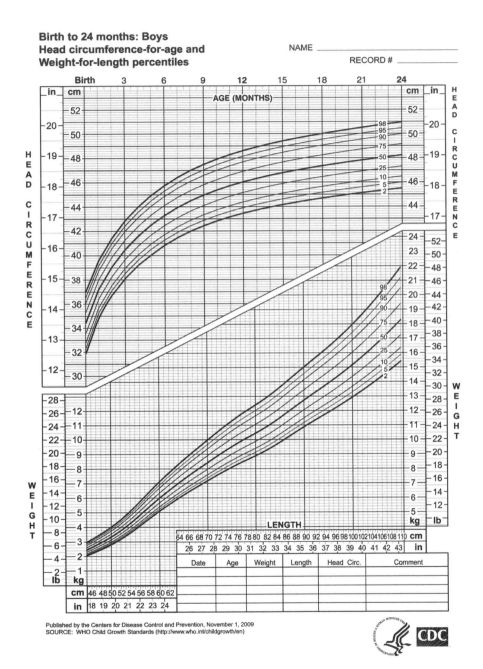

Birth to 24 months: Boys
Head circumference-for-age and
Weight-for-length percentiles

NAME _____

RECORD # _____

WHO boys weight-for-length percentiles and head circumference-for-age.

GROWTH CHART FOR PREMATURE INFANTS

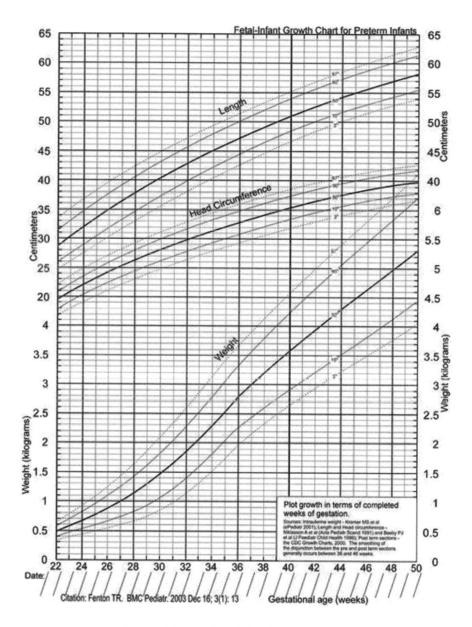

Preterm infant male and female growth chart.

What to Feed Your Baby

GROWTH CHARTS FOR INFANTS AND TODDLERS
WITH DOWN'S SYNDROME

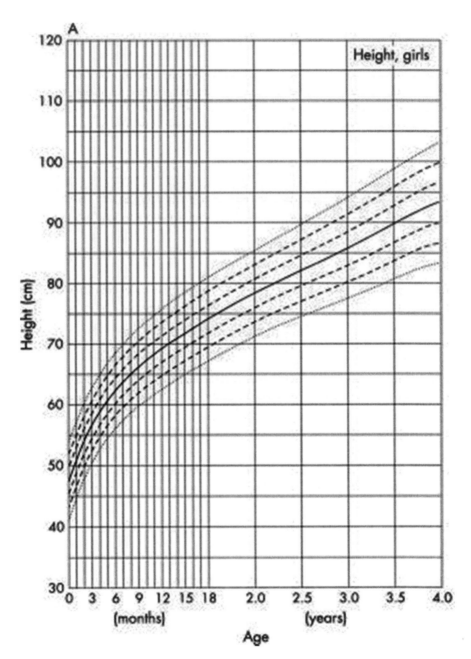

Height of girls with Down's syndrome (0 to 4 years).

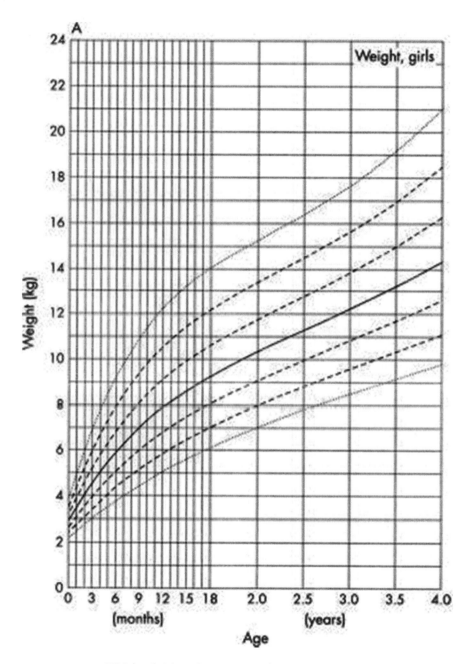

Weight of girls with Down's syndrome (0 to 4 years).

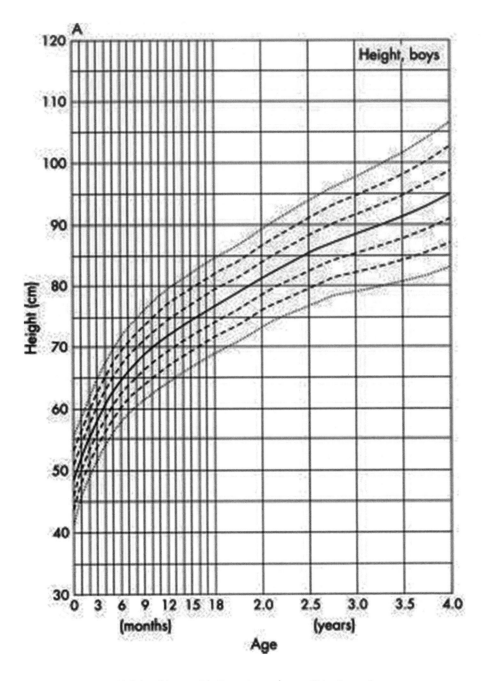

Height of boys with Down's syndrome (0 to 4 years).

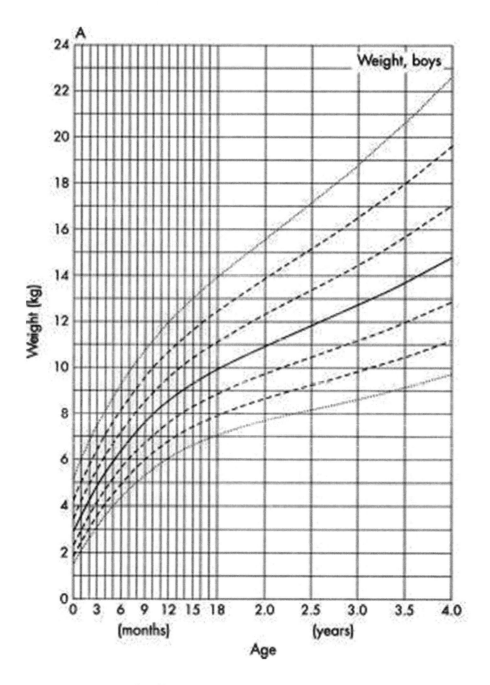

Weight of boys with Down's syndrome (0 to 4 years).

INFANT FORMULA RESOURCE

Table A.1. Part 1: Term Infant

Tier	Formula Category	WIC-Approved Formula[a]	Manufacturer	Composition	Indication/ICD-9[d]
Tier 1	"Routine" cow's milk	Enfamil Lipil Premium	Mead Johnson	20 kcal/fl. oz., whey 60 percent/casein 40 percent, lactose, prebiotics, DHA/ARA	Healthy term infants who are not exclusively breastfed
		Enfamil Lipil Newborn	Mead Johnson	20 kcal/fl. oz., whey 80 percent/casein 20 percent, lactose, prebiotics, DHA/ARA	
		Similac Advance	Abbott	20 kcal/fl. oz., whey 60 percent/casein 40 percent, lactose, prebiotics, DHA/ARA, lutein	
	Rice starch	Enfamil AR	Mead Johnson	20 kcal/fl. oz., whey 20 percent, casein 80 percent, DHA/ARA, lactose, rice starch, maltodextrin, prebiotics	Gastroesophageal reflux disease (GERD)/530.81
		Similac for Spit Up	Abbott	20 kcal/fl. oz., corn syrup solids, DHA/ARA, prebiotics, lutein	
Tier 2	Soy	Gerber Good Start Soy	Nestlé	20 kcal/fl. oz., soy-protein isolate, methionine lactose free, DHA/ARA	Cow's-milk allergy/558.3 Lactose intolerance/271.3 Galactosemia/271.1 Vegetarian/vegan families Parental request
		Enfamil Soy	Mead Johnson	20 kcal/fl. oz., soy-protein isolate, methionine lactose free, DHA/ARA	
		Similac Soy	Abbott	20 kcal/fl. oz., soy-protein isolate, methionine lactose free, DHA/ARA	

Table A.1. Part 1: Term Infant (*continued*)

Tier	Formula Category	WIC-Approved Formula[a]	Manufacturer	Composition	Indication/ICD-9[d]
Tier 3	Partially hydrolyzed whey	Gerber Good Start[b]	Nestlé Nutrition	20 kcal/fl. oz., 100 percent whey protein partially hydrolyzed, lactose, prebiotics, probiotic, DHA/ARA	Infants with family history of allergy Irritability/colic
	Extensively hydrolyzed casein containing MCT oil	Pregestamil	Mead Johnson Nutrition	20 kcal/fl. oz, hypoallergenic lactose free, DHA/ARA	Cow's-milk allergy/558.3 Soy-protein allergy/693.1
	Casein hydrolysate	Nutramigen	Mead Johnson Nutrition	20 kcal/fl. oz , hypoallergenic lactose free, corn syrup solids/modified corn starch, probiotic, DHA/ARA	Malabsorption/579.00[c] Food-protein–induced enterocolitis (FPIES)/558.41
		Similac Expert Care Alimentum	Abbott Nutrition	20 kcal/fl. oz., hypoallergenic whey 70 percent, casein 30 percent lactose free, sucrose and modified tapioca starch, 33 percent MCT, DHA/ARA	
Tier 4	Amino acid elemental	EleCare	Abbott Nutrition	20 kcal/fl. oz., amino acids; lactose-, sucrose-, soy-, and gluten-free; DHA/ARA; hypoallergenic; 33 percent MCT	Short bowel syndrome/ ICD-9 579.3
		Puramino	Mead Johnson Nutrition	20 kcal/fl. oz., 100 percent free amino acids; 5 percent of fat is MCT; DHA/ARA	Necrotizing enterocolitis/ ICD-9 777.50
		Neocate Infant DHA/ARA	Nutricia	20 kcal/fl. oz., DHA/ARA	Eosinophilic esophagitis/ ICD-9 530.13 Severe allergy to cow's milk with failure of Tier 3 formula/ICD-9 558.3 Multiple food-protein intolerance/ICD-9 558.1 Malabsorption/ICD-9 579

Table A.1. Part 2: Premature Infant Formulas

Category	WIC-Approved Formula	Composition	Indication/ICD-9
Human-milk fortifier	Enfamil Human Milk Fortifier Acidified Liquid	Commercially sterile liquid, DHA/ARA, milk and soy ingredients	For breastfed babies who were born prematurely or with a low birth weight Prematurity/low birth weight 765.1
	Similac Human Milk Fortifier (powdered)	Milk and soy ingredients	Breastfed babies with a low birth weight *Powdered formulas are not sterile and should not be fed to premature infants or infants who might have immune problems unless directed and supervised by a physician.* Low birth weight 765.1
	Gerber Good Start Premature 24	100 percent whey protein partially hydrolyzed, corn maltodextrin, lactose, DHA/ARA, MCT oil, increased calcium, phosphorus, and vitamin D	Very low-birth-weight infants with increased protein requirements Prematurity 765.1 Very low birth weight V21.3
Predischarge premature formulas (24 cal.)	Gerber Good Start Premature 24 High Protein	100 percent whey protein partially hydrolyzed, protein-to-energy ratio of 3.6g/100 kcal, DHA/ARA, MCT oil, corn maltodextrin, lactose, increased calcium, phosphorus, and vitamin D	Prematurity/low birth weight 765.1
	Enfamil Premature 24 with Iron	Corn syrup solids, MCT oil, lactose, increased calcium, phosphorus and vitamin D, DHA/ARA	Prematurity/low birth weight 765.1
	Similac Special Care 24	Corn syrup solids, MCTs, lactose, lutein, DHA/ARA	Prematurity/low birth weight 765.1

Table A.1. Part 2: Premature Infant Formulas (*continued*)

Category	WIC-Approved Formula	Composition	Indication/ICD-9
Postdischarge transitional formulas (22 cal.)	Gerber Good Start Nourish	100 percent whey protein partially hydrolyzed. protein, calcium, phosphorus, DHA/ARA, lactose, corn maltodextrin, MCT oil	Prematurity/low birth weight 765.1
	Enfamil EnfaCare	2.8g protein/100 cal., DHA/ARA, MCT oil, corn syrup solids, lactose, increased calcium and phosphorus	Prematurity/low birth weight 765.1
	Similac Expert Care Neosure	3g protein/100 cal., MCT oil, lutein, and DHA, corn syrup solids, lactose	Prematurity/low birth weight 765.1
Postdischarge formulas (20 cal.)	Enfamil Premature 20 with Iron	3g protein/100 cal., levels of calcium, phosphorus, and vitamin D, corn syrup solids, MCTs, lactose	Prematurity/low birth weight 765.1
	Similac Special Care 20	2.8g protein/100 cal. and ratio (1.8:1) DHA and ARA, corn syrup solids, MCTs, lactose	Prematurity/low birth weight 765.1

[a]These are formulas approved by the Georgia WIC Program. Store brands similar to these products are available.

[b]Several varieties of this formula are available containing different probiotics (please see text).

[c]Malabsorption is not an indication for Nurtramigen.

[d]ICD-9 codes, where available, are provided for healthcare workers to assist their efforts in prescribing these formulas

Source: Adapted from S. A. Cohen and K. Crane, *An Evidence-Based, Cost-Sensitive infant Formula Algorithm for the Infant on Georgia's WIC.* Georgia Department of Public Health, American Academy of Pediatrics Georgia Chapter, Georgia WIC. Special Edition Newsletter, 2013.

Table A.2. Milk Alternative Comparison Chart

Brand	Various	Meyenberg	Silk Soy Milk	Silk Soy Milk	Silk Soy Milk	Silk Soy Milk	Silk Soy Milk
Product	Whole Cow's Milk	Whole Goat's Milk	Plain	Vanilla	Very Vanilla	Chocolate	Vanilla + Fiber
Serving size	8 fl. oz.	8 fl. oz.	8 fl. oz.	8 fl. oz.	8 fl. oz.	8 fl. oz.	8 fl. oz.
Nutrients per serving							
Calories	150	142	100	100	130	140	100
Fat	8g	7.2g	4g	3.5g	4g	3.5g	3.5g
Protein	8g	8.45g	7g	6g	6g	5g	6g
Cholesterol	33 mg	25.2 mg	0 mg	0 mg	0 mg	0 mg	0 mg
Fiber	0g	0g	1g	1g	1g	2g	5g
Calcium	292 mg	307 mg	300 mg	300 mg	350 mg	300 mg	300 mg
Vitamin D	100 IU	100 IU	60 IU	60 IU	60 IU	60 IU	60 IU
Notes	18.8 cal./oz.	17.8 cal./oz.; most kids with milk-protein allergy will not tolerate	12.5 cal./oz.; lactose- and dairy-free; low fat	12.5 cal./oz.; lactose- and dairy-free; low fat	16.3 cal./oz.; lactose- and dairy-free; low fat	17.5 cal./oz.; lactose- and dairy-free; low fat	17.5 cal./oz.; lactose- and dairy-free; low fat

Table A.2. Milk Alternative Comparison Chart (continued)

Brand	Rice Dream Rice Drink	Rice Dream Rice Drink	Rice Dream Rice Drink	Rice Dream Rice Drink	Rice Dream Rice Drink	Rice Dream Rice Supreme	Rice Dream Horchatta
Product	Enriched Original	Enriched Vanilla	Enriched Chocolate	Vanilla	Carob	Vanilla Hazelnut	N/A
Serving size	8 fl. oz.	8 fl. oz.	8 fl. oz.	8 f. oz.	8 fl. oz.	8 fl. oz.	8 fl. oz.
Nutrients per serving							
Calories	120	130	160	130	150	140	130
Fat	2.5g	2.5g	3g	2.5g	2.5g	3g	4g
Protein	1g	1g	2g	1g	1g	2g	7g
Cholesterol	0 mg	0 mg	0 mg	0 mg	0 mg	0 mg	0 mg
Fiber	0g	0g	<1g	0g	<1g	<1g	2g
Calcium	300 mg	300 mg	300 mg	20 mg	0 mg	300 mg	40 mg
Vitamin D	50 IU	50 IU	50 IU	0 IU	0 IU	50 IU	0 IU
Notes	15 cal./oz.; very low protein and fat; lactose- and soy-free	16.3 cal./oz.; very low protein and fat; lactose- and soy-free	20 cal./oz.; very low protein and fat; lactose- and soy-free	15 cal./oz.; very low protein and fat; lactose- and soy-free	18.75 cal./oz.; very low protein and fat; lactose-, dairy-, and soy-free; not enriched!	17.5 cal./oz.; very low protein and fat; lactose-, dairy-, and soy-free; not enriched!	16.3 cal./oz.; lactose-, dairy-, and soy-free; not enriched!

232

What to Feed Your Baby

Table A.2. Milk Alternative Comparison Chart (*continued*)

Brand	Kidz Dream Smoothie	Kidz Dream Smoothie	Darifree Potato Milk	Darifree Potato Milk	Blue Diamond Almond Breeze	Blue Diamond Almond Breeze	Blue Diamond Almond Breeze
Product	Orange Cream	Berry Blast	Original	Chocolate	Original	Vanilla	Chocolate
Serving size	1 container	1 container	8 fl. oz.	8 fl. oz.	8 fl. oz.	8 fl. oz.	8 fl. oz.
Nutrients per serving							
Calories	120	100	70	70	60	90	120
Fat	2g	2g	0g	0g	2.5g	2.5g	3g
Protein	4g	4g	0g	0g	1g	1g	2g
Cholesterol	0 mg	0 mg	0 mg	0 mg	0 mg	0 mg	0 mg
Fiber	<1g	1g	0g	1g	1g	1g	1g
Calcium	350 mg	350 mg	300 mg	300 mg	200 mg	200 mg	200 mg
Vitamin D	60 IU	60 IU	30 IU	30 IU	50 IU	50 IU	50 IU
Notes	Fortified blend of fruit juice and soy milk; lactose- and dairy-free; enriched	Fortified blend of fruit juice and soy milk; lactose- and dairy-free; enriched	8.8 cal./oz.; very low calorie with no fat or protein; a powder you mix with water; lactose-, dairy-, soy-, and gluten-free	8.8 cal./oz.; very low calorie with no fat or protein; a powder you mix with water; lactose-, dairy-, soy-, and gluten-free	7.5 cal./oz.; very low calorie, protein, and fat; dairy-, soy-, and gluten-free	11.3 cal./oz.; very low calorie, protein, and fat; dairy-, soy-, and gluten-free	15 cal./oz.; very low calorie, protein, and fat; dairy-, soy-, and gluten-free

Table A.2. Milk Alternative Comparison Chart (*continued*)

Brand	Living Harvest Hemp Milk	Living Harvest Hemp Milk	Living Harvest Hemp Milk	So Delicious Coconut Milk	So Delicious Coconut Milk	So Delicious Coconut Milk	Pacific Oat Milk
Product	Original	Vanilla	Chocolate	Original	Unsweetened	Chocolate	Original
Serving size	8 fl. oz.	8 fl. oz.	8 fl. oz.	8 fl. oz.	8 fl. oz.	8 fl. oz.	8 fl. oz.
Nutrients per serving							
Calories	130	130	150	80	50	90	130
Fat	3g	3g	5g	5g	5g	5g	2.5g
Protein	4g	4g	4g	1g	1g	1g	4g
Cholesterol	0g	0g	0g	0g	0g	0g	0g
Fiber	1g	1g	1g	0g	0g	0g	2g
Calcium	460 mg	460 mg	460 mg	100 mg	100 mg	100 mg	350 mg
Vitamin D	50 IU	50 IU	50 IU	60 IU	60 IU	60 IU	50 IU
Notes	16.3 cal./oz.; low in protein and fat; increased omega-3 and -6 fatty acids; dairy-, soy-, and gluten-free	16.3 cal./oz.; low in protein and fat; increased omega-3 and -6 fatty acids; dairy-, soy-, and gluten-free	18.8 cal./oz.; low in protein and fat; increased omega-3 and -6 fatty acids; dairy-, soy-, and gluten-free	10 cal./oz.; dairy-, lactose-, soy-, and gluten-free; rich in medium-chain fatty acids	6.25 cal./oz.; dairy-, lactose-, soy-, and gluten-free; rich in medium-chain fatty acids	11.3 cal./oz.; dairy-, lactose-, soy-, and gluten-free; rich in medium-chain fatty acids	16.3 cal./oz.; dairy-, lactose-, and soy-free

Source: Bailey Koch, RD, CSP, www.nutrition4kids.com.

Notes

CHAPTER 1: FIRST DECISIONS

1. E. E. Birch et al., "A Randomized Control Trial of Early Dietary Supply of Long-Chained Polyunsaturated Fatty Acids and Mental Development in Term Infants," *Developmental Medicine & Child Neurology* 42, no. 3 (2000): 174–81.

2. S. A. Cohen, *Start Right: Feeding Babies and Young Children* (London: Sidgewick & Jackson, 1983).

3. J. Dobbing and J. Sands, "Quantitative Growth and Development of Human Brain," *Archives of Diseases in Childhood* 48 (1973): 757–67.

4. Babies and children are referred to with the masculine pronoun in *What to Feed Your Baby* in order to ease reading, since often I speak about breastfeeding mothers using the feminine pronoun. In that same vein, I often write about parents as mothers, not to ignore the fathers but to simplify reading.

5. In *What to Feed Your Baby*, I often refer to pediatricians as the usual providers for children. This is meant to simplify the reading and is not meant to diminish the important role that many family physicians, physicians assistants, and nurse practitioners have in the care of children in various communities.

6. V. Oliveria, E. Frazão, and D. Smallwood, *The Infant Formula Market: Consequences of a Change in the WIC Contract Brand*, ERR-124 (Washington, DC: US Department of Agriculture, Economic Research Service, 2011).

7. Personal communication, T. Stormant, Georgia WIC Program with K. Crane, 2012.

CHAPTER 2: BACK TO THE BREAST

1. US Department of Health and Human Services, *The Surgeon General's Call to Action to Support Breastfeeding* (Washington, DC: US Department of Health and Human Services, Office of the Surgeon General, 2011).

2. National Immunization Survey, Center for Disease Control and Prevention, US Department of Health and Human Services, 2003.

3. S. A. Cohen, *Healthy Babies, Happy Kids: A Commonsense Guide to Nutrition for the Growing Years* (New York: Delilah Books, 1982).

4. American Academy of Pediatrics and the American College of Obstetricians and Gynecologists, *Breastfeeding Handbook for Physicians* (Washington, DC: American Academy of Pediatrics and the American College of Obstetricians and Gynecologists, 2006).

5. World Health Organization, "Breastfeeding Key to Saving Children's Lives," press release, July 30, 2010, http://www.who.int/mediacentre/news/notes/2010/breastfeeding_20100730/en.

6. J. Dobbing and J. Sands, "Quantitative Growth and Development of Human Brain," *Archives of Diseases in Childhood* 48 (1973): 757–67.

7. US Department of Health and Services, *Healthy People 2020*, Office of Disease Prevention and Health Promotion, Publication No. B0132, November 2010, available at http://www.healthypeople.gov/2020/topicsobjectives2020/objectiveslist.aspx?topicId=26 (accessed October 11, 2012).

8. US Department of Health and Health Services, *Healthy People 2010. With Understanding and Improving Health and Objectives for Improving Health*, 2nd ed. (Washington, DC: US Government Printing Office, 2000).

9. US Department of Health and Human Services, *The Surgeon General's Call to Action to Support Breastfeeding* (Washington, DC: US Department of Health and Human Services, Office of the Surgeon General, 2011).

10. US Department of Health and Human Services, Office of Women's Health, *Your Guide to Breastfeeding* (Washington, DC: US Government Printing Office, 2011).

11. CDC, "Hospital Support for Breastfeeding," *Vital Signs*, August 2011, http://www.cdc.gov/vitalsigns/breastfeeding.

12. American Academy of Pediatrics, "Breastfeeding and the Use of Human Milk," *Pediatrics* 129 (2012): e827–e841.

13. American Academy of Family Physicians, "Breastfeeding (Policy Statement)," 2012, http://www.aafp.org/online/en/home/policy/policies/b/breastfeedingpolicy.html (accessed September 30, 2012).

14. American Dietetic Association, "Position of the American Dietetic Association: Promoting and Supporting Breastfeeding," *Journal of the American Dietetic Association* 109 (2009): 1926–42.

15. American Public Health Association, "A Call to Action on Breastfeeding: A Fundamental Public Health Issue," Policy Number 200714, November 6, 2007, www.apha.org/advocacy/policy/policysearch/default.htm?id=1360 (accessed September 30, 2012).

16. WHO-UNICEF, "Global Policy on Infant and Young Child Feeding," 2003, www.unicef.org/nutrition/index_breastfeeding.html (accessed September 30, 2012).

17. R. J. Schandler, ed., *Breastfeeding Handbook for Physicians* (Elk Grove Village, IL: American Academy of Pediatrics and the American College of Obstetricians and Gynecologists, 2006), 19–36.

18. R. K. Chandra, "Food Hypersensitivity and Allergic Diseases," *European Journal of Clinical Nutrition* 56 (Suppl. 3) (2002): S54–S56.

19. This is my own summation of the data on intestinal barrier development, with much of that work done by Dr. Allan Walker's laboratories. A particularly good article

that Dr. Walker often cites is E. J. Eastham et al., "Antigenicity of Infant Formulas: Role of Immature Intestine on Protein Permeability," *Journal of Pediatrics* 93 (1978): 561–64.

20. CDC, "Hospital Support for Breastfeeding."

21. E. E. Birch et al., "Visual Acuity and Cognitive Outcomes at 4 Years of Age in a Double-Blind, Randomized Trial of Long-Chain Polyunsaturated Fatty Acid–Supplemented Formula," *Early Human Development Journal* 83 (2007): 279–84.

22. E. E. Birch et al., "Visual Maturation of Term Infants Fed Long-Chain Polyunsaturated Fatty Acid–Supplemented or Controlled Formula for 12 Mo.," *American Journal of Clinical Nutrition* 81 (2005): 871–79.

23. L. J. Horwood and D. M. Furgusson, "Breastfeeding and Later Cognitive and Academic Outcomes," *Pediatrics* 101 (1998): e9.

24. E. L. Mortensen et al., "The Association between Duration of Breastfeeding and Adult Intelligence," *Journal of the American Medical Association* 287 (2002): 2365–71.

25. E. E. Birch et al., "Visual Acuity and the Essentiality of Docosahexaenoic Acid and Arachidonic Acid in the Diet of Term Infants," *Pediatric Research* 44 (1998): 201–9.

26. A. Qawassami, "Meta-analysis of Long-Chain Polyunsaturated Fatty Acid Supplementation of Formula and Infant Cognition," *Pediatrics* 129 (2012): 1141–49.

27. Whole Food Catalog, at http://wholefoodcatalog.info (accessed July 23, 2012).

28. "What You Need to Know about Mercury in Fish and Shellfish," EPA and FDA advisory, EPA, http://water.epa.gov/scitech/swguidance/fishshellfish/outreach/advice_index.cfm (accessed July 23, 2012).

29. T. Hale, *Medications and Mother's Milk*, 14th ed. (Amarillo, TX: Hale Publishing, 2010).

30. US Breastfeeding Committee, "Workplace Accommodations to Support and Protect Breastfeeding 2010," www.usbreastfeeding.org (accessed December 28, 2012).

CHAPTER 3: BREASTFEEDING IS ALMOST AS SIMPLE AS IT LOOKS

1. A. S. Matthiesen et al., "Postpartum Maternal Oxytocin Release by Newborns: Effects of Infant Hand Massage and Sucking," *Birth* 28 (2001): 13–19.

2. La Leche League USA, at http://www.lllusa.org (accessed July 30, 2012).

3. S. Cohen, *Healthy Babies, Happy Kids: A Commonsense Guide to Nutrition for the Growing Years* (New York: Delilah Books, 1982), 23. I have attempted to find the study that I originally referenced to reconfirm this, since breastfeeding texts do not approach this in the same way; I have also looked for studies refuting this, but I have been unable to find either.

4. Stanford School of Medicine, "Hand Expression of Breastmilk," 2012, http://newborns.stanford.edu/Breastfeeding/HandExpression.html.

5. Ameda, "Your Baby Knows How to Latch On," 2010, http://www.ameda.com/resources/video.

6. K. M. Berchelmann, "Have You Had Trouble Breastfeeding?," St. Louis Children's Hospital, 2012, http://www.stlouischildrens.org/articles/wellness/have-you-had-trouble-breastfeeding (accessed July 24, 2012).

7. A wonderful term I adopted from Susan Boekel, RD, a lactation consultant at Children's Healthcare of Atlanta.

8. H.R. Res. 3590, Section 4207, Session March 2010.

9. L. M. Wolfe, "Activities to Burn 700 Calories a Day," 2011, http://www.livestrong .com/article/517013-activities-to-burn-700-calories-a-day (accessed July 13, 2012).

10. US Department of Health and Human Services, Office of Women's Health, *Your Guide to Breastfeeding* (Washington, DC: US Government Printing Office, 2011).

11. Institute of Medicine, National Academy of Sciences, "Dietary Reference and Intake Tables," 2012, http://www.iom.edu/Activities/Nutrition/SummaryDRIs/DRI-Tables.aspx.

12. S. Cohen, "Blastfax: New AAP Vitamin D Recommendation," American Academy of Pediatrics, 2008.

13. CDC, "Hospital Support for Breastfeeding," *Vital Signs*, August 2011, http://www .cdc.gov/vitalsigns/breastfeeding.

14. C. X. Zhao et al., "[Effects of Nonnutritive Sucking on Gastric Emptying and Gastroesophageal Reflux in Premature Infants (in Chinese)]," *Zhonghua Er Ke Za Zhi* 42, no. 10 (2004): 772–76.

CHAPTER 4: IF YOU CHOOSE TO USE A BOTTLE

1. P. C. Jeans and W. M. Marriott, *Infant Nutrition*, 4th ed. (St. Louis: C. V. Mosby, 1947), 178.

2. L. E. Holt Jr. and R. McIntosh, *Holt's Diseases of Infancy and Childhood*, 11th ed. (New York: Appleton-Century, 1940), 188.

3. Quoted in S. Cohen, *Healthy Babies, Happy Kids: A Commonsense Guide to Nutrition for the Growing Years* (New York: Delilah Books, 1982), 13. Unhappily, I have been unable to find that quote again.

4. E. E. Stevens, T. E. Patrick, and R. Pickler, "A History of Infant Feeding," *Journal of Perinatal Education* 18 (2009): 32–39.

5. S. Cohen, *Healthy Babies, Happy Kids: A Commonsense Guide to Nutrition for the Growing Years* (New York: Delilah Books, 1982).

6. A. Lucas et al., "Breast vs Bottle: Endocrine Responses Are Different with Formula Feeding," *Lancet* 315 (1980): 1267–69.

7. N. Stetler et al., "Rapid Weight Gain during Infancy and Obesity in Young Adulthood in a Cohort of African Americans," *American Journal of Clinical Nutrition* 77 (2003): 1374–78.

8. N. Karaolis-Danckert et al., "How Early Dietary Factors Modify the Effect of Rapid Weight Gain in Infancy on Subsequent Body-Composition Development in Term Children Whose Birth Weight Was Appropriate for Gestational Age," *American Journal of Clinical Nutrition* 86 (2007): 1700–1708.

9. J. Trabulsi et al., "Effect of an α-Lactalbumin-Enriched Infant Formula with Lower Protein on Growth," *European Journal of Clinical Nutrition* 65 (2011): 167–74.

10. Cohen, *Healthy Babies, Happy Kids*, 12–14.

11. US Department of Health and Human Services, Office of Women's Health, *Your Guide to Breastfeeding* (Washington, DC: US Government Printing Office, 2011).

12. CDC, "Hospital Support for Breastfeeding," *Vital Signs*, August 2011, http://www.cdc.gov/vitalsigns/breastfeeding.

13. World Health Organization, "Breastfeeding," 2012, http://www.who.int/topics/breastfeeding/en.

14. AllianceSUD, "Babymilk: Protest against Nestle in Laos," June 21, 2011, http://www.alliancesud.ch/en/policy/other/babymilk-protest-against-nestle-in-laos (accessed July 26, 2012).

15. V. Oliveria, E. Frazão, and D. Smallwood, *The Infant Formula Market: Consequences of a Change in the WIC Contract Brand,* ERR-124 (Washington, DC: US Department of Agriculture, Economic Research Service, 2011), quoting 2007 statistics.

16. L. Bode, "Recent Advances on Structure, Metabolism, and Function of Human Milk Oligosaccharides," *Journal of Nutrition* 136 (2006): 1227–30.

17. ISAPP, "FDA Update, ISAPP Meeting, June 26, 2007," http://www.isapp.net/docs/13%20-%20sanders.pdf (accessed July 26, 2012).

18. E. N. Baker and H. M. Baker, "Molecular Structure, Binding Properties and Dynamics of Lactoferrin," *Cellular and Molecular Life Sciences* 62 (2005): 2531–39.

19. E. E. Birch et al., "The Impact of Early Nutrition on Incidence of Allergic Manifestations and Common Respiratory Illnesses in Children," *Journal of Pediatrics* 156 (2010): 902–6.

20. A. Qawassami, "Meta-analysis of Long-Chain Polyunsaturated Fatty Acid Supplementation of Formula and Infant Cognition," *Pediatrics* 129 (2012): 1141–49; J. Colombos and S. E. Carlson, "Is the Measure the Message? The BSID and Nutritional Interventions," *Pediatrics* 129 (2012): 1166–67; S. J. Meldrum et al., "Effects of High-Dose Fish Oil Supplementation during Early Infancy on Neurodevelopment and Language: A Randomised Controlled Trial," *British Journal of Nutrition* 108 (2012): 1443–54.

21. N. Auestad et al., "Growth and Development in Term Infants Fed Long-Chain Polyunsaturated Fatty Acids: A Double-Masked, Randomized, Parallel, Prospective, Multivariate Study," *Pediatrics* 106 (2001): 372–81.

22. E. E. Birch et al., "Visual Acuity and the Essentiality of Docosahexaenoic Acid and Arachidonic Acid in the Diet of Term Infants," *Pediatric Research* 44 (1998): 201–9.

23. C. Barber, vice president of regulatory, medical, and clinical affairs, Perrigo Nutritionals, personal communication, October 17, 2012.

24. Common Dreams, "Group Exposes Practice of Adding Synthetic Preservatives to 'Organic' Baby Formula: Cornucopia Institute Files Legal Complaint against Manufacturers," August 9, 2012, https://www.commondreams.org/headline/2012/08/09-1 (accessed October 26, 2012).

25. C. L. Wagner and F. R. Greer, American Academy of Pediatrics, Section on Breastfeeding and Committee on Nutrition, "Prevention of Rickets and Vitamin D Deficiency in Infants, Children, and Adolescents," *Pediatrics* 122, no. 5 (2008): 1142–52.

26. S. J. Fomon, *Infant Nutrition*, 2nd ed. (Philadelphia: W. B. Saunders, 1974).

27. L. Szabo, "Europe Votes to Ban Chemical from Baby Bottles," *USA Today*, November 29, 2010, 1.

28. US Food and Drug Administration Public Health Focus, "Bisphenol A (BPA): Use in Food Contact Application: Update on Bisphenol A (BPA) for Use in Food Contact Applications," January 2010, www.FDA.gov (accessed July 28, 2012).

CHAPTER 5: SPECIALTY FORMULAS
FOR BABIES WITH PROBLEMS

1. S. A. Cohen and K. Crane, "An Evidence-Based, Cost-Sensitive Infant Formula Algorithm for the Infant on Georgia's WIC," Georgia Department of Public Health, American Academy of Pediatrics Georgia Chapter, Georgia WIC, Special Edition Newsletter, 2013.

2. Cynthia Barber, PhD, vice president of regulatory, medical, and clinical affairs, Perrigo Nutritionals, personal communication, October 17, 2012.

3. B. L. Strom et al., "Exposure to Soy-Based Formula in Infancy and Endocrinological and Reproductive Outcomes in Young Adulthood," *Journal of the American Medical Association* 286 (2001): 807–14.

4. A. L. McCartney and G. R. Gibson, "The Normal Microbiota of the Human Gastrointestinal Tract: History of Analysis, Succession, and Dietary Influences," in *Gastrointestinal Microbiology*, ed. A. Ouwehand and E. Vaughan (New York: Taylor and Francis Group, 2006), 51–73.

CHAPTER 6: GASTROESOPHAGEAL REFLUX

1. "The Seven Ages of Man," Jaques's speech, in William Shakespeare, *As You Like It*, II:vii.

2. P. M. Sherman et al., "A Global Evidence-Based Consensus on the Definition of Gastroesophageal Reflux Disease in the Pediatric Population," *American Journal of Gastroenterology* 104 (2009): 1278–95.

3. American Academy of Pediatrics, "AAP Expands Guidelines for Infant Sleep Safety and SIDS Risk Reduction," HealtyChildren.org, October 18, 2011, http://www.aap.org/en-us/about-the-aap/aap-press-room/pages/AAP-Expands-Guidelines-for-Infant-Sleep-Safety-and-SIDS-Risk-Reduction.aspx?nfstatus=401&nftoken=00000000-0000-0000-0000-000000000000&nfstatusdescription=ERROR%3a+No+local+token (accessed July 28, 2012).

4. S. A. Cohen and K. Crane, "An Evidence-Based, Cost-Sensitive Infant Formula Algorithm for the Infant on Georgia's WIC," Georgia Department of Public Health, American Academy of Pediatrics Georgia Chapter, Georgia WIC, Special Edition Newsletter, 2013.

5. B. D. Gold, "Epidemiology and Management of Gastro-Esophageal Reflux in Children," *Alimentary Pharmacology & Therapeutics* 19 (Suppl. 1) (2004): 22–27.

6. A. J. Martin et al., "Natural History and Familial Relationships of Infant Spilling to 9 Years of Age," *Pediatrics* 109 (2002): 1061–67.

CHAPTER 7: COLIC AND FUSSINESS

1. P. Zwart, M. G. Vellema-Goud, and P. L. Brand, "Characteristics of Infants Admitted to Hospital for Persistent Colic, and Comparison with Healthy Infants," *Acta Paediatrica* 96 (2007): 401–5.

2. P. Coccorullo et al., "*Lactobacillus reuteri* (DSM 17938) in Infants with Functional Chronic Constipation: A Double-Blind, Randomized, Placebo-Controlled Study," *Journal of Pediatrics* 157 (2010): 598–602.

3. F. Savino et al., "*Lactobacillus reuteri* (American Type Culture Collection Strain 55730) versus Simethicone in the Treatment of Infantile Colic: A Prospective Randomized Study," *Pediatrics* 119 (2007): e124–e130.

CHAPTER 8: POOPING PROBLEMS

1. S. A. Cohen, *Healthy Babies, Happy Kids: A Commonsense Guide to Nutrition for the Growing Years* (New York: Delilah Books, 1982).

CHAPTER 9: ARE ALLERGIES EVERYWHERE?

1. J. Bousquer and N. I. Kjellman, "Predictive Value of Tests in Childhood Allergy," *Journal of Allergy and Clinical Immunology* 78 (1986): 1019–22.
2. S. Halken and A. Host, "The Lessons of Noninterventional and Interventional Prospective Studies on the Development of Atopic Disease during Childhood," *Allergy* 55 (2000): 793–802.
3. L. Seidu, personal communication, October 13, 2012; G. J. Rennick, E. Moore, and D. C. Orchard, "Skin Prick Testing to Food Allergens in Breastfed Young Infants with Moderate to Severe Atopic Dermatitis," *Australasian Journal of Dermatology* 47, no. 1 (February 2006): 41–45.
4. R. L. Bergmann et al., "Predictability of Early Atopy by Cord Blood-IgE and Parental History," *Clinical & Experimental Allergy* 27, no. 7 (July 1997): 752–60.
5. B. P. Vickery, S. Chin, and A. W. Burke, "Pathophysiology of Food Allergy," *Pediatric Clinics of North America* 58 (2011): 363–76.
6. American Academy of Pediatrics, Committee on Nutrition: J. Bhatia and F. R. Greer, "Use of Soy Protein-Based Formulas in Infant Feeding," *Pediatrics* 121, no. 5 (May 2008): 1062–68.
7. S. Koletzko et al., "Diagnostic Approach and Management of Cow's Milk Protein Allergy in Infants and Children: ESPGHAN GI Committee Practical Guidelines," *Journal of Pediatric Gastroenterology and Nutrition* 55 (2012): 221–29.
8. American Academy of Pediatrics, Section on Breastfeeding, "Breastfeeding and the Use of Human Milk," *Pediatrics* 129 (2012): e827–e841.
9. E. E. Birch et al., "The Impact of Early Nutrition on Incidence of Allergic Manifestations and Common Respiratory Illnesses in Children," *Journal of Pediatrics* 156 (2010): 902–6.
10. A. von Berg et al., "The Effect of Hydrolyzed Cow's Milk Formula for Allergy Prevention in the First Year of Life: The German Infant Nutritional Intervention Study, a Randomized Double-Blind Trial," *Journal of Allergy and Clinical Immunology* 111 (2003): 533–40.

CHAPTER 10: UNDERWEIGHT OR UNDERGROWN

1. S. A. Cohen, *Healthy Babies, Happy Kids: A Commonsense Guide to Nutrition for the Growing Years* (New York: Delilah Books, 1982).
2. M. Winick, "Nutrition and Prenatal Growth," in *The Underweight Infant, Child, and Adolescent*, ed. S. A. Cohen (Norwalk, CT: Appleton-Century-Crofts, 1986), 51–56.

3. Centers for Disease Control and Prevention, National Center for Health Statistics, "WHO Growth Standards Are Recommended for Use in the U.S. for Infants and Children 0 to 2 Years of Age," CDC, September 9, 2010, http://www.cdc.gov/growthcharts/who_charts.htm (accessed July 29, 2012).

4. Growth charts for Down Syndrome are included in the appendix. However, there is controversy regarding former versions of the cerebral palsy growth charts and the newer iterations, which also account for the degree of disability but do not begin until two years of age and therefore are not included here. They can be found at J. Brooks, S. Day, R. Shavelle, and D. Strauss, "Low Weight, Morbidity, and Mortality in Children with Cerebral Palsy: New Clinical Growth Charts," *Pediatrics* (2011): 128, e299.

5. Your pediatrician will often measure your baby's head circumference as well, which is an indicator of brain growth. While head and brain growth can be affected as a late stage of malnutrition, they can also be affected by numerous other factors. As a result, they are not the focus of our attention here (but they are included in the appendix, so you can use them to track your pediatrician's measurements).

6. I. J. Griffin and R. J. Cooke, "Development of Whole Body Adiposity in Preterm Infants," *Early Human Development Journal* 88 (Suppl. 1) (2012): S19–S24.

CHAPTER 11: THE PREMATURE INFANT

1. ESPGHAN Committee on Nutrition: P. J. Aggett et al., "Feeding Preterm Infants after Hospital Discharge: A Commentary by the ESPGHAN Committee on Nutrition," *Journal of Pediatric Gastroenterology and Nutrition* 42 (2006): 596–603.

2. R. A. Ehrenkranz et al., "Growth in the Neonatal Intensive Care Unit Influences Neurodevelopmental and Growth Outcomes of Extremely Low Birth Weight Infants," *Pediatrics* 115 (2006): 1253–61.

3. E. E. Ziegler, "Meeting the Nutritional Needs of the Low-Birth-Weight Infant," *Annals of Nutrition and Metabolism* 58 (Suppl. 1) (2011): 8–18. E-published June 21, 2011.

4. R. S. Cohen and K. R. McCallie, "Feeding Premature Infants: Why, When, and What to Add to Human Milk," *Journal of Parenteral and Enteral Nutrition* 36 (Suppl. 1) (2012): 20S–24S.

5. B. E. Stephens et al., "First-Week Protein and Energy Intakes Are Associated with 18-Month Developmental Outcomes in Extremely Low Birth Weight Infants," *Pediatrics* 104 (2009): 1337–43.

6. B. Koletzko et al., "Long Chain Polyunsaturated Fatty Acids (LC-PUFA) and Perinatal Development," *Acta Paediatrica* 90 (2001): 460–64.

7. Food and Agricultural Organization/World Health Organization Joint Expert Consultation, "Lipids in Early Development," *FAO Food and Nutrition Paper* 57 (1994): 49–55.

8. M. V. Dhobale et al., "Reduced Levels of Placental Long Chain Polyunsaturated Fatty Acids in Preterm Deliveries," *Prostaglandins, Leukotrienes and Essential Fatty Acids* 85, no. 3–4 (September–October 2011): 149–53.

9. C. J. Valentine, "Maternal Dietary DHA Supplementation to Improve Inflammatory Outcomes in the Preterm Infant," *Advances in Nutrition* 3 (2012): 370–76.

10. J. Neu and W. Mihatsch, "Recent Developments in Necrotizing Enterocolitis," *Journal of Parenteral and Enteral Nutrition* 36 (Suppl. 1) (2012): 30S–35S.

11. Committee on Nutrition, American Academy of Pediatrics, "Soy Protein-Based Formulas: Recommendations for Use in Infant Feeding," *Pediatrics* 101 (1996): 148–53.

12. N. K. Goyal, A. G. Fiks, and S. A. Lorch, "Persistence of Underweight Status among Late Preterm Infants," *Archives of Pediatrics & Adolescent Medicine* 166 (2012): 424–30.

CHAPTER 12: OVERWEIGHT OR JUST PLAIN HEALTHY?

1. M. S. Randall et al., "Hispanic and Black US Children's Paths to High Adolescent Obesity Prevalence," *Pediatric Obesity* 7, no. 6 (December 2012): 423–35. E-published ahead of print on August 1, 2012.

2. L. M. Wier and W. Encinosa, "Obesity in Children: Hospitalizations from 2000–2009," HCUP Statistical Brief 138, July 2012, Agency for Healthcare Research and Quality, Rockville, MD.

3. A. G. Tsai, D. F. Williamson, and H. A. Glick, "Direct Medical Cost of Overweight and Obesity in the USA: A Quantitative Systematic Review," *Obesity Reviews* 12 (2011): 50–61.

4. S. A. Cohen, "Changing the Outcomes of Obesity: Developing a Model for Use in Healthcare Settings, Including the WIC Program," Report to Georgia WIC Program, July 2002.

5. National Research Council, Institute of Medicine: Leann L. Birch, Lynn Parker, and Annina Burns, eds., *Early Childhood Obesity Prevention Policies* (Washington, DC: National Academies Press, 2011).

6. D. Dabalea, "The Predisposition to Obesity and Diabetes in Offspring of Diabetic Mothers," *Diabetes Care* 30 (Suppl. 2) (2007): S169–S174.

7. J. Armstrong and J. J. Reilly, "Breastfeeding and Lowering the Risk of Childhood Obesity," *Lancet* 359 (2002): 2003–4.

8. L. Shields et al., "Breastfeeding and Obesity at 14 Years: A Cohort Study," *Journal of Paediatrics and Child Health* 42 (2006): 289–96.

9. T. L. Crane et al., "Selective Protection against Extremes in Childhood Body Size, Abdominal Fat Deposition, and Fat Patterning in Breastfed Children," *Archives of Pediatrics & Adolescent Medicine* 166 (2012): 437–43.

10. M. C. Neville et al., "Lactation and Neonatal Nutrition: Defining and Refining the Critical Questions," *Journal of Mammary Gland Biology and Neoplasia* 17 (2012): 167–88. E-published July 1, 2012.

11. J. G. Woo et al., "Human Milk Adiponectin Is Associated with Infant Growth in Two Independent Cohorts," *Breastfeeding Medicine* 4 (2009): 101–9.

12. M. Weyermann, H. Brenner, and D. Rothenbacher, "Adipokines in Human Milk and Risk of Overweight in Early Childhood: A Prospective Cohort Study," *Epidemiology* 18 (2007): 722–29.

13. J. G. Woo et al., "Human Milk Adiponectin Affects Infant Weight Trajectory during the Second Year of Life," *Journal of Pediatric Gastroenterology and Nutrition* 54 (2012): 532–39.

14. S. G. Hassink, ed., *A Parent's Guide to Childhood Obesity: A Road Map to Health* (Elk Grove Village, IL: American Academy of Pediatrics, 2006).

15. B. E. Ginsburg et al., "Plasma Valine and Urinary C-Peptide in Breastfed and Artificially Fed Infants Up to 6 Months of Age," *Acta Paediatrica* 73 (1984): 213–17.

16. A. Lucas et al., "Breast vs Bottle: Endocrine Responses Are Different with Formula Feeding," *Lancet* 315 (1980): 1267–69.

17. J. Trabulsi et al., "Effect of an α-Lactalbumin-Enriched Infant Formula with Lower Protein on Growth," *European Journal of Clinical Nutrition* 65 (2011): 167–74.

CHAPTER 13: INFANT FOODS AND HOW TO INTRODUCE THEM

1. W. A. Walker, "Development of the Intestinal Mucosal Barrier," *Journal of Pediatric Gastroenterology and Nutrition* 34 (2002): S33–S39.

2. Adverse Reactions to Foods Committee, American College of Allergy, Asthma and Immunology: A. Fiocchi et al., "Food Allergy and the Introduction of Solid Foods to Infants: A Consensus Document," *Annals of Allergy, Asthma and Immunology* 97 (2006): 10–20.

3. J. A. Boyce et al., "5.3.4. Guideline 40," in "Guidelines for the Diagnosis and Management of Food Allergy in the United States: Summary of the NIAID-Sponsored Expert Panel Report," NIH Publication No. 11-7700, December 2010, http://www.niaid.nih.gov/topics/foodallergy/clinical/documents/faguidelinesexecsummary.pdf.

4. C. L. M. Joseph, D. R. Ownby, and S. L. Haystad, "Early Complementary Feeding and Risk of Food Sensitization in a Birth Cohort," *Journal of Allergy and Clinical Immunology* 127 (2011): 1203–10.e5.

5. H. Wasser et al., "Infants Perceived as 'Fussy' Are More Likely to Receive Complementary Foods before 4 Months," *Pediatrics* 127, no. 2 (February 2011): 229–37.

6. ESPGHAN Committee on Nutrition: C. Agostoni et al., "Complementary Feeding: A Commentary by the ESPGHAN Committee on Nutrition," *Journal of Pediatric Gastroenterology and Nutrition* 46 (2008): 99–110.

7. A. A. Kuo et al., "Introduction of Solid Food to Young Infants," *Maternal and Child Health Journal* 15, no. 8 (November 2011): 1185–94.

8. F. R. Greer, S. H. Sicherer, and A. W. Burks, "Effects of Early Nutritional Interventions on the Development of Atopic Disease in Infants and Children: The Role of Maternal Dietary Restriction, Breastfeeding, Timing of Introduction of Complementary Foods, and Hydrolyzed Formulas," *Pediatrics* 121, no. 1 (2008): 183–91.

9. B. J. Stordy, A. M. Redfern, and J. B. Morgan, "Healthy Eating for Infants—Mothers' Actions," *Acta Paediatrica* 84, no. 7 (July 1995): 733–41.

10. J. M. Norris et al., "Timing of Initial Cereal Exposure in Infancy and Risk of Islet Autoimmunity," *Journal of the American Medical Association* 290, no. 17 (2003): 13–20.

11. A. G. Ziegler et al., "Early Infant Feeding and Risk of Developing Type 1 Diabetes–Associated Antibodies," *Journal of the American Medical Association* 290 (2003): 1721–28.

12. G. M. Maloney et al., "Food Allergy and the Introduction of Solid Food to Infants: A Consensus Document," *Annals of Allergy, Asthma and Immunology* 97 (2006): 559–60.

13. ESPGHAN Committee on Nutrition, "Complementary Feeding."

14. LISA Study Group: A. Zutavern et al., "Timing of Solid Food Introduction in Relation to Atopic Dermatitis and Atopic Sensitization: Results from a Prospective Birth Cohort Study," *Pediatrics* 117, no. 2 (February 2006): 401–11.

15. N. D'Vaz et al., "Postnatal Fish Oil Supplementation in High-Risk Infants to Prevent Allergy: Randomized Controlled Trial," *Pediatrics* 130 (2012): 674–82.

16. K. Beyer et al., "Effects of Cooking Methods on Peanut Allergenicity," *Journal of Allergy and Clinical Immunology* 107 (2001): 1077–81.

17. G. Lack et al., "Factors Associated with the Development of Peanut Allergy in Childhood," *New England Journal of Medicine* 348 (2003): 977–85.

18. G. Du Toit et al., "Early Consumption of Peanuts in Infancy Is Associated with a Low Prevalence of Peanut Allergy," *Journal of Allergy and Clinical Immunology* 122, no. 5 (November 2008): 984–91.

19. J. M. Norris et al., "Risk of Celiac Disease Autoimmunity and Timing of Gluten Introduction in the Diet of Infants at Increased Risk of Disease," *Journal of the American Medical Association* 293 (2005): 2343–51.

20. E. Hoffenberg, personal communication, April 8, 2012.

21. A. Fasano, personal communication, April 9, 2012.

22. WHO Global Data Bank on Infant and Young Child Feeding (IYCF), World Health Organization (accessed August 2, 2012).

23. A. Ivarsson et al., "Epidemic of Coeliac Disease in Swedish Children," *Acta Paediatrica* 89 (2000): 165–71.

24. A. Ivarsson et al., "Breastfeeding Protects against Celiac Disease," *American Journal of Clinical Nutrition* 75 (2002): 914–21.

25. ESPGHAN Committee on Nutrition, "Complementary Feeding."

CHAPTER 14: TRANSITIONING TO THE REAL STUFF

1. If your baby has not mastered these skills, he may have some developmental issues that will likely also delay his readiness for solids and his ability to proceed safely. If you have any questions about his abilities and/or the timing for these nest steps, please discuss this with your primary care provider before initiating any of the suggestions here.

2. A. Peyser, "Intolerant Lacto-Nuts," *New York Post*, March 11, 2010, http://www.nypost.com/p/news/national/intolerant_lacto_nuts_FfIYeztglYmuvPJ0BObcqJ.

3. S. Koletzko et al., "Diagnostic Approach and Management of Cow's Milk Protein Allergy in Infants and Children: ESPGHAN GI Committee Practical Guidelines," *Journal of Pediatric Gastroenterology and Nutrition* 55 (2012): 221–29.

4. J. D. Skinner et al., "Meal and Snack Patterns of Infants and Toddlers," *Journal of the American Dietetic Association* 104 (2004): 65–70.

5. M. K. Fox et al., "Feeding Infants and Toddlers Study: What Foods Are Infants and Toddlers Eating?," *Journal of the American Dietetic Association* 104 (2004): s22–s30.

6. ESPGHAN Committee on Nutrition: C. Agostoni et al., "Complementary Feeding: A Commentary by the ESPGHAN Committee on Nutrition," *Journal of Pediatric Gastroenterology and Nutrition* 46 (2008): 99–110.

7. D. Benton, "Role of Parents in the Determination of the Food Preferences of Children and the Development of Obesity," *International Journal of Obesity* 28 (2004): 858–69.

8. K. E. Rhee et al., "Parenting Styles and Overweight Status in First Grade," *Pediatrics* 117 (2006): 2047–54.

CHAPTER 15: ESSENTIAL NUTRIENTS

1. J. J. Otten, J. P. Hellwig, and L. D. Meyers, eds., *Dietary Reference Intakes: The Essential Guide to Nutrient Requirements* (Washington, DC: National Academies Press, 2006).

2. C. L. Wagner and F. R. Greer, "Prevention of Rickets and Vitamin D Deficiency in Infants, Children, and Adolescents," *Pediatrics* 122 (2008): 1142–52.

3. The source material for this chapter is a compilation of J. J. Otten, J. P. Hellwig, and L. D. Meyers, eds., *Dietary Reference Intakes: The Essential Guide to Nutrient Requirements* (Washington, DC: National Academies Press, 2006); American Academy of Pediatrics Committee on Nutrition: R. Kleinman, ed., *Pediatric Nutrition Handbook*, 5th ed. (Elk Grove Village, IL: American Academy of Pediatrics, 2004); and S. Cohen, *Healthy Babies, Happy Kids: A Commonsense Guide to Nutrition for the Growing Years* (New York: Delilah Books, 1982), which are really compilations of other source materials that have informed these recommendations and the text.

4. Reginald C. Tsang, *Nutrition of the Preterm Infant: Scientific Basis and Practical Guidelines* (Cincinnati, OH: Digital Educational Publishing, 2005), 417–18.

5. American Academy of Pediatrics Committee on Nutrition: R. Kleinman, ed., *Pediatric Nutrition Handbook*, 5th ed. (Elk Grove Village, IL: American Academy of Pediatrics, 2004), 325–42.

6. J. L. Coulehan et al., "Vitamin C and Acute Illness in Navajo School Children," *New England Journal of Medicine* 295, no. 18 (1976): 973–77.

7. M. F. Holick, "The D-Lightful Vitamin D for Child Health," *Journal of Parenteral and Enteral Nutrition* 36, no. 1 (2012): 9S–19S.

8. M. F. Holick et al., "Evaluation, Treatment, and Prevention of Vitamin D Deficiency: An Endocrine Society Clinical Practice Guideline," *Journal of Clinical Endocrinology and Metabolism* 96 (2011): 1911–30.

9. A. C. Looker et al., "Vitamin D Status: United States, 2001–2006," *NCHS Data Brief* 59 (2011): 1–8.

10. Y. Dong et al., "Low 25-Hydroxyvitamin D Levels in Adolescents: Race, Season, Adiposity, Physical Activity, and Fitness," *Pediatrics* 125 (2010): 1104–11.

11. C. M. Gordon et al., "Prevalence of Vitamin D Deficiency among Healthy Adolescents," *Archives of Pediatrics & Adolescent Medicine* 158 (2004): 531–37.

12. S. S. Sullivan et al., "Adolescent Girls in Maine at Risk for Vitamin D Insufficiency," *Journal of the American Dietetic Association* 105 (2005): 971–74.

13. M. Urashima et al., "Randomized Trial of Vitamin D Supplementation to Prevent Seasonal Influenza A in Schoolchildren," *American Journal of Clinical Nutrition* 91 (2010): 1255–60.

14. E. Hypponen et al., "Intake of Vitamin D and Risk of Type 1 Diabetes: A Birth-Cohort Study," *Lancet* 358 (2001): 1500–1503.

15. Y. Dong et al., "A 16-Week Randomized Clinical Trial of 2,000 IU Daily Vitamin D_3 Supplementation in Black Youth: 25-Hydroxyvitamin D, Adiposity, and Arterial Stiffness," *Journal of Clinical Endocrinology and Metabolism* 95 (2010): 4584–91.

16. C. L. Wagner et al., "Vitamin D and Its Role during Pregnancy in Attaining Optimal Health of Mother and Fetus," *Nutrients* 4, no. 3 (2012): 208–30.

17. S. Cohen, "Blastfax: New AAP Vitamin D Recommendation," American Academy of Pediatrics, Georgia Chapter, 2008.

18. P. M. Brannon and M. F. Picciano, "Vitamin D in Pregnancy and Lactation in Humans," *Annual Review of Nutrition* 31 (2011): 89–115 (an excellent review of the current literature).

19. T. M. Ferguson, "Vitamin D: On the Double," Healthy Children, December 11, 2012, http://www.healthychildren.org/English/healthy-living/nutrition/Pages/Vitamin-D

-On-the-Double.aspx?nfstatus=401&nfstatus=401&nftoken=00000000-0000-0000-0000
-000000000000&nfstatusdescription=ERROR%3a+No+local+token (accessed August 3, 2012).

20. Food and Nutrition Board, Institute of Medicine of the National Academies: A. C. Ross et al., eds., *DRI Dietary Reference Intakes Calcium Vitamin D: Committee to Review Dietary Reference Intakes for Vitamin D and Calcium* (Washington, DC: National Academies Press, 2011).

21. American Academy of Pediatrics and the American College of Obstetricians and Gynecologists, *Breastfeeding Handbook for Physicians* (Washington, DC: American Academy of Pediatrics and the American College of Obstetricians and Gynecologists, 2006).

CHAPTER 16: TRANSITIONING TO TODDLERHOOD

1. K. E. Rhee et al., "Parenting Styles and Overweight Status in First Grade," *Pediatrics* 117 (2006): 2047–54.

Glossary

Definitions and Abbreviations

absorption/malabsorption: the ability (or inability) of the intestine to absorb or take in one or many nutrients.

accretion rate: the rate at which a human or animal accumulates a nutrient.

adequate intake (AI): the estimate of what constitutes a sufficient intake when an Estimated Average Requirement and Recommended Daily Allowance are not available.

allergen (allergenic): the part of a protein (from a food or the environment) that causes an allergy.

amino acid: the building block of protein.

anemia: a decrease in red blood cells or in the hemoglobin those cells contain to transport oxygen.

antibody: the substance with which the body responds to an antigen.

antigen: a foreign material (usually a protein) that creates an allergic or immune response in the body.

antioxidant: a molecule that interferes with the (damaging) occurrence of oxidation; includes vitamins C and E.

arachidonic acid (ARA): one of the (omega-6) long-chain polyunsaturated fatty acids that is important to ensure an infant's growth.

atopy (atopic): condition encompassing airborne and food allergy, eczema, and asthma.

bilirubin: hemoglobin's normal breakdown product, which causes jaundice when it accumulates.

bioavailable (bioavailability): usable by man or animal.

bolus feeding: an entire feeding given all at once or over a short period, usually through a feeding tube.

breastmilk jaundice: jaundice caused by high bilirubin levels in a breastfed baby when there is no other cause.

calorie (actually kilocalorie or large calorie): the unit of energy measured in food or activity.

carbohydrate: sugars, starch, and fiber as a group.

carcinogen: cancer-causing substance. A carcinogen is a substance that will not necessarily cause cancer itself but will promote the growth of cancer in combination with another cancer-inciting factor.

casein: the predominant protein from cow's milk and present at lower levels in breastmilk; assists with calcium absorption.

celiac disease: a food intolerance to a certain protein (gluten) in wheat.

cholesterol: a substance found in animal fat and converted in our bodies into steroids. When present in excess, cholesterol may increase the risk of heart disease and gallstones.

cofactor: a chemical needed for another chemical's biological function.

colostrum: the thick, yellowish milk with immune properties provided during breastfeeding in the first days before breastmilk fully comes in.

conditionally essential nutrient: a necessary nutrient that the body can make but not in enough quantity all the time. Examples include docosahexaenoic acid and niacin.

deficiency: an inadequate amount of a particular nutrient, with the potential to cause clinical illness or symptoms.

diabetes: a condition in which the pancreas does not produce adequate insulin; often referred to as sugar diabetes.

Dietary Reference Intakes (DRI): a composite of a certain population's (e.g., 6- to 12-month-old infants or breastfeeding mothers) estimated need for a nutrient, established by the Food and Nutrition Board of the Institute of Medicine of the National Academies (US) and Health Canada.

digestion: the grinding up and transformation of food into absorbable subunits.

direct bilirubin: the chemically bound fraction of bilirubin that elevates in the blood when it cannot be eliminated by the liver.

docosahexaenoic acid (DHA): a (omega-3) long-chain polyunsaturated fatty acid that helps in brain, eye, and immune development.

donor milk: human milk provided by one woman for another's child, possibly stored in a donor bank for children who need breastmilk.

dysmature infant: a term or preterm infant who is smaller than expected at birth.

enteral feeding: nutrition given through a feeding tube that goes to the stomach or intestine.

enzyme: a substance that speeds up a chemical reaction.

essential nutrient: a necessary nutrient the body cannot make, so it must be eaten.

Estimated Average Requirement (EAR): the amount of a specific nutrient needed by at least half of a particular population. See *Dietary Reference Intakes.*

eustachian tubes: the tubes that connect the middle ear and the nose/throat, equalizing air pressure and draining fluid from the ear.

extrusion reflex: an automatic response when food enters a baby's mouth and he pushes it out with his tongue.

factor: a substance usually used in a nutritional context as a body chemical that participates in a chemical reaction or body function.

first-degree relative: a parent or full sibling (biological brother or sister).

fissure: a torn area of skin, often in the rectum or anus.

food allergy: a particular immunologically based pattern that your body develops whenever you are exposed to an offending substance or allergen.

food intolerance: a patterned or repeated reaction to a food that is often dose related.

food-protein-induced enterocolitis syndrome (FPIES): a condition in which one or more food proteins cause a severe intestinal reaction in an infant, often with diarrhea, vomiting, possibly bleeding, and even a shock-like reaction.

fortification: the addition of a nutrient to a food (e.g., iron-fortified cereal).

fructose: a sugar from fruit and one-half of table (or raw) sugar.

galactogue: medication that stimulates breastmilk production.

gastroenteritis: illness (usually with diarrhea and/or vomiting, with or without a fever) caused by an infection in the intestinal tract.

gastroesophageal reflux: the return of food or stomach contents from the stomach into the esophagus.

gastroesophageal reflux disease: gastroesophageal reflux that results in a significant problem (e.g., asthma, sinus problems, or decreased weight gain).

gestational diabetes: diabetes that occurs only during pregnancy.

glucose: the simple sugar that is usually part of the complex sugars that we eat.

hindmilk: the last phase of breastmilk containing a higher fat content.

histamine: the chemical released in IgE allergies that then is responsible for the symptoms that develop.

hydrolysis, full or partial: the process of breaking down a protein or other chemical completely or in part (with water actually breaking the chemical bonds).

hyperalimentation: nutrition that comes into the body from someplace other than the alimentary or gastrointestinal tract; variably called parenteral nutrition.

hypoallergenic: having a low risk of causing an allergy.

ideal weight: the average weight for a particular height and body build.

immune globulin: protein involved in immune defense; also known as gamma globulin; the different types are represented as IgA, IgE, IgG, and IgM.

international unit (IU): the standard unit of measurement for some vitamins.

intrauterine growth rate: the rate at which a baby is growing while in the womb.

isoflavone: part of soy and other vegetables that also functions as very weak (1/1,000) estrogen.

lactose: the sugar in mammalian milk.

late preterm: babies born between 34 and 36 weeks.

legume: a fruit of woody plants (or the plants themselves), including peas, peanuts, soy, lentils, and beans.

letdown reflex: an automatic response releasing milk from one or both breasts.

lipid: scientific term for fat(s).

lysozyme: an enzyme in breastmilk that helps protect the baby from certain bacteria.

macronutrient: nutrient required in large amounts, often measured in grams.

meconium: an infant's first stool, containing the intestine's content from before birth.

mediator: the chemical or enzyme that facilitates or carries forward a reaction.

megavitamin: a vitamin given in very large amounts.

metabolism: (1) the process making energy available to the body, or (2) the steps in the breakdown of a substance.

microflora (microbiota): the bacteria and other organisms that inhabit our intestines (they are 10 to 100 times the number of cells in our bodies).

microgram (µg): one millionth of a gram.

micronutrient: nutrient needed in minute quantities, often measured in milligrams, micrograms, or international units.

milk bank: a place that provides milk to mothers who are unable to use their own breastmilk.

milligram (mg): 1/1,000th of a gram.

mineral: an (inorganic) element that serves as a nutrient (has other chemical meanings as well).

Montgomery glands: glands in the breast around the areola that provide moisture to the nipple area of the breast.

moro reflex: an early reflex in babies where the head snaps back and arms jerk forward.

nucleotide: building block of DNA.

nutrient: a substance that provides nourishment or is needed by the body.

nutritional value: what a food offers an individual.

obesity: the condition of being overly fat, usually increasing one's weight at least 20 percent above their ideal weight, and increasing the risk of additional health problems.

oligosaccharide: sugar chain (present in breastmilk).

organic chemical: substance containing carbon, and various other elements.

organic food: food grown and processed by agricultural techniques, with certification now required by the US Department of Agriculture.

osteopenia: low mineral density of bone; less severe than osteoporosis.

osteoporosis: loss of calcium in bones resulting in a weakened bone.

outcome: the clinical result or consequence of a procedure or treatment.

parenteral nutrition: nutrition that comes into the body in ways other than the alimentary or gastrointestinal tract (through nutritionally dense intravenous fluids).

peptide: a protein fraction made up of several amino acids.

pincer grasp: grasp (helpful for self-feeding) between thumb and forefinger; infants usually develop this capacity at seven to eight months of age.

polyunsaturated fat: fat with several double bonds.

prebiotic: poorly digested oligosaccharides and fiber that promote the growth of desirable strains of bacteria (probiotics).

premature formula: a milk-based formula designed for the early premature infant while still in the hospital. These are liquid and sterile.

premature infant: infant born at less than 37 weeks inside the womb.

probiotic: strains of bacteria provided by diet or a supplement to provide a health benefit.

processed food: food that has been altered by chemical reactions, often with the addition of chemicals intended to prolong shelf life or enhance the appeal of the food.

protein: complex substances containing nitrogen that are made of amino acids.

pyloric stenosis: a complete blockage of the stomach outlet; vomiting, and often forceful vomiting, is the norm.

Recommended Daily Allowance (RDA): the amount approximately 97 percent of a particular population needs of a specific nutrient. See *Dietary Reference Intakes*.

rehydration: replenishment of the body with fluids (and salts).

saturated fat: fat that has no double bonds between the carbon atoms.

silent reflux: return of stomach contents into the esophagus without vomiting.

store: storage of a nutrient.

sucrose: table sugar; breaks down into fructose and glucose.

sufficiency: having enough of a nutrient for healthy maintenance of the body and its functions.

sugar: simple carbohydrate made up of one or two molecules; usually sweet.

synthesis: the formation of a chemical molecule.

term (or full term) gestation: generally a 38 to 40-week pregnancy.

thrush: a yeast infection in the mouth of infants.

total parenteral nutrition (TPN): provision of nutrition solely via intravenous fluids.

toxic: having the effect of a poison.

transitional formula: formula designed for premature infants once they leave the hospital. These formulas have higher levels of certain nutrients than term or routine infant formulas.

trophic feeding: minimal feeding through a tube down the nose to the stomach to stimulate intestinal development.

type 1 diabetes: diabetes that requires insulin shots or infusion and often presents in childhood.

type 2 diabetes: diabetes that does not require insulin and may be caused by dietary factors.

unsaturated fat: fat with double bonds between the carbon atoms.

upper limit (UL): the amount above which adverse or toxic reactions might occur.

vitamin: an organic substance required, in small amounts, by the body.

whey: a combination of various proteins in breastmilk and other mammalian milks.

Resources

Books and Trusted Websites

BOOKS

Green, Peter H. R., and Rory Jones. *Celiac Disease (Revised and Updated Edition): A Hidden Epidemic*. New York: William Morrow, 2010.

Hale, Thomas W. *Medications and Mothers' Milk*. 15th ed. Amarillo, TX: Hale Publishing, 2012. Updated every several years.

Hassink, S. G., ed. *A Parent's Guide to Childhood Obesity: A Roadmap to Health*. Elk Grove Village, IL: American Academy of Pediatrics, 2006.

Institute of Medicine. *Dietary Reference Intakes*. Washington, DC: National Academies Press, 2006.

Joneja, Janice Vickerstaff. *Dealing with Food Allergies in Babies and Children*. Boulder, CO: Bull Publishing, 2007.

Korn, Danna. *Kids with Celiac Disease: A Family Guide to Raising Happy, Healthy, Gluten-Free Children*. Bethesda, MD: Woodbine House, 2001.

Spangler, Amy. *Breastfeeding*. 9th ed. N.p.: Amy Spangler, 2010.

US Department of Health and Human Services, Office of Women's Health. *Your Guide to Breastfeeding*. Washington, DC: US Government Printing Office, 2011.

Vartabedian, Bryan. *Colic Solved: The Essential Guide to Infant Reflux and the Care of Your Crying, Difficult-to-Soothe Baby*. New York: Ballantine Books, 2007.

WEBSITES

babygooroo.com (Baby Gooroo)
US government websites
wholefoodcatalog.info (Whole Food Catalog)
www.aap.org and www.healthychildren.org (American Academy of Pediatrics)
www.ccdhc.org (the Children's Center for Digestive Health Care)

www.celiac.org (the Celiac Foundation) and www.celiaccentral.org (National Foundation for Celiac Awareness)

www.foodallergy.org (Food Allergy and Anaphylaxis Network)

www.ibreastfeeding.com (Hale Publishing)

www.llli.org (La Leche League International)

www.nutrition4kids.com

www.what2feedyourbaby.com

Index

allergies, 3, 64, 85, 111–21, 215; bleeding from, 105; breastmilk, prevention of, 10, 59, 115, 119; cow's-milk allergy (*see* cow's milk, allergy); family history of, 112, 119, *120*, 168–71; hydrolysates and, 68–69; infant foods and, 158–63, 168, 169–71, 174, 175; irritability from, 52, 96, 97; peanut allergy, 119, 158, 164, 170, 175; pre- and probiotics, prevention of, 73; reflux and, 85; soy allergy, 68; switching formulas, 66
amino acid formulas. *See* elemental formulas
antibodies, 10, 158; allergies, 115–16; mother's, 10, 21, 25
ARA, 13, 45, 48, 50–51, 143, 190

bacteria: breastmilk protection, 10; breastmilk transfer, 15; diarrhea, 106–7; *Enterobacter sakazakii*, 54; folate and, 197–98; gas and, 92; lactoferrin and, 208–9; in mouth, caries, 179; premature infant susceptibility, 140–41, 145; well water, 55–56. *See also* intestinal bacteria; probiotics
bolus feeding, 145
botulism, 174–75
bowel movements (stool), 101–9; blood in, 81, 112, 116, 117; in breastfed infants, 14, 23, 36–37; cereal and, 161, 167;

evaluation of, 132, 146; fiber and, 189; formulas and, 46; removal of bilirubin, 39
BRAT diet, 108
breastmilk/breastfeeding, 7–42; advantages/benefits, 7–14, *9*, *13*; allergy prevention, 10, 59, 115, 119; bowel movements, 37, 102–4; compared to formulas, 43–48, 51, 58–59, 71; contraindications, 14–16; during diarrhea, 107; fussy infants and, 94; Healthy People 2020 Goals, *8*; introducing solids, 157–62, 166–69; jaundice, 39–40; latching on, 20–21, *21*; medications, *15*; nutrient requirements, *34*, 185–88, 190, 191, 195, 199, 200, 208–9, 210, 211, 212; obesity decrease, 153; pacifier use and, 22, 40; premature infants and, 41, 140–41, 143, 145–46; pre- and probiotics, 72–74; storage, *27*; support, 16–17; techniques, 19–38; thrush, 38; vitamins, 33–36; weaning, 58–59
burping, 58, 91, 93

calcium, *206*, 206–7; breastmilk, 33, 44; dairy, 178; fluoride and, 211; formulas, 46, 51, 68, 69, 70, 96, 108, 176; lactose and, 66; premature infants and, 139, 140, 141, 148; reflux medication and, 86; vitamin D and, 193, 201–2, 203–4